T0295717

WEB-SCALE DISCOVERY SERVICES

Chandos Information Professional Series

WEB-SCALE DISCOVERY SERVICES

Principles, Applications, Discovery Tools and Development Hypotheses

ROBERTO RAIELI

TRASLATED BY

ELENA CORRADINI

Chandos Publishing is an imprint of Elsevier
50 Hampshire Street, 5th Floor, Cambridge, MA 02139, United States
The Boulevard, Langford Lane, Kidlington, OX5 1GB, United Kingdom

ISBN: 978-0-323-90298-4

For information on all Chandos Publishing publications visit our website at https://www.elsevier.com/books-and-journals

Publisher: Glyn Jones
Editorial Project Manager: Ivy Dawn Torre
Production Project Manager: Nirmala Arumugam
Cover Designer: Greg Harris

Typeset by TNQ Technologies

This book is the adaptation of the Italian version for an international audience: Roberto Raieli, Web-scale discovery services: principi, applicazioni e ipotesi di sviluppo. Roma, AIB, 2020 (ISBN: 978-88-7812-295-6).

Contents

Preface

More and more often, browsing the websites of both Italian and foreign universities, the section dedicated to libraries is unfortunately often absent from the main menus and those who manage to reach it no longer find a well-highlighted link to the online catalog, but a "Google-like" search box that allows you to enter one or more terms. This is also without neither the possibility of specifying whether they refer to authors, titles, subjects or anything else, nor connecting them with the Boolean operators. The result is a very long list of document descriptions, of which in some cases, depending on one's access rights, it is possible to read the full text online or locate it in the physical collections of the libraries of that university.

To such software packages, which are part of the broader family of the so-called Web-scale discovery services and which are mainly referred to—after an initial period of uncertainty—as discovery tools (while there are still those who call them, more generically, "portals," specifying only sometimes "for bibliographic research"), and which in some countries for some years have also been spreading to other types of libraries, Roberto Raieli has dedicated this very clear, complete, updated, and documented book, which was in fact needed, and which also includes rather broad and relevant considerations on related issues such as open access, the semantic web, linked data, and information literacy.

The popularity of discovery tools among users is considerable and growing, so much so that the vast majority of libraries that adopt them put them in full evidence compared with the traditional online catalog, which is sometimes, when not abandoned, just transformed into a link to a collective OPAC to which the library adheres. The main reasons for this success are, in my opinion, three:

(1) The exceptional ease of use, modeled on the one typical of generalist Web search engines and which users no longer know how to do without, especially the younger ones.

(2) The vastness of the average results obtained, which goes beyond the size of the local (both physical and digital) collection as reflected by the OPAC, with the possibility of identifying even less traditional documents and reducing the risk of frustrating searches with few or no results, without, however, experiencing the risk of running into even more numerous and often poor quality documents offered by generalist search engines.

(3) The illusory but widespread perception that the exclusive use of one of these tools allows an exhaustive bibliographic search, in any case sufficient for most of the needs of—let us say—an average university student, exempting him from identifying, learning to use, and finally interrogating other research tools.

Despite these advantages, there are those who, especially among librarians and library and information scientists, also notice numerous defects, or issues, some of which paradoxically caused and supported by the librarians themselves who have the task of adapting the discovery tools to the needs of each specific library or university, while on other aspects the possibilities for local staff to develop the software, often purchased from large international companies, are objectively limited. Among these critical issues, I would like to mention at least the following:

(A) It is extremely difficult, not only for users but even for librarians, to know with absolute certainty which databases and other sources are exactly covered by the discovery tool index purchased, also because they often change according to the commercial agreements between the discovery tool producer and the bibliographic sources suppliers.

(B) Even more inscrutable are the criteria with which the discovery tool sorts the results of the searches carried out, which in general are inspired by the relevance ranking algorithms typical of generalist search engines, originally conceived to be applied to unstructured full texts of various nature and quality produced by anyone (such as web pages) and not to homogeneous and structured metadata sets created by professionals (such as those often found in bibliographic databases). Only sometimes librarians are able to change these criteria a priori, for example, by valorizing the local resources cataloged in the OPAC, and users are allowed to change them after their search, rearranging the list of results by date or author.

(C) Since sometimes the company that produces the discovery tool also distributes bibliographic sources, the suspicion may arise that they are privileged in the ranking or otherwise valued in some way compared with those distributed by competing companies.

(D) Although the advertisements of the producers sometimes seem to suggest the opposite, since no discovery tool includes in its index either all the databases and other bibliographic sources existing on the market or openly accessible, it often happens that a library pays the subscription for information sources that are not covered by the index of the discovery tool adopted. In this case, those sources will have to be queried by users through their native interface, or the library will have to provide another search tool, to be managed in parallel with the discovery tool, in both cases with the risk that the sources in question are underused.

(E) Conversely, the index of each discovery tool almost certainly also covers full-text information sources to which the single library is not subscribed. Deselecting them from the index itself with the aim of making them invisible to their users would be a too demanding and not always possible job for librarians. A job in any case would deprive users of pure bibliographic metadata, in some cases useful, anyway. On the other hand, the decision not to deselect them would increase the percentage of bibliographic descriptions retrieved during the search that do not lead to the full text of the document described and, therefore, the frustration of users.

(F) To try to reduce the risks associated with points D and E, some libraries may be tempted to acquire mainly information sources marketed by the same company that produces their discovery tool or, at least, included in the index of the discovery tool itself. In the long term, this could lead to a distortion of the collections or, at least, to the penalization and progressive marginalization of precious information sources published by small publishers.

(G) The doubly hybrid nature of the discovery tools (partly bibliographies of the existing and partly catalogs of owned resources, but also repertories of both paper documents, of which they always provide only metadata, and digital documents, of which sometimes also offer the full text), combined with the second horn of the dilemma described under point E, reduces the percentage of resulting documents whose full digital text users can immediately access to. This can, paradoxically, be particularly frustrating precisely for the younger users whose needs discovery tools would like to preferentially meet and for whom what is not immediately usable on the screen is almost nonexistent.

(H) The discovery tool search algorithms favor the boolean OR operator over the AND operator and, more generally, recall over precision, producing extremely long lists of results, which, after a moment of relief for "finding something," generate in users (especially the older ones) first an "information overload" anxiety and then irritation due to the significant percentage of documents traced that turn out to be completely irrelevant.

(I) The "advanced" search form of the discovery tools, which would allow to increase precision and reduce recall, is often extremely less rich and sophisticated than that of the best OPACs and is always much less visible than the Google-style single search box, which instead automatically triggers the "result multiplier" algorithms.

(J) The metadata present in the discovery tool index are heterogeneous and often both qualitatively worse and quantitatively lower than those of the original databases from which they come. Furthermore, their transfer to the index is not always simultaneous and timely. This produces dysfunctions both in the search mechanisms and in the descriptions of the documents and, in particular, the filters that can be applied subsequently to the list of results are less effective to try to segment it into coherent sets of documents.

(K) In addition to searching on their entire index, discovery tools often also allow you to investigate only some of its subsets that should be mutually excluded, but irrational segmentations and ambiguous terminologies (often depending more by local librarians than by software companies) make this option risky. For example: if the choice is between "paper resources" and "online resources," where are CDs and DVDs? And if the alternatives include "electronic journals" and "articles," where should I look for an article published in an electronic journal?

(L) The imaginative names with which each library or institution names its discovery tool make it more difficult for users to understand that it is always the same type of tool and sometimes underline (as in the case of "All" or "One for All") precisely that claim of research exhaustiveness that librarians should warn against.

(M) The discovery tools bring to a stop and favor a backward process in the progressive increase of hypertextualization (and, therefore, of the contextualization of documents and the freedom of choice among different bibliographic navigation paths by users) that has accompanied the evolution of the various generations of OPACs from their birth up to today: both the list of results and the descriptions of the individual documents recovered generally from discovery tools have fewer links than the more recent OPACs.

(N) Discovery tools are tools designed for bibliographic research and not for a more comprehensive management of bibliographic documents.

They are therefore often lacking in services typically offered to users by OPACs, such as loan management, personalized reporting of new acquisitions, maintaining a "personal virtual shelf," etc.

To try to counterbalance at least part of these issues, Raieli proposes various strategies, among which I summarize the main ones here:

(I) Discovery tools should be used mainly in the initial phase of bibliographic research, to then move on to OPACs (assuming they have not been discontinued in the meantime) and to specialized databases for subsequent investigations.

(II) The success of "friendly" tools such as discovery tools does not reduce the importance of information literacy, in which it is necessary to continue to invest so that everyone knows the costs, limits, and illusions of such friendship, as well as the entire range of means and research techniques and, above all, information selection and evaluation.

(III) Although search algorithms and user interaction interfaces are important in any digital bibliographic tool, not even those of discovery tools can work miracles when the raw material to which they are applied is of poor quality and too heterogeneous. To improve the effectiveness and reliability of the discovery tools, it would therefore be essential, first of all, to increase the quality level and homogeneity of the metadata that are put into their indexes.

(IV) Librarians should not fancy that the expensive (in financial terms) purchase of a discovery tool exempts them from the additional cost (in terms of human resources) of a demanding and constant implementation and customization work with respect to their specific users and the local collection.

(V) Not only should librarians be more involved and engaged in information literacy, in the production and control of metadata and in software implementation, but, more generally, it should be recognized, valued, and enhanced—as Raieli writes in the last lines of the first part of the book—"the need for library knowledge in every phase of the creation, structuring, archiving, research, and visualization of data" managed by the discovery tools. Such knowledge will, for example, be particularly valuable in ensuring the appropriateness and consistency of the terms used to indicate to users the available functions, segmentations, operators, filters, and search masks.

All these suggestions are correct and shareable, but personally I am perhaps a little more pessimistic than Raieli about their effectiveness, because it will be increasingly difficult for a professional category facing a growing (numerical, economic, cultural, identity, etc.) crisis to significantly affect the interests, orientations and behaviors of users, supplier companies, and even their own institutions. In particular, in my role as a professor who teaches university students also basic level courses on bibliographic research, I encounter considerable difficulties in teaching them to understand and make the best use of such inscrutable and scarcely "orientable" tools such as discovery tools.

In any case, bibliography teachers and librarians must necessarily get to know discovery tools and strive to convey to students and users what they learn from books such as what you are about to read and from their experiences both in front of and behind the interfaces of discovery systems, realistically taking into account the climate created both by the sociocultural context (i.e. what those who carry out bibliographic searches, rightly or wrongly, prefer) and the economic–technological one (i.e., the powerful pressures of companies on the IT market in general and on library software in particular).

I conclude this preface with a final, short, list of quick considerations:

- Given the preliminary and introductory nature that bibliographic searches carried out with discovery tools should cover, I believe it would be more correct (but, I understand, even less captivating) to call them "exploration" rather than "discovery" tools.
- It is paradoxical (although understandable from a technological and economic point of view) that the success of discovery tools was born and still stands out in the university environment, where researchers and students should not be too frightened by the complexities of bibliographic research, given that for the former it is a relevant part of their work and skills and for the latter it is one of the main things they are trying to learn (but which they are unlikely to really learn if it is overly simplified and automated).
- Perhaps the discovery tools could be a good example, in the context of bibliographic research, of what is expressed in general terms by the aphorism traditionally attributed to Albert Einstein according to which "everything should be made as simple as possible, but not one bit simpler."

Riccardo Ridi
Università Ca' Foscari, Venezia
October 2019

PART ONE

CHAPTER 1

Introduction: scope, tools, actors, and values of knowledge discovery

1.1 The space of information and knowledge

In the universe of information and knowledge, which exploded and began to expand uncontrollably at the dawn of the development of human intelligence, libraries and other institutes concerned with the preservation and dissemination of knowledge have always tried to define a specific galaxy, a "space" in which to live and develop organically, taking and exchanging the essential elements for tangible and cultural existence.

Therefore, such a space was conceived to give birth to a given library and its specific mission, which was not easy to define or theorize, ineffable in its logical and technical essence. In the past decades, this space has been redefined and restructured, as it is normally happening in a healthy organic system.[1] This redefinition, which bears the features of a revolution, often appears as if it was happening outside control, which means in a way inextricably connected to a series of developments concerning the universe of which the "cutout" space is part: the information society in its various aspects, and, generally speaking, the Internet, the World Wide Web, the Information and Communication Technology (ICT).

Consequently, the selection, organization, mediation, and retrieval of information and knowledge resources available to libraries and cultural institutes, the characteristics of the tools and services that they make available for research activities, the specific role and the scope of application of each of these tools and services are constantly changing, and so are the methodologies that must be applied in the specific mediation activities, and

[1] A general review of the library organic system is presented by Giovanni Solimine, *Introduzione allo studio della biblioteconomia: riflessioni e documenti*. Manziana: Vecchiarelli, 1995 (especially p. 195—209).

Web-Scale Discovery Services
ISBN 978-0-323-90298-4
https://doi.org/10.1016/B978-0-323-90298-4.02003-6

in the activities of "education" towards users and people. All these are changes and lines of development, which must be evaluated through an objective consideration of the social and economic changes that characterize today's society, and which are interwoven with ICT developments.[2]

With regard to the space to which today's research and discovery activities apply, which can no longer be strictly defined as a "documentary," or "collections" space, it is necessary to adhere to a "long-term perspective," which can enable the organization of a library structure—and not only—to continue today the original mission of connecting information with people's knowledge needs.[3] The same concept of "owned" physical resources to be made available—for more or less known users—has been facing evolution, and for much longer than the tools of its connection with people. This space has been expanded to include not only what is not physically owned, although still acquired as a service, but also what is "merely" selected on the web and widely mediated as a "resource," provided it has the characteristics of a sufficiently structured, coherent, and recognizable object of knowledge: in short, being reliable and trustworthy. You could be tempted to take on an extreme stance, wondering if mediation can also include resources such as simple projects, programs, tags or hashtags of social websites, etc.[4]—which can stretch to the boundaries of the "bibliographic" galaxy.

In this regard, and assuming that, no matter how large, the reliable space of libraries will always be a "bounded" and "safe" place, which even the less experienced researcher can approach with confidence, it is worth remembering David Weinberger's essay titled *Too big to know*.[5] Already from the clear richness of the title—and above all of the subtitle: *rethinking knowledge now that the facts aren't the facts, experts are everywhere, and the smartest person in the room is the room*—the author explains which are the reasons for

[2] As an example for this, cf.: IFLA Trend Report: Riding the Waves or Caught in the Tide? 2013. http://trends.ifla.org/insights-document.

[3] Vivarelli, M., 2015. C'è bisogno di collezioni? Teorie, modelli, pratiche per l'organizzazione di spazi documentari connessi e condivisi, Bibl. Oggi 1(1), 18–29. http://www.bibliotecheoggi.it/trends/article/view/38. This complex matter is discussed more deeply in the paragraph 3.3 in this book, where I further refer to this article by Vivarelli.

[4] Cf. DeZelar-Tiedman, C., 2016. Redefining library resources in discovery systems. In: Spiteri, L.F. (Ed.) Managing Metadata in Web-Scale Discovery Systems. Facet, London, pp. 91–112.

[5] Weinberger, D., 2012. Too Big to Know: Rethinking Knowledge Now That the Facts Aren't the Facts, Experts Are Everywhere, and the Smartest Person in the Room Is the Room. Basic books, New York.

the astonishment, or the sense for "sublime,"[6] which it is legitimate to prove in front of the size of the Web. Weinberger argues that, given the growing amount of information contained on the Internet and the Web, we are less and less sure of what we know, of knowing something, of who it is who really knows something, and we are not even sure of the very concept of knowledge. In any case, the Internet represents a fundamental revolution regarding the methods and logic we adopt to understand the world we live in, even allowing people to process information faster and more completely than traditional—or past—resources and sources of knowledge.

In the dimension of the Internet, the issue of finding a unique method, or tool, to tackle the boundless space of research should not be decisive either. In a recent article published in *Avvenire*, an Italian newspaper, the question is explained to the general public in terms of the risk of homologation of intelligence and knowledge.[7] With regard to the diffusion of big data, the author comments that if the algorithms and other tools that guide our actions on the Internet, as for the management and research of data, propose an infallible path, a continuous facilitation to achieve the result, the consequent great disadvantage would be a "one-way" world, with no room for the unexpected and, essentially, for the freedom of human beings. People would adopt the same thinking strategies, all problems would be faced in the same way—and it is not certain that it would be the best way—research in every field would all be the same and would lead to similar results. The solution, enhancing the meaning and value of the Humanities, would be to spread throughout the curricula basic courses in Philosophy, Art, Literature, and Poetry, even in the scientific disciplines, as these subjects may allow to develop resilient and flexible minds, capable of creating unexpected, individual, innovative, and revolutionary solutions.

From these writings, a renewed interest for the primacy of the researcher's "mind" emerges. This mind is considered able to create, invent, and—why not?—even neglect and lose some information. The research path is addressed in various ways, even "thoughtless," sifting through

[6] For a classical explanation of the concept of "sublime," which is equally captivating and horrible, cf. Burke, E., 1759. A Philosophical Enquiry into the Origin of Our Ideas of the Sublime and Beautiful. Dodsley, London.

[7] Paliaga, S., 2018. Big data. Ecco perché le discipline umanistiche governeranno il digitale. Avvenire.it 23 gennaio 2018. https://www.avvenire.it/agora/pagine/algoritm-c69cd26cfb864b589e128b2611bc932f.

millions of information resources "by eye," through an infinity that attracts, a sublime that does not scare, strengthened by one's own vocation to know.

Therefore, the boundless space of information and knowledge should not be feared: it is possible to venture into it with the enthusiasm of discovery, with "serendipity," as human beings have always done in the infinite space of nature, in the world, in the universe. For this adventure, you can choose the reassuring guide of the library and other cultural institutes, their "point of view" that defines a given information space—which, however expanded, is always a "restriction" on the entire web—or let yourself go.

Returning to the logic of the reliable, bounded, and safe expansion of the space provided by libraries and their mediation, a not too vague example is that of the discussions on the cataloging of open access (OA) resources. By underlining the role that libraries can have in the knowledge circuit, and the functions they can claim, we can first of all justify the value that the cataloging of OA resources, e-books, and e-journals assumes. If a library chooses certain resources, and inserts them in the catalog, it implicitly and explicitly establishes their cultural value. For example, specialized libraries collect, evaluate, select, and make available within their catalogs the relevant resources for each sector of interest, separating them from all the rest of the editorial production. These operations have a high bibliographic value, also because specific semantic accesses are created, or access points linked to specific standards or reference books.[8] The reason for cataloging OA resources, available elsewhere, is even stronger than simply addressing them by listing the sites from which they are accessible: it serves to give authority to the resource, to provide it with a list of accesses usually exploited in case of more traditional resources, and to expand what can be defined as the "owned," to the advantage of both the resource and the space of the library.[9]

[8] Cf. to this point: Osservazioni conclusive in: Robbio, A.D., 2007. Analisi citazionale e indicatori bibliometrici nel modello open access. p. 1–36: p. 32. http://eprints.rclis.org/10686/1/valutazione-23gennaio2008.pdf.

[9] It would be fascinating to follow the debate concerning the preservation of the digital copy of cataloged OA resources: the library would take back again old functions, even in the current digital environment, thus ensuring the preservation of the knowledge products, especially when these are not issued by publishers that are capable of granting their permanence. For this discussion, I owe my thanks to the colleagues Mattia Vallania and Maura Quaquarelli, Sistema bibliotecario Sapienza (SBS), Rome, Italy.

Even while cataloging the most varied resources, not only just addressing them in different ways, greatly strengthens the sense of expanding the "librarian" space. Moreover, in the new logic of researching in this space, the sense of the "discovery" of new information and resources in the context of broader research paths is increasingly present. Among the tools that the library maintains or offers to users, therefore, there are new tools whose effectiveness has yet to be evaluated and improved, and tools born outside the library environment and of even more problematic integration, all, however, aimed at mediating a wide and variable heritage and the knowledge that contextualizes it. In this system, even the catalog, which traditionally is the main tool for identifying and accessing documents, is often put to the test and must demonstrate the evidence of being still needed as a reliable means of finding, identifying, selecting, obtaining resources, and navigating among them.[10]

It is therefore necessary to question in depth the nature of the different search engines available today. The need for this debate can also be introduced by reporting traces of a brief discussion that took place on the list of Italian librarians AIB-CUR in April2016.[11] We complain, in fact, of the unconscious use, taken for granted, of various search engines, without ever bothering to verify their neutrality, or the "political" line, or the history of their foundation—often obscure, too. These tools should have been created by libraries, since they have among their main tasks precisely that of indexing and making information resources available, in addition by

[10] Cf.: Riva, P., Le Boeuf, P., Žumer, M., 2017. IFLA Library Reference Model: A Conceptual Model for Bibliographic Information. IFLA. https://www.ifla.org/publications/node/11412; International Federation of Library Associations and Institutions, 1998. Study group on the functional requirements for bibliographic records, Functional Requirements for Bibliographic Records: Final Report. Saur, München (current text available at the: http://www.ifla.org/publications/functional-requirements-for-bibliographic-records); IFLA Cataloguing Section; IFLA Meetings of Experts on an International Cataloguing Code, Statement of international cataloguing principles (ICP) 2016: IFLA cataloguing principles: statement of International cataloguing principles (ICP) and its glossary, edited by Barbara Tillett, Ana Lupe Cristán. München: Saur, 2009, http://www.ifla.org/files/assets/cataloguing/icp/icp_2009-en.pdf.

[11] The discussion was named *Biblioteche e motori di ricerca, una riflessione storica.* The excerpts are taken from e-mails written by Beppe Pavoletti (April 1, 2016) and Raffaele Messuti (April 2, 2016).

selecting them, and instead a large part of this role was left in the hands of commercial enterprises.[12] The search engines of today's systems used in the library risk, like others, to escape completely from being understood in the library field, and to act in the context of the bibliographic resources themselves with assumptions that are not only unclear, but would not even be acknowledged by librarians and professionals who care for free and objective information.

Together with the various thoughts on the role that libraries could or may have, the need for a discussion on the "meaning" of new and different research tools is therefore present, but at the same time with the awareness that, even if they so wish, librarians—and other colleagues in related sectors—do not intervene too much in the design of these tools. This could be fine, given that technology specialists, engineers, and computer scientists design and propose new means certainly not hindering the collaboration of information professionals. The point is precisely to grasp the possibilities of collaboration, and to participate in the processes of creation and experimentation of the different tools, above all by taking care of "understanding" them in depth, knowing how to conceive them and, in any case, knowing how to prepare and manage the whole context, not only connected to librarianship, to be able to integrate or reject them: consciously.

1.2 OPAC, discovery tools, and information literacy

In addition to the OPAC interface of the catalog, which is seriously questioned even when the catalog itself is not, and beyond the interfaces of individual specific tools such as databases, perhaps destined for a longer stay, the various tools nowadays used aim to create a unified and univocal point for research and access to discover the space managed by all library activities. These interfaces are designed on the basis of what appear to be the essential principles of libraries, revised in the light of today's possibilities: to lead end users to everything that a library can ascertain to be reliable for the information needs of different types of people, and to make this the more efficient and "comfortable" path of research and discovery.[13]

[12] A role more or less consciously delegated to other levels, as almost was the case for databases about 60 years ago, but this issue needs further investigation.

[13] Cf.: Bianchini, C., 2012. Dagli OPAC ai library linked data: come cambiano le risposte ai bisogni degli utenti. AIB Studi 52 (3), 303–323, https://aibstudi.aib.it/article/view/8597.

Well before the launch of the new solutions, more than 10 years ago, the first voices emerged in favor of the development of research interfaces in the aforementioned direction, thus prompting a transformation according to principles connected to Web 2.0 and, also, the Semantic Web toward extreme friendliness and usability, interactive and collaborative organization, interoperability, and granularity of information and data.[14] At that time, however, a crucial question was overlooked, which even today does not seem to be a concern: whether, while being an innovation enthusiast, one does not run too much of the risk of following the Web trends uncritically, just obtaining that some rules and the good name of libraries would survive deprived of "personality." On the other hand, some scholars argue that a commitment to develop historically established library theories and library methods would be more productive to transform these principles toward the future direction of information science, better responding to people's future needs.[15]

Beyond this theoretical awareness, however, the need was indicated to critically welcome the new tools suggested by the Web, proposing them as a starting point for a broad discovery of information and resources, to be further explored with more specific research services offered by the library, starting with the OPAC and databases first. The new tools are modeled in a friendly and technologically updated way on a system that allows for the construction of a single index of all the available resources, in which it is possible to search for any piece of information available in an organic and straightforward way, instead of looking in each database separately, following the Web-scale technology of the main general search engines. If, however, the generalist engines build a generic index of the most disparate contents of the Web, the new discovery systems constitute their own index based on the resources to which the library has access, or which in any case it deems useful for research. These systems, therefore, make available to people, in a way that is easy to understand and use, the vast potential of a unified index together with the good quality of the results found. Much of their effectiveness, however, depends on the attention and competence

[14] Among others: Calhoun, K., 2006. The Changing Nature of the Catalog and its Integration with Other Discovery Tools: Final Report. Library of Congress, Washington. http://www.loc.gov/catdir/calhoun-report-final.pdf.

[15] Cf. for a summary of discussions: Richardson, H.A.H., 2013. Revelations from the literature: how web-scale discovery has already changed us. Comput. Libr. 33 (4), 12—17, http://www.infotoday.com/cilmag/may13/Richardson–How-Web-Scale-Discovery-Has-Already-Changed-Us.shtml.

with which a library is able to implement them, consciously defining the "boundaries" of the application space, depending on its mission and the target audience.[16]

The research and discovery systems on which the greatest trust and the related technical—if not theoretical—attention is still placed, are those generally referred to as Web-scale discovery services (WSDS), and in particular the related broad subset of tools called discovery tools. These services have so far shown a good ability to respond practically to the specific new information needs expressed by different types of people. Beyond this, from a more theoretical point of view, the WSDS seem to have the chance of being well integrated among the other consolidated tools of the library, even if they require a sound and well-thought implementation to be "accepted." It would be a mistake to approve and introduce these technologies uncritically, just considering the extent of their diffusion.[17]

To circumscribe the idea of "valid development," I would propose that these tools do not necessarily have the aim to replace the OPAC and other specific "research" interfaces, but can for now be placed at the more basic and general level of "discovery" of information and resources, when it is needed to begin a wide-ranging research, especially in the academic field, where at the moment the WSDS are mainly in place. Over time, hopefully thanks to the improvement of the technology and methodologies of the WSDS, it will be possible to embrace more radical choices, such as the setting up of a single tool for each type of research and its use at every level, even for the most specialized and in-depth investigations.

Placing themselves alongside the more "durable" tools of information retrieval (IR), these information discovery tools, in any case, do not offer access to the entire Web in which the library must still be integrated, but rather point toward the resources that the library has decided to select and make available. Information discovery tools act, with the "democratic" simplicity of a generalist search engine but with more "richness," within a

[16] In this regard, cf.: Luther, J., Kelly, M.C., 2011. The next generation of discovery. Libr. J. 136 (5), 66–71. https://www.libraryjournal.com/?detailStory=the-next-generation-of-discovery; Moore, K.B., Greene, C., 2012. Choosing discovery: a literature review on the selection and evaluation of discovery layers. J. Web Librariansh. 6 (3) 145–163, https://www.tandfonline.com/doi/full/10.1080/19322909.2012.689602.

[17] On the debate related to this, cf. the essays contained In: Pagliero Popp, M., Dallis, D. (2012) *Planning and Implementing Resource Discovery Tools in Academic Libraries*. IGI Global, Hershey.

bounded and safe universe, both vast, as it is not limited to "typical" documents, but offers all kinds of resources; and, at the same time, not extended to infinite possibilities, because these are carefully validated by the library which has made this universe a constitutive part of its cultural space.

This matter leads to various discussions regarding the perspective that considers discovery tools as a possible "single point" to carry out effective research, and the consequent access, which include all the resources mediated by a library. The main issue consists in the fact that a real and overall change in the organization of the various databases to which the WSDS must be applied has not yet been achieved, and many of them are really similar to "silos," that is, closed and independent repositories.[18] There is no doubt that the problem cannot be solved by transforming the search interfaces without modifying the databases. The new access tools must be applied to new data indices. Structurally, they take after the new semantic Web, which is expandable, interoperable, granular, integrable, complex, and significant at any time. But this is also part of the weaknesses of current research tools due to the context in which Web-oriented interfaces have been developed and that need to be applied to data that are still closed in silos produced exclusively, or only, by a few communities.

Although in-depth discussions abound on this matter, before redesigning the tools to achieve precise bibliographic and organizational objectives, it is still necessary to fully regain awareness of which are these same objectives, in the light of the current societal and technological developments. Essentially, WSDS should be structured to be implemented in a library, or other cultural institution, which has undertaken a conceptual reorganization according to the principles contained in guidelines such as IFLA LRM,[19] RDA,[20] RDF,[21] Linked Open Data,[22] and also BIBFRAME (bibliographic framework initiative).[23] Therefore, these discovery services

[18] Cf. again: Bianchini, C., Dagli OPAC ai library linked data cit., p. 308–317.

[19] Riva, P., Le Boeuf, P., Žumer, M., IFLA Library Reference Model cit.

[20] Joint steering committee for development of RDA [et al.], 2014. RDA: Resource Description & Access. American Library Association, Chicago; RDA Toolkit, www.rdatoolkit.org.

[21] Resource Description Framework (RDF). http://www.w3.org/RDF.

[22] World Wide Web Consortium, 2011. Library Linked Data Incubator Group Final Report. W3C. http://www.w3.org/2005/Incubator/lld/XGR-lld-20111025.

[23] Library of Congress, 2012. Bibliographic framework as a web of data: linked data model and supporting services. Library of Congress, Washington. http://www.loc.gov/bibframe/pdf/marcld-report-11-21-2012.pdf. Cf. the second part of this book for further discussion on this topic.

may have the task of managing a universe of resources safely bounded inside the vast information space of a library, but the metadata and data that compose this universe must first be suitably arranged, also considering the options of creating data, connecting existing data right inside the semantic Web, and managing them with new processing and searching tools.[24]

This issue is connected to the overall technological innovation toward the future of information and cultural services to people, and for the progress of society. If cultural institutes really want to meet the needs of research and information, as understood in a renewed way by Library and Information Science (LIS) and by society, they should continue to maintain their specific role in the path of general cultural innovation and provice more powerful and semantically organized tools that will ensure to really meet people's needs.[25]

In particular, therefore, it is necessary to continue to think about the role that WSDS are expected to have, critically framing their acceptance among library services and mediation tools. This goes not without mentioning the role that every new information mediation tool must play not only for the libraries themselves but also by inserting them in the more general context of institutions and cultural mediation bodies, such as

[24] The convergence among libraries and semantic web has been the main topic of the international seminar: "Global interoperability and linked data in libraries" (Florence, 18–19 June 2012), http://www.linkedheritage.eu/linkeddataseminar; Cf. also the papers published in: Global interoperability and linked data in libraries: special issue. JLIS.it, 4 (2013) (1). http://leo.cineca.it/index.php/jlis/issue/view/536. Another international conference on the topic was: "Convegno AIB CILW 2016. La rinascita delle risorse dell'informazione: granularità, interoperabilità e integrazione dei dati" (Rome, 21 October 2016), https://www.aib.it/attivita/congressi/aib-cilw-2016-conference/2016/56896-convegno-aib-cilw-2016-programma/; the conference papers and other essays are published in: *Progressi dell'informazione e progresso delle conoscenze: granularità, interoperabilità e integrazione dei dati*, a cura di Roberto Raieli. Roma: AIB, 2017; some articles have been also published in: L'universo delle risorse culturali: lampi di genio e azioni concrete. Lightning talks presentati al Convegno AIB CILW 2016, a cura del Gruppo di studio AIB CILW, AIB Studi, 57 (2017) (1), 91–117, https://aibstudi.aib.it/article/view/11569.

[25] This aspect has been also discussed during an international congress, "FSR 2014," in which the role and coherence of the existing tools used by libraries for information intermediation has never been under discussion, despite the need for their further development: "Faster, smarter and richer. Reshaping the library catalogue. FSR 2014. International conference" (Roma, 27–28 febbraio 2014), http://www.aib.it/attivita/congressi/c2014/fsr2014. Per gli interventi del convegno, vedere inoltre: Special issue: FSR 2014. JLIS.it 5 (2). http://leo.cineca.it/index.php/jlis/issue/view/651.

museums, archives, galleries, and so on: in a nutshell, everything that can be integrated into the broader Italian MAB (Museums, Archives, Libraries),[26] or else at the international LAM (Library, Archives, Museums)[27] context. In addition to MAB and LAM, other kinds of organizations and stakeholders may be taken into account, with at least a certain degree of reliability, when talking about the Web of data, where the data circulate richly in form of "absolute value," validated by the authority that produced them, and are widely reusable by all those who can make profitable use, and not only culturally.

Essentially, libraries still have to definitely get used to not having absolute ownership of the resources to which they allow access. Moreover, they must consider the possibility of not even owning all the data with which they define such access,[28] as well as accept the consequent "alienation" of the bibliographic record, increasingly pushed toward the boundaries of the bibliographic universe that contextualizes its origin and history. The practice of enriching "open" silos, in fact, aims to catalog or describe resources by harvesting the open data present on the Web, when their origin is clear and authoritative, and following the new methods of aggregation of linked data that structure the network of open relations of the Semantic Web. Therefore, the bibliographic records themselves would consist of the dynamic relationships between different "triples," which in turn connect one to another the data created by libraries and by other kinds of organizations.[29]

The spirit of improving access to information and knowledge resources is closely linked to that of disseminating it to all individuals, all levels of society, all societies, in close relationship with the progress of information technologies and communication, so that cultural organizations and new technologies together can really contribute to the development, for every

[26] The Italian acronym used for Libraries, Museums, Archives (LAM) is Musei Archivi Biblioteche (MAB). http://www.mab-italia.org.

[27] Cf.: International Federation of Library Associations and Institutions. Libraries, Archives, Museums, Monuments & Sites (LAMMS). http://www.ifla.org/lamms.

[28] Cf.: Bianchini, C. *Dagli OPAC ai library linked data* cit., p. 316. Il testo di Bianchini cita a sua volta: Coyle, K., 2013. Library linked data: an evolution. JLIS.it 4 (1), 53–61. http://leo.cineca.it/index.php/jlis/article/view/5443.

[29] Cf.: Guerrini, M., Possemato, T., 2013. Linked data: a new alphabet for the semantic web. JLIS.it 4 (1), 67–90; Coyle, K., Library Linked Data: An Evolution cit.

citizen, of the possibility of exercising civil, political, economic, social, and cultural rights.[30] It is along this line that the innovation of information management research systems and knowledge resources must be implemented: a profound, organic, and balanced innovation, not only involving the catalog and the OPAC, but also databases, institutional repositories, open-access archives, and related interfaces.

This social spirit is bound to an appropriate implementation, as well as a time for "learning" any new or revamped tool made available by libraries. Even in the case of a thoughtful and adequate implementation, followed by an effective use of these tools, each library, therefore, will have to take care not only of incorporating them in the most appropriate way but also of ensuring that users learn how to discover their potential and usefulness, compared with traditional tools. It will be necessary to clarify the features that make them distinct tools for different purposes, as well as to explain which search strategies can be performed, how to critically evaluate results obtained, and the risks of excessive disintermediation. Then, it will also be necessary to define to which level discovery tools seem to remain in any case limited to being basic tools for a first univocal research and discovery of resources, and, vice versa, when they can allow to yield an exhaustive research.[31]

In this context, a renewed role for information literacy will be a priority. Much must be invested in the activities and principles that concern it, and much be investigated about the meaning of its developments toward digital literacy and the broad landscape it covers.[32] This area remains a primary, distinctive, and qualifying activity of the library,[33] in particular to facilitate the use and evaluation of all information retrieval and discovery tools, and above all the evaluation of resources obtained through the searches, to guide each individual toward discovering the advantages of new research methods and systems. In the end, the aim is to instill critical thinking while dealing with results often too easily achieved.

[30] This direction is supported by the Lyon declaration, launched officially by IFLA in August 2014: The Lyon Declaration on Access to Information and Development. http://www.lyondeclaration.org.

[31] Cf.: Fagan, J.C. 2011. Discovery tools and information literacy. J. Web Librariansh. 5 (3), 171–178. https://www.tandfonline.com/doi/full/10.1080/19322909.2011.598332.

[32] To this point, cf.: Gilster, P. 1997. Digital Literacy. Wiley, New York. For further discussion, cf. Chapter 4 in this book.

[33] Cf., for instance: David Lankes, R. 2011. The Atlas of New Librarianship. MIT, Cambridge, pp. 72–77.

Finally, it is a matter of empowering people, even outside libraries, in the society of which they are part and make them conscious of the implicit critical issues and disadvantages of not well aware attitudes and behaviors while navigating the universe of information and, even more, of knowledge.[34]

1.3 Enduring values

Any issue related to change fundamentally requires a solid basis from which to start, even for revolutionary changes, and this basis cannot be constituted only by the negativity of the things to be changed, but must include above all of the things that deserve permanence, the "good" that has been gained and strengthened through years of experience, which must be maintained and even more strengthened, while pursuing change—leaving out things that are just an obstacle, and can only be eliminated.

Over time, Michael Gorman has raised the attention on then "enduring values," to be safeguarded while facing any change.[35] In an article published in 2015 on *JLIS.it*, the author summarizes the meaning of his latest book, in which lasting values in general and librarianship values are reviewed and reaffirmed in the light of today's experience.[36]

The values that Gorman deals with all benefit from the general technological innovations of today's society,[37] but in the context of the discourse on WSDS, it can be said that especially freedom of thought, rationalization of actions, literacy, learning, equal opportunities for access to information, democracy, and the common good are, more or less, positively affected by these innovations. This is because libraries and related services exist and interact fully in the context of society, and changes in

[34] Information literacy, intended for people as citizens, can be part of a general educational project in the line of the so-called "social" librarianship. On this point, cf.: Di Domenico, G., 2015. Un'identità plurale per la biblioteca pubblica. AIB Studi 55 (2), 235–246; Solimine, G., 2013. Nuovi appunti sulla interpretazione della biblioteca pubblica, AIB Studi, 53 (3), 261–271. https://aibstudi.aib.it/article/view/9132.

[35] The main essays on the topic are: Gorman, M., 2000. Our Enduring Values: Librarianship in the 21st Century. American Library Association, Chicago; *id.*, Our Enduring Values Revisited: Librarianship in an Ever-Changing World. American Library Association, Chicago, 2015.

[36] Gorman, M., 2015. Revisiting enduring values. JLIS.it. 6 (2), 13–33. https://www.jlis.it/article/view/10907.

[37] The values Gorman affirms are: stewardship, service, intellectual freedom, rationalism, literacy and learning, equity of access, privacy, and democracy as a common good.

technology, politics, and lifestyle are fully reflected in them. Given the many uncertainties of these evolutions, it is therefore necessary to define some permanent foundations, which can be discussed at length, but on which it is possible to base the development of the library profession and library science, as well as of the future service for society.

Gorman, however, argues that people are naturally inclined to find principles, ethical lines, beliefs, and values that not only frame a given conduct of existence but also allow them to face any kind of change with strength and optimism. In the same way, libraries, which are a microcosm of the world, and are involved in the stressful rapid change due to new technologies, economic-political events, new needs of people, need to realign their principles and values to face, understand and plan change in the best possible way.

It can be confirmed that the current situation of change is more radical and faster than those previously experienced by humanity and its own institutions, again due to the growing acceleration that the development of basic technologies for progress is having, at least since the years following the conquest of the Moon.[38]

If during the first 30 of these 50 years of development progress seemed to be governable, since 2000, its widespread and even democratic diffusion has instead strengthened the sense of global bewilderment, the need to "run" in every situation, as well as the need to find immediate solutions even if not well thought out.

Sharing Gorman's vision, the solution for libraries and librarianship is to plan and, as far as possible, drive change, based on a clear and conscious principle. The question remains how to evaluate the ideas and forecasts of innovation linked to society's expectations, starting with the most radical ones that envisage a rapid obsolescence and the end of libraries and related practices and theories. In this, it is first of all necessary to eliminate any degree of misunderstanding of the actual role of libraries. If many are led to think that the Web contains many more books than any library, in a way that they are easy to find, and many with immediate access, it is necessary to reiterate with the example of the right point that libraries are not just collections of books: essential places, and irreplaceable in the context of the Web, they are also the space, which has developed a functional and updated

[38] Luciano Floridi, referring to our era, has defined the concept of «hyperhistory»: Floridi, L., 2012. Hyperhistory and the philosophy of information policies. Philos. Technol. 25 (2), 129–131. https://link.springer.com/article/10.1007/s13347-012-0077-4.

bibliographic architecture, in which competent staff works. Together with a rich collection of resources, these library elements are the basis of any retrieval, research and discovery system, and also of guidance, as they are responsible for organizing the resources and data, which allow them to be found and recovered.[39]

Other values that Gorman discusses—to be kept in mind in the perspective of the WSDS—are the importance of the "human record" and "cultural heritage," as contents of the mediation that libraries have always had among their primary qualities. The objects in which human knowledge is recorded—more or less traditional documents or resources—are fundamental for learning, and their transmission is crucial for the progress and development of civilization; hence, the role they have always played libraries for management, organization, conservation, and dissemination can only be confirmed as one of the values to be kept central.

Human records and the tangible and intangible cultural heritage that they record interact continuously, so the role of libraries, but also of archives, museums, and other institutions, in the management and dissemination of records, also becomes crucial in the conservation and development of cultural heritage itself, of which records are a part, all the more so when the new technologies through which culture spreads are accepted and mastered. Mastering current information technologies also means, however, effectively understanding the meaning of what information is, not uncritically accepting the all-encompassing definitions spread through technologies, which would lead to the acceptance of every information object as part of the cultural heritage to be mediated, thus accepting a scale of values foreign to librarianship, which instead has always supported the convinced selection of the resources to be protected and promoted.[40]

Regarding the role of the library in the world of information, however, it is essential to understand that information itself is not the main value on which the library is founded, but the library virtues are founded on much more complex purposes than the simple preservation and dissemination of the library information as suggested by ICT. Communication technologies are only a tool to operate in the field of cultural progress, mediating objects of knowledge, but also fully playing the role of a cultural institution that

[39] Cf.: Gorman, M., Revisiting Enduring Values cit., p. 19–20.
[40] *Id.*, p. 21–24.

works to promote education, learning, social cohesion, access to knowledge, democracy, and other high human aspirations.

Therefore, among the values to be maintained, the concentration on the "contents" of the culture with which the library has to do can also be indicated, a value that goes far beyond the simple methods of communicating such contents, to the heart of the virtue of a cultural institute capable of making a society grow, growing with it. From this point of view, therefore, it is possible to deal with the change and development of new systems proposed by technologies, such as the WSDS, in a healthy way, to "also" play the role of mediation of information, but not forgetting that "beyond" the information research and mediation service, it is necessary to maintain a role of critical approach and guide to knowledge.

CHAPTER 2

The evolution of the search systems

2.1 The renewal of the OPACs (Online Public Access Catalog)

Still today, the catalog, as it is properly understood, is a very useful tool to access library resources, and to start to build one's knowledge around a topic through the research paths it makes possible. In this, however, libraries had to cope with the evolving concept of "owned resources" to be made available, by including what is not materially owned or acquired as a service, but also selected and mediated as a "document," as traditionally intended in the library context. Even more widely, this could include any "resource," provided it is accomplished and reliable. Therefore, the catalog is one of the tools available to the library, together with other newer and no less problematic ones, to be used to mediate a large and varied cultural heritage assets and their contextual knowledge. However, the catalog continues to maintain the dignity of the first and main tool to allow identification and access to documents,[1] that is, to allow you to find, identify, select, and obtain resources and navigate between them.[2] As such, the many ongoing discussions on the possibility of achieving fast, reliable, contextualized, and democratic access to knowledge resources start from the catalog and its history and theory.

A comprehensive framing of the topic is not quickly achieved either by resolving once again some aspects of the overall issue of ownership versus

[1] I would like here to remind to some often discussed classic works on the topic: Charles A. Cutter, *Rules for a printed dictionary catalogue*. Washington: Government printing office, 1876; Seymour Lubetzky, *Cataloging rules and principles: a critique of the A.L.A. rules for entry and a proposed design for their revision*. Washington: Library of Congress (1953); as well as the 91 rules of Antonio Panizzi published in: British museum. Department of printed books, *Catalogue of printed books in the British museum*. London, 1841.

[2] Similarly, it is necessary to refer again to FRBR, ICP e IFLA-LRM (Cf. previous notes).

Web-Scale Discovery Services
ISBN 978-0-323-90298-4
https://doi.org/10.1016/B978-0-323-90298-4.00005-7

access or by differentiating between either local or remote resources, which are, in any case, provided and suitable to be included in the catalog, or else online, volatile resources, which are preferably to be linked via the library website or gateway. Nor is it appropriate to try not to differentiate at all between the resources included in a specific catalog and those coming from various databases, repositories, e-journals, or from the entire Web. Several tools, as the so-called next-generation catalogs (NGCs),[3] have been designed to create a unified and univocal starting point for end users, as to guide them to perform searches and have access to resources that a library can validate as useful and relevant to the needs expressed by different types of people.[4]

Tracing back the history of libraries, their original aim was to mediate between the growing availability of recorded information and supports that record them and the specific needs of each person wishing to increase their knowledge. As the discussion widens, it is preferable to take into account "people" in general, of all the people toward whom the cultural action of mediation is directed, not simply of specific "users" of a given service or system. In fact, only at this level can the issue of the validity and usefulness of each cultural expression can be addressed again, despite the different types of resources and tools most suitable for the treatment of each of them.

Today, among the various systems whose actual purpose is the mediation of information and knowledge resources, those generally referred to as web-scale discovery services (WSDS), and specifically discovery tools, seem to be the tools on which, for various reasons, it is possible to base a specific theoretical and "uncertain" discourse, aimed at highlighting the pros of their valid and conscious development as library tools, and the cons of an uncritical acceptance as technologies that are especially worthy of being adopted just because of their wide diffusion.

An intermediate and wiser stance, which may also be dictated by the current state of WSDS technologies, is to argue that these tools must not

[3] Next-generation catalogs (NGCs) are often compared with broader Web-Scale Discovery Service tools, but there is no agreement on the adaptability of the definition, as the "grade" of NGCs should be lower, because they can be applied only to catalog databases and some institutional repositories. To this point, cf. Eric Lease Morgan, *Next generation library catalog*. 2007, http://infomotions.com/musings/ngc/.

[4] A summary of this development is offered in: Paul G. Weston; Salvatore Vassallo, *"... e il navigar m'è dolce in questo mare": linee di sviluppo e personalizzazione dei cataloghi*. In: *La biblioteca su misura: verso la personalizzazione del servizio*, a cura di Claudio Gamba, Maria Laura Trapletti. Milano: Bibliografica, 2007, p. 130–167: p. 146–163. More also in: Andrea Marchitelli; Giovanna Frigimelica, *OPAC*. Roma: AIB, 2012, p. 34–54.

necessarily aim to replace the OPAC and other specific "research" interfaces, but they can care for a more basic, or more general, level of "discovery" of information and resources. In addition, it must be clear that the discovery tools do not offer access to the entire Web in which the library must be integrated, but rather to what it has specifically selected and made available. Although thanks to the "democratic" simplicity of a generalist search engine, discovery tools operate within a "bounded" and "safe" universe: a broader "docuverse" as it is not limited to "documents" but extended to all kinds of resource—more or less within the "bibliographic" space[5]—and at the same time not extended to everything because it is validated by the authoritativeness that library institutions have always maintained.[6]

Operating within a quantitatively limited, but organized and known world, allows each information and resource mediation tool to be coherent, punctual, and reliable, even in the case of a broad and casual and serendipitous search, which can produce, nonetheless, the desired results.[7] This approach is in line with the principles and paradigms to which the development of such tools must belong, that is, the same underpinning bibliographic and library history, up to the current discussions in the field of Library and Information Science. In the same way, mediation tools can and must innovate their aspect and functionality accordingly, adopting user-friendly interfaces and web-scale structures, realizing in various ways the trend toward a "democracy of access," simplifying access, as well as by possibly creating a single access for resources of all kinds.

Returning to the OPACs, especially in the past 10 or 15 years, a series of considerations particularly in favor of the development of interfaces in line with Web 2.0 and the Semantic Web principles has often been voiced to support features such as maximal friendliness and usability, interactive and collaborative organization, interoperability, and granularity of information and data. The most enthusiastic stance among these opinions poses decisive

[5] For a clarification regarding the bibliographic space and the possibility of crossing its boundaries, cf. below at paragraph 3.3.

[6] That is, the space where Web-Scale Discovery Services play a role can be much wider than the universe of documents described long ago by Ted Nelson (Cf. Theodor Holm Nelson, *Literary machines*. Sausalito: Mindful, 1990), but not indefinitely merged into the Web of Data as already defined by Tim Berners-Lee (Cf. Tim Berners-Lee; Mark Fischetti, *Weaving the Web*. San Francisco: Harper, 1999). About these scholars, their relationships and the idea of docuverse, cf. Paola Castellucci, *Dall'ipertesto al Web: storia culturale dell'informatica*. Roma: Laterza, 2009.

[7] On this point, Carlo Revelli's idea of "oxymoron" referred to the "open shelving" that "offers the great possibility of a controlled serendipity" is worth a reading: Carlo Revelli, *Il catalogo*. Milano: Bibliografica, 2004, p. 451.

questions such as follows: How can a coherent idea of a catalog be maintained in a world of atomized and shared data? Will information retrieval systems be crumbled into a series of information discovery practices? Is the role of the library going to be still decisive for the mediation of resources?

The issues that emerged in the years between 2011 and 2015, when WSDS actually began to spread are still not completely resolved, at least not with the growing awareness that one would have expected after the first experimentation. Today, discovery tools are accepted as a factual reality, indispensable also because users "like" it and allow the search for everything "needed." Thus, in the changing world of the Web, a negative response to the defeatist perplexities regarding the role of librarianship principles is not yet to be taken for granted.

In some fairly recent columns, written by John Akeroyd, we wonder whether the time may have come when discovery tools are able to replace not only the OPAC and other search interfaces but also the entire library.[8] If the spirit of discovery has spread widely in everyday life as well as in academic circles, this does not mean that the resources to be discovered are adequately recovered from every tool used, which is why, despite the spread of generalist search engines, in library environments there has been a rapid shift toward more specialized web-scale systems. After the academic libraries, recently also the public ones have begun to approach the WSDS,[9] whose success is due to the simple—and usual—reason that such systems can be used with ease and immediacy, "like Google."[10] All this has led to an increasingly reduced use of specific library interfaces.

At the moment, anyway, this is not enough to replace specialized bibliographic systems, especially because the quality of the metadata that allow the management and retrieval of resources, and the role of the catalog and other tools maintained by libraries still seems to be under control. However, the need and implementation of new functions is growing in the fields of artificial intelligence, text mining, and semantic research. These fields are already imposing a radical change in the way of rendering library service. This situation often entails that users are diverted, through a sort of

[8] John Akeroyd, *Discovery systems: are they now the library?*, "Learned publishing," 30 (2017), n. 1, p. 87–89, https://onlinelibrary.wiley.com/doi/full/10.1002/leap.1085.

[9] Cf., for example, the project *Access to research*: http://www.accesstoresearch.org.uk/.

[10] Regarding the functions, and the specific "effects," of the search engines of the Google family and the like, cf.: John Battelle, *The search: how google and its rivals rewrote the rules of business and transformed our culture*. London: Brealey, 2005.

encroachment, to other nonlibrary sources, other platforms or publishers' sites, where they can redefine the search, or access the full text, unknowingly leaving the constitutive functions of library mediation, such as guidance in the choice of resources,[11] or the availability of access to them. All this without not only users but also librarians being able to understand these other tools and start a productive "collaboration" with them.[12]

In his columns, in fact, Akeroyd wonders if this is the reason why the WSDS have not already, "in fact, become the library," excluding only the role in metadating resources with quality data, which for contingent reasons remains exclusively a library function. The purpose of the development of the library service should certainly be to master the use of discovery tools and consequently provide people with the guide to use them, but as library tools, not substituting the richness of the library itself.

Libraries—and librarianship—must seriously consider issues like the one mentioned here. It is essential to know how to intervene in current research and discovery processes, follow the developments of the WSDS, and understand them, to be able to be valid advisors in the critical use of all the tools that a library can deliver to people. In the face of the new scenarios, it is also essential to care more about the production of metadata. This library role seems not to have been usurped yet. Moreover, the environments of the Semantic Web and linked data confirm with confidence that cultural institutions have always maintained it with competence. However, this role could progressively be reduced only to materials that are owned by a library.

Even more concern is expressed by William Breitbach in his report, which goes so far as to point to WSDS as a possible nightmare.[13] Starting

[11] To this point, I would like to draw the attention to an essay discussing the risks involved in the "selection" mechanism which is almost exclusively the preserve of specific algorithms connected to either commercial interests or anyway "unclean" aims: Paola Castellucci, *Formiche virtuali o virtuose? Verso un'etica dell'accesso*, "AIB studi," 57 (2017), n. 1, p. 51–62, https://aibstudi.aib.it/article/view/11555.

[12] The terms of this collaboration, essentially between human intelligence and "artificial intelligence," are rather indefinite and very delicate to define. To this end, some cues are given in a recent editorial written by the Italian scholar Alfredo Serrai, *Linguaggi, codici e informazione*, "Bibliothecae.it," 8 (2019), n. 1, p. 1–3, https://bibliothecae.unibo.it/article/view/9495/9283.

[13] William Breitbach, *Web-scale discovery: utopian dream or dystopian nightmare (or maybe something in between)?*, report submitted to the "California Academic & Research Libraries 2016 Conference," March 31–April 2, 2016, Costa Mesa, California, http://conf2016.carl-acrl.org/wp-content/uploads/2016/05/Breitbach-Web-scale-discovery-FINAL.pdf.

Figure 2.1 The "wheel of books" by Agostino Ramelli[16].

from the 16th-century "wheel of books" by Agostino Ramelli,[14] through the Memex created by Vannevar Bush,[15] following the history of discovery tools and the services implemented through them, he argues that we can identify a research path that had started almost 500 years before, as the fulfillment of the dream of making the various information media accessible with ease and from a single access point made over time. In a sort of ideal history of library automation, other objectives can be added to this, such as extracting a unique meaning from a complex whole, guiding the choice of resources, and so on (Fig. 2.1).

[14] Cf. the entry *Agostino Ramelli*, in *Wikipedia, the free enciclopedia*, https://en.wikipedia.org/wiki/Agostino_Ramelli.

[15] Vannevar Bush, *As we may think*, "The Atlantic monthly," 176 (1945), n. 1, p. 101–108.

[16] Illustration no. CLXXXVIII published in: Agostino Ramelli, *Le diverse et artificiose machine del capitano Agostino Ramelli dal Ponte della Tresia ingegniero del christianissimo re di Francia e di Pollonia*. Milano: Maestri, 1981 (ed. originale 1588).

But if we follow Aaron Tay, and his view that the WSDS, like any other technological tool, are subject to a development cycle that begins with a "peak of inflated expectations," we realize that after an initial enthusiasm reaching its peak around 2012,[18] a predictable path of disillusionment follows, until reaching a common process of using the tools.[19] At the moment, it is more useful to take into account the phase of disillusionment, in which discovery tools still seem far from the goal of representing a reliable platform for the search and discovery of information and knowledge.

One of the main reasons for Breitbach's disappointment is that the WSDS lack any means of contextualizing resources, which, on the contrary, is precisely one of the strengths of specialized databases and specific metadating. In the operations of mixing and normalization of data, necessarily following the creation of the single index of discovery tools, any descriptive specificity is mitigated and any disciplinary area is eliminated, thus waiving the boundaries between the different subjects and the appropriate treatment that the different resources may have[20]. The remedy, however, appears worse than the damage: the search interfaces offer a series of facets to guide a path through different categories and subcategories of topics, but the resources are forced into each category by the reindexing system itself, and the latter they are often too "crowded" with references. At this point, any search always returns a very large number of results, favoring "recall" rather than "precision." Many results are of little relevance to the actual user's needs. As a consequence, both, the user who already knows how to use specific search terms, and even more so the one who uses broader terms, would find better help from the system if the result would be less if not close to zero: this would push the researcher to better formulate his own strategy, or to seek advice.

The failure of these objectives, and of the utopian dream of the WSDS, is dryly treated by Breitbach with the conclusion that libraries could continue to deal with specialized databases, providing correct metadata, which, like the catalog, can also grant access to selected available resources, leaving the task

[17] V. Bush, *As we may think* cit., p. 107.

[18] This enthusiastic peak is confirmed by some literature reviews on discovery tools: Nadine P. Ellero, *Integration or disintegration: where is discovery headed?* "Journal of library metadata," 13 (2013), no. 4, p. 311–329, https://www.tandfonline.com/doi/full/10.1080/19386389.2013.831277; H. Richardson, *Revelations from the literature* cit.

[19] Aaron Tay, *Four possible web scale discovery future scenarios*, 2014, http://musingsaboutlibrarianship.blogspot.com/2014/12/four-possible-web-scale-discovery.html#.Vvrov-IrJpg.

[20] Cf. William Breitbach, *Web-scale discovery: a library of babel?* In: *Planning and implementing resource discovery tools in academic libraries* cit., p. 641–649.

of a wider range discovery, and the accessibility of every traceable resource, to general search engines, without having to force "mixed" systems to perform a function that does not belong to either of the two areas.[21]

Without having to get to the drastic rejection of a now clearly widespread reality, Breitbach's provocation demonstrates how necessary it is to further understand and deepen the knowledge about WSDS, to maximize their strengths, anticipate, and intervene to implement useful corrections to their innovations. The new systems are not to be totally rejected, because there is a clear difference between them and the generalist search engines. Furthermore, they can be employed in different areas of application, and there are various expectations expressed by people using different tools. However, it is necessary to avoid the risk that WSDS totally replace specialized databases, methodologies created to produce metadata, or, essentially, the library itself.

In any case, at least in recent years the point of view of the more or less provocative, more or less reflective writings related to WSDS has become more critical, more "investigative," and closer to the actual object on which to reflect, compared with articles written in the previous years, at the moment of the greatest enthusiasm.

In the years closest to the debut of discovery tools, the central question always appears to be the same, as shown, for example, by the columns on *Information today* written by Barbara Quint and entitled *Attacking our problems*: the first problem to be faced is still that of acknowldging and satisfying the concrete needs of users, "real people," far from sterile theory, to reaffirm the survival of libraries, librarians, and information professionals.[22] The point, rather, should be how much Web trends should be followed to survive with a part of the historical apparatus of rules and reputation of libraries, which fortunately "still has authority," and how much more effective, instead, it is to develop library theories and library methods historically established and carry out evolutions of the relative principles that will allow better living and managing the future of information.

The first attitude, however, is also confirmed in more reasoned and summarized essays, such as the one written by Hillary Richardson, who

[21] A similar experiment, on which I will return in this book, is described in: Simone Kortekaas, *Thinking the unthinkable: a library without a catalogue. Reconsidering the future of discovery tools for Utrecht University library*, paper presented to "LIBER 41st Annual Conference" (27–30 June 2012, Tartu, Estonia), http://www.uttv.ee/naita?id=12538.

[22] Barbara Quint, *Attacking our problems*, "Information today," 31 (2014), n. 2, p. 8.

draws the attention toward a specialist literature that seems to be animated mainly with practical concerns, motivated by emergencies, and with few reflections, split into different short articles or essays, which try to theorize the principles by which these impulses for transformation could be accepted within a scientific framework in LIS.[23]

The first general consideration, which the author draws from the literature examined, concerns the usual observation of the fact that an "Internet-like" search, through a single and simple interface, attracts users much more than the specialized research to be carried out on different and complex systems. Obviously, the problem must be posed as to how to welcome this impulse also in library systems without rejecting the coherence and specificity of the wealth of information tools they provide. However, this issue seems far from having been further addressed, and indeed, sometimes the tendency to give priority to Google-like systems over other search interfaces, including OPAC, prevails. Anyway, some changes, seem to point to the right direction. This is the case, for example, of the definition of new terms appropriate to the LIS vocabulary,[24] decisive for the development of a first theoretical framework; the influence on new professional best practices[25] and information literacy,[26] which tends to thoughtfully redefine practice; the development of an awareness, if not of a theoretical issue, about the need to critically welcome the new tools suggested by the Web, as a "starting point" to discover information and resources to be further explored with the more specific research services offered by the library.[27]

[23] H. Richardson, *Revelations from the literature* cit.

[24] Cf. Athena Hoeppner, *The ins and outs of evaluating Web-Scale Discovery Services*, "Computers in libraries," 32 (2012), no. 3, p. 6—10, http://www.infotoday.com/cilmag/apr12/Hoeppner-Web-Scale-Discovery-Services.shtml; cf. also Jason Vaughan, *Web scale discovery services.* Chicago: American library association, 2011 (also published in: "Library technology reports," 47 (2011), no.1).

[25] Ana Guthrie; Rhonda McCoy, *A glimpse at discovery tools within the HBCU library landscape*, "College & undergraduate libraries," 19 (2012), no. 2/4, p. 297—311, https://www.tandfonline.com/doi/full/10.1080/10691316.2012.693437.

[26] Beth Thomsett-Scott; Patricia E. Reese, *Academic libraries and discovery tools: a survey of the literature*, "College & undergraduate libraries," 19 (2012), no. 2/4, p. 123—143, https://www.tandfonline.com/doi/full/10.1080/10691316.2012.697009.

[27] Nancy Fawley; Nikki Krysak, *Information literacy opportunities within the discovery tool environment*, "College & undergraduate libraries," 19 (2012), no. 2/4, p. 207—214, https://www.tandfonline.com/doi/full/10.1080/10691316.2012.693439.

Reviewing the terms in which the question was posed in the period anticipating the debut of discovery tools,[28] the incitements to new ways of setting up catalogs such as Roy Tennant's *MARC must die*,[29] and Tim Burke, *Burn the catalog*[30], appear rather provocative. Positions of this kind can be misunderstood by those who approach this issue only from an implementation's point of view, that is, the development of new interfaces without a thorough reasoning on how to get there, without reflecting on the current evolution and development, of guidelines, methods, and principles created on the basis of specific historical, past situations. It is easier to put aside traditional criteria and methods by considering them just out-of-date, rather than picking up the question from the origins, realizing that these apparatuses were in turn the result of an attitude of innovation and adaptation to the times, and that now, with the same spirit, these can be adapted once again dynamically to the current paradigms.[31]

Again, other utterances by Tennant himself are very clear, such as *Lipstick on a pig*, or *Fixing library discovery*, where a valid point of view is exposed on the uselessness of external changes of the OPAC interfaces not supported by a profound redesign of the catalog itself.[32] In particular, with regard to "cosmetic" operations, assuming that one can approach the implementation of an interface similar to the one the user would prefer, one does not do his "good" anyway until he gets a hand on a "systematic" reorganization of the rules and methods for producing the data to which the interface activity must then be applied.

[28] Previously, among the pioneers who promoted one of the precursors of the expansion of the catalog Cf. William Gray Potter, *Expanding the online catalog*, "Information technology and libraries," 8 (1989), no. 2, p. 99–104, https://www.questia.com/library/journal/1G1-13823201/expanding-the-online-catalog. For the "debut" period, cf. Marshall Breeding, *The state of the art in library discovery 2010*, "Computers in libraries," 30 (2010), n. 1, p. 31–35, https://librarytechnology.org/repository/item.pl?id=14574.

[29] Roy Tennant, *MARC must die*, "Library journal," 127 (2002), no. 17, p. 26–27, https://www.libraryjournal.com/?detailStory=marc-must-die.

[30] Timothy Burke, *Burn the catalog*, 20 January 2004, http://www.swarthmore.edu/SocSci/tburke1/perma12004.html.

[31] This "dynamic" spirit can be found in the reflections of today's most attentive scholars and professionals, as Rachel Clarke, Karen Coyle, Carlo Bianchini and Mauro Guerrini; cf. the aforementioned conference FSR 2014.

[32] Roy Tennant, *Lipstick on a pig*, "Library journal," 130 (2005), no. 7, p. 34–37; *id.*, *Fixing library discovery*, "Library journal," 131 (2006), n. 11, p. 30–31.

The well-known and disputed report by Karen Calhoun prepared in 2006 for the Library of Congress is part of the same climate,[33] and so the previous University of California Bibliographic Services Report.[34] These studies indicate the lines of action to reform cataloging practices, review missions and objectives, welcome technological innovations, and digitize assets. Regarding the difficulty of using many catalogs, and their remoteness from the new habits of people accustomed to the Web, it is proposed to upgrade to simple and fast interfaces, which include spell check, search suggestions, indexes, abstracts and reviews, covers, and links to external pages. In this regard, concerning even more crucial issues about building catalogs, it is suggested, for example, to replace the subject matter with the use of keywords, to redefine the workflows with reference to a limited number of data that can also be produced automatically and on the basis of new standards, and to use managerial models to evaluate the use of resources, following the research habits of people in general rather than those of specialist users.

It is clear that the most "daring" theses attracted not only objections, coming from the more "conservative" circles, but also encouraged lucid and productive positions such as those of Thomas Mann,[35] just balanced by other more accomodating opinions.[36] In any case, if the aforementioned reports propose a new bibliographic librarian world, at the basis of any change, even revolutionary, there must always be a careful examination of the proposals, and a rigorous comparison between "old" and "new,"[37]

[33] K. Calhoun, *The changing nature of the catalog and its integration with other discovery tools* cit.

[34] The University of California libraries. Bibliographic services task force, *Rethinking how we provide bibliographic services for the University of California: final report*. Berkeley: University of California (2005), http://libraries.universityofcalifornia.edu/groups/files/bstf/docs/Final.pdf.

[35] Thomas Mann, *Il catalogo e gli altri strumenti di ricerca: un punto di vista dalla Library of Congress*, "Bollettino AIB," 46 (2006), no. 3, p. 186–206, https://bollettino.aib.it/article/view/5154. Cf. also the original English text of Mann's "critical review" to Calhoun's report: http://www.guild2910.org/AFSCMECalhounReview.pdf, and the following essay: *id.*, *What is going on at the Library of* Congress?, 2006, http://www.guild2910.org/AFSCMEWhatIsGoingOn.pdf.

[36] Deanna B. Marcum, *The future of cataloging*, "Library resources & technical services," 50 (2006), no. 1, p. 5–9, https://www.questia.com/library/journal/1G1-141577373/the-future-of-cataloging.

[37] Among the essays underpinning this discussion, even if an almost opposite nature, cf., for example: International Federation of Library Associations and Institutions, *Guidelines for online public access catalogue (OPAC) displays: final report*. München: Saur, 2005; Christopher Harris, *Catalog manifesto*, "Infomancy," June 14, 2007, http://schoolof.info/infomancy/?p=388.

above all to evaluate the specific impact that the various changes in the current reality, not only at technological, but also at social and economic level, will have on libraries.[38] Furthermore, the surveys carried out at that time on people's information searching strategies performed through the new Web tools should be taken into consideration,[39] as well as the type of tool that could be made available by libraries[40], to favor the more "hasty" and more "social" needs of many people while preserving the principles of accuracy required by other specialist users and librarians.

A balanced position is the one expressed by John Byrum Jr. at the 2005 IFLA Congress in Oslo.[41] Starting again from the new expectations of access to information not met by the "traditional" bibliographic library systems, Byrum turns to national bibliographic agencies, to entrust them with the task of achieving two important objectives, in dialogue with information professionals, system users, and developers: to ensure access to very broad content, and implement a new generation of OPACs with powerful features inspired by "Web search engine standards and online libraries." Although ISBD and MARC have been models and standards of great value in innovating the

[38] The point about this general situation is also presented in *IFLA trend report: Riding the waves or caught in the tide?*, 2013 http://trends.ifla.org/insights-document.

[39] Among these: Online Computer Library Center, *Perceptions of libraries, 2010: context and community. A report to the OCLC membership*. Dublin: OCLC, 2011, http://oclc.org/reports/2010perceptions.en.html; *id.*, *Perceptions of libraries and information resources: a report to the OCLC membership*. Dublin: OCLC, 2005, http://oclc.org/reports/2005perceptions.en.html.

[40] About this: University College London, *Information behaviour of the researcher of the future*. London: University College, 2008, http://www.jisc.ac.uk/media/documents/programmes/reppres/gg_final_keynote_11012008.pdf; Karen Calhoun [et al.], *Online catalogs: what users and librarians want*. Dublin: OCLC, 2009, http://www.oclc.org/content/dam/oclc/reports/onlinecatalogs/fullreport.pdf; Kathryn Zickuhr [et al.], *Library services in the digital age*. Washington: Pew Internet & American life project, 2013, http://libraries.pewinternet.org/2013/01/22/library-services.

[41] John D. Byrum, *Raccomandazioni per miglioramenti urgenti dell'OPAC: il ruolo delle agenzie bibliografiche nazionali*, "Biblioteche oggi," 23 (2005), no. 10, p. 5–14, http://www.bibliotecheoggi.it/2005/20051000501.pdf. The article is the translation of the original report: *id.*, *Recommendations for urgently needed improvement of OPAC and the role of the National bibliographic agency in achieving it*, presented at the "71st IFLA General conference and council" (Oslo, 14–18 agosto 2005) http://www.ifla.org/IV/ifla71/papers/124e-Byrum.pdf.

production and exchange of catalog descriptions, they no longer correspond to the needs expressed in the dissemination of data on the network.

The experience of the Bibliographic Enrichment Advisory Team (BEAT),[42] established by the Library of Congress in 1992, demonstrated how bibliographic records can be "enriched" with a series of data, information, and resources already freely available on the Web, simply by connecting them to bibliographic descriptions via links displayed in special interfaces. The OPACs, thus, expand, including the table of contents (TOC), which allow the user to better determine the content of the resources, as well as allowing a more precise search, if integrated into the fields of the records, as they are practically composed of keyword. Another extension is to link, or to integrate in the records, the reviews or extracts contained, for example, in the sites of the publishers.[43] Not to mention the links that can be established with the full text of the digital editions, as with the images accompanying the texts or simply those of the covers.

In addition to the expansion of content, the new generation of OPACs must be equipped with web-scale functionality. Referring to the "IFLA Cataloging Code, under development," Byrum lists the five fundamental functions of the catalog—search, identify, select, obtain, and navigate—warning that the traditional OPAC can no longer perform them satisfactorily in relationship to the increase in digital resources, especially with regard to "obtaining" and "navigating." Thus, around 2000, "federated search engines" were developed, which, in part imitating the method of web search engines, can connect the user, from a single query point, with all the resources that the library has decided to indicate and mediate through the catalog and through other databases, repositories, e-journals, open archives, websites, and so ob. In addition to being integrated into this system, the OPAC will have to offer a number of other possibilities that "apply a mental model typical of Web search engines to the library catalog"[44]: suggestions, error correction, menu proposal, browsing options and faceted grouping, relevance orders, graphical representations of results, recommendation options, and natural language search.

[42] Website of the Bibliographic Enrichment Advisory Team: http://www.loc.gov/catdir/beat.

[43] To this, you can add some social websites dedicated to books, and also Google's cultural projects Web pages.

[44] Byrum cites widely from: Holly Yu; Margo Young, *The impact of Web search engines on subject searching in OPAC*, "Information technology and libraries," 23 (2004), no. 4, p. 168–181, https://ejournals.bc.edu/index.php/ital/article/view/9658.

Indications on the key points for the renewal of the OPACs are also suggested by Giovanni Bergamin in a summary written in response to some provocations[45] from the Web to highlight the shortcomings of OPACs in the face of the ease and efficiency of search engines in everyday life.[46] Just as it is certain that new technologies can improve the service of OPACs to people, one must not exaggerate in "purism" with respect to the bibliographic record, accepting even profound reformulations of cataloging methodologies precisely to avoid a "ridiculous" disconnect[47] between the "reform" of the interface and that of the data to which it applies.

The three novelties of the interface that deserve careful consideration, therefore, are indicated as: the dynamic grouping of the results, or faceted browsing, or filter, which allows to establish an organic "point of view" to those who are still defining a research idea, based on quality data entered in the record fields; suggestions regarding the search terms typed, indications such as "maybe you were looking for" by Google, which can be so useful when they are not intrusive and the more they are based on thesauri; ordering of results based on relevance, or relevance ranking, in which technology can collaborate in a "transparent" way with careful preparation of metadata.

2.2 Search, interaction, and discovery scenarios

Many of the objectives identified during the development of catalogs, OPACs, and other information mediation tools have always been among the constitutive purposes of librarianship paradigms. It is easily observed that behind a careful and conscious development of these elements, there may well be the exaltation of the classical principles of library work, as well as of bibliographic work, which "agreeing" with technologies find the direction to best apply themselves to today's reality and the transformations of society.

[45] Giovanni Bergamin, *OPAC: migliorare l'esperienza degli utenti*, "Bibliotime," 11 (2008), no. 1, http://www.aib.it/aib/sezioni/emr/bibtime/num-xi-1/bergamino.htm.

[46] Cf., for example, the video *The OPAC sucks*, available on Youtube: http://www.youtube.com/watch?v=tJD-safYEb0. In comparison, cf. Karen G. Schneider, *How OPACs suck, part 2: the checklist of shame*, "ALA TechSource," April 3, 2006, http://www.alatechsource.org/blog/2006/04/how-opacs-suck-part-2-the-checklist-of-shame.html.

[47] The reference is taken from: R. Tennant, *Lipstick on a pig* cit.

Much could be added, of course, on the characteristics of the new mediation systems of information and resources, and the arguments that support their validity, much could be added, of course, and the picture would never be complete. At least, among the reflections of the beginnings, noteworthy are reviews with programmatic titles such as *Defrosting the digital library*, which express the need to revamp scientific biomedical digital libraries and make them more friendly and interactive through specific Web-based applications,[48] and more general recapitulations such as *The state of the art in library discovery 2010*[49] that, like others[50], explains the new tools and compares different approaches to setting up WSDS.

Further expanding the perspectives, it is also possible to evaluate the first arguments regarding the social networks OPAC, or SOPAC, which represent a season not yet concluded, and sometimes enriched with new intentions. Social OPACs are defined in this way because they are developed based on the comparison with social networks and social cataloging applications,[51] enriching them with functions usually used in everyday life by the network communities, to be even closer to the habits and needs of the new user communities.[52] The OPAC can thus reveal another vocation, together with the entire library, that of aggregator of a community—either of citizens or other people. The aim is to call users to participate in the enrichment of the catalog, without distorting it, adding open and flexible tools to the rigorous professional structure, to allow users to also be creators of part of the content. Thus, quality information can coexist, controlled and

[48] Duncan Hull [et al.], *Defrosting the digital library: bibliographic tools for the next generation Web*, "PLoS computational biology," 4 (2008), no. 10, http://www.ploscompbiol.org/article/info%3Adoi%2F10.1371%2Fjournal.pcbi.1000204.

[49] M. Breeding, *The state of the art in library discovery 2010* cit.

[50] Cf., for example, the essays contained in: *Discovery tools: the next generation of library research*, "College & undergraduate library,—" 19 (2012), no. 2/4. Si veda anche: K. B. Moore; C. Greene, *Choosing discovery* cit.

[51] Among the first experiments: Library thing: http://www.librarything.com; Anobii: http://www.anobii.com; Goodreads: https://www.goodreads.com.

[52] For a reconnaissance of the topic, cf.: Andrea Marchitelli; Tessa Piazzini, *OPAC, SOPAC e social networking: cataloghi di biblioteca 2.0?*, "Biblioteche oggi," 26 (2008), no. 2, p. 82–92, http://www.bibliotecheoggi.it/2008/20080208201.pdf; cf. also: Cristina Bambini; Tatiana Wakefield, *La biblioteca diventa social*. Milano: Bibliografica, 2014.

guaranteed by the catalogers' experience, and information created by users, free but verifiable, shareable together with catalographic descriptions.[53]

Comments, reviews, folksonomies, and tags, autonomously produced by users and then entered directly in the appropriate fields suggested by the OPAC or linked from external sites, enrich catalog records through a new communicative dimension that responds to multiple cognitive needs, and which is added to descriptions and classifications that are reliable, but complicated and not really "open."[54] Community members who use library resources can endow them with a new "expressiveness," in addition to that of the catalog record, and by doing this they serve the community itself, whether a scientific or civic one, adding features such as virtual shelf organization, tagging and simplified classification services, review, evaluation, and suggestion, each interacting with the catalog and, through the catalog, mutually.[55] The activities performed by users visiting the OPAC are technically controllable by the library that holds even elementary advice on the use of resources, on studying or reading, it is preferable that the library plays the mediator's role, rather than commercial sites or sites managed at random or in an opaque way.

In the line of today's development of the WSDS, relevant is the next issue to be addressed, that is, the usefulness of such systems for public libraries, given that academic libraries, although pioneering partners, are not

[53] To explore the topic of this coexistence, cf.: Marieke Guy; Emma Tonkin, *Folksonomies tidying up tags?* "D-Lib magazine," 12 (2006), no. 1, http://www.dlib.org/dlib/january06/guy/01guy.html; Brian Matthews [et al.], *An evaluation of enhancing social tagging with a knowledge organization system*, "Aslib proceedings," 62 (2010), no. 4/5, p. 447–465, https://www.emerald.com/insight/content/doi/10.1108/00012531011074690/full/html; Sharon Q. Yang, *Tagging for subject access*, "Computers in libraries," 32 (2012), no. 9, p. 19–23, https://www.questia.com/magazine/1P3-2816646581/tagging-for-subject-access; Sachin Katagi; Bhakti Gala, *Social tags of select books written by Mahatma Gandhi: a comparative study of Library Thing tags and OCLC Fast Subject Headings*, "DESIDOC Journal of Library & Information Technology," 40 (2020), no. 1, p. 34–39, https://publications.drdo.gov.in/ojs/index.php/djlit/article/view/15138.

[54] Regarding the need for a great opening toward simple and interactive communication with users, cf. also: Online Computer Library Center, *Sharing, privacy and trust in our networked world: a report to the OCLC membership*. Dublin: OCLC, 2007, https://eric.ed.gov/?id=ED532599.

[55] To embrace a view of "participatory" librarianship, cf. R. David Lankes [et al.], *Participatory networks: the library as conversation*, "Information research,"– 12 (2007), n. 4, http://www.informationr.net/ir/12-4/colis/colis05.html.

necessarily the single perspective for these services, which tend to widen their scope. An experience of this kind can involve a public library even simply starting from the establishment of a consortium with an academic library, which allows both to optimize their efforts and to improve services, sharing a tool that can meet the needs both of common people, as well as students and researchers. A clarifying example can be that of the Library Consortium of Vigo County, which has structured a technological and communicative collaboration between libraries with diverse missions and objectives.[56]

Beyond "enthusiastic" and popular arguments, also more technical visions on the general issue of research and discovery of information have emerged, some of which compare the possibilities offered by new technological models within old organizational paradigms.[57] The necessary changes, and the line of changes, must be evaluated through an objective consideration of the social and economic changes that characterize today's society, and that mutually impact on the developments in ICT.[58] In the field of information and knowledge, new tools and methods of creation, recording, dissemination, research, and use have been adopted for some time, converging toward digital and multimedia, in a perspective centered on the general type of "resource" and on the network. To this library, models cannot fail to respond, by "decentralizing," in terms of data openness, interoperability and integration, usability, friendliness, and sharing. Anyway, they would serve as gatekeepers for data reliability, scalability, and sustainability.

With regard to the convergence of knowledge resources toward digital and multimedia, now an irreplaceable reality in the world of information, it

[56] Tim Gritten; Alberta Comer, *Venturing across the borders: collaborating on a new discovery system between academic and public libraries*, presented at the "IFLA WLIC 2017. Libraries, solidarity, society. Section S10, Satellite Meeting: Reference and Information Services and Information Technology Sections," http://library.ifla.org/id/eprint/1813.

[57] First of all, cf. Valdo Pasqui, *Evoluzione dei sistemi di gestione bibliotecaria tra vecchi e nuovi paradigmi*, "Bollettino AIB," 49 (2009), no. 3, p. 289–306, https://bollettino.aib.it/article/view/5455.

[58] Cf., for example: Lorcan Dempsey, *Always on: libraries in a world of permanent connectivity*, "First Monday,–" 14 (2009), no. 1/5, http://firstmonday.org/article/view/2291/2070. Cf. also: *IFLA trend report: Riding the waves or caught in the tide?* cit.

can be noted that precisely this technological development recovers and confirms the role of libraries as a place where convergence can take place fully and can be well managed[59]. Libraries have always been open to innovations and the management of the development of various information media, always attentive to proposed innovations and looking for the best way to develop their mission by adapting it to the era in which they operate. In an era of converging resources, where the digital structure and the multimedia form become characteristics shared by every kind of information resource, and where also basic distinctions fade away, such as those between text and image, or between paper and magnetic support, every opportunity may be good to reiterate the need for mediation as a relevant activity of differentiation, selection, and choice among everything that "flows" in the digital data flows.

Given these views, libraries can "reposition themselves" in the new information scenario at their ease by rediscussing the form and function of their main mediation tools, and related services, also enriching themselves with new coherent methodologies, as has always been the case, meeting the needs for information and knowledge of the society in which they interactively operate and grow.[60] Indeed, the study of people's research behavior, assimilated to daily iterative cognitive processes, can inspire the new ways of organizing and mediating OPACs.[61] In this way, it is possible to facilitate more spontaneous forms of research, interaction, navigation, browsing, and discovery of information, without the risk of uncritically pursuing new "ways" instinctively developed on the Web, and without betraying what should be the basic library principles, but instead being based on conceptual models such as, for example, FRBR for some time.[62]

[59] Cf. Rosa Maiello, *Le biblioteche per la convergenza digitale*, "Biblioteche oggi," 53 (2017), no. 4, p. 22–29. Cf. also Giovanni Solimine, *La biblioteca: scenari, culture, pratiche di servizio*. Roma: Laterza, 2004, p. 6–11.

[60] About this topic, cf. Giovanni Solimine, *Verso una biblioteconomia 2.0?*, "Bollettino AIB," 47 (2007), no. 4, p. 433–434, https://bollettino.aib.it/article/view/5250.

[61] A classical example is reported in: Marcia J. Bates, *The design of browsing and berrypicking techniques for the online search interface*, "Online review," 13 (1989), no. 5, p. 407–424, https://www.emerald.com/insight/content/doi/10.1108/eb024320/full/html.

[62] Cf. Antonella Iacono, *Opac, utenti, rete. Prospettive di sviluppo dei cataloghi elettronici*, "Bollettino AIB," 50 (2010), no. 1/2, p. 69–88: p. 75–81, https://bollettino.aib.it/article/view/5295.

Through a "safe" evolution, library mediation tools such as those of similar or allied institutions will be able to effectively place themselves in the context of Web 2.0 and the Semantic Web, and maintain the authoritative position they have always had in society; indeed, they will be able to contribute to the new web with the undisputed authority of bibliographic data and information issued by librarians.

Obviously, at the time of the first widespread diffusion of discovery tools, there were not only more or less enthusiastic acceptances but also reasoned and critical opposing proposals, which discussed the very nature of WSDS, suggesting alternatives that originated from different considerations about the principles upon which library mediation services should be based.

An experience showing contradictory aspects, but nonetheless usefully provocative, is that of the Utrecht University Library,[63] whose managers argue that the library can certainly do without a discovery tool, as well as a catalog, focusing all its efforts on the service of making available both paper and electronic resources. Given that other actors are able to produce good information search services, it is better not to invest in the implementation of your own system, letting the data be traced with other tools and ensuring, instead, that the discovered resource is actually accessible at the library.[64]

The principle underlying this way of seeing the library service is to evaluate the "discovery" and "delivery" of resources separately, focusing only on delivery only, and collaborating with other libraries, publishers, and service providers, to provide a truly extensive discovery service. Thus, after having collaboratively defined who the best suppliers of the research and discovery service are, always collaboratively, each library will be able to make available their share of actually accessible resources.

Since 2002, alongside the catalog of printed materials, the library of the University of Utrecht has also made available a first discovery system for the search for articles published in electronic journals called Omega. The diffusion of the discovery tools of the big producers then overshadowed the value of this pioneering tool, but it was above all the realization that users

[63] Utrecht University Library: https://www.uu.nl/en/university-library.

[64] Simone Kortekaas; Bianca Kramer, *Thinking the unthinkable: doing away with the library catalogue*, "Insights," 27 (2014), no. 3, p. 244–248 https://insights.uksg.org/articles/10.1629/2048-7754.174/. Cf. also: S. Kortekaas, *Thinking the unthinkable: a library without a catalogue* cit.

reached the magazines purchased by the university through even larger search engines, such as Google Scholar, to push to reconsider the issue from another perspective. Access statistics showed the library that while the use of the Omega catalog and discovery tool remained stable, access to licensed e-journals increased significantly, almost certainly through access from either network search engines or special and general databases purchased by the University.

The issue has long been well known in international studies: users, students, and scholars tend to move further and further away from library catalogs and search systems, preferring web search engines or specialized databases, and return to the library only for obtaining final access to their purchased (and accessible) resources.[65] This fact, stigmatized by many as an absolutely negative one, is to be solved by letting users walk again into the library thanks to customized WSDS. At Utrecht University, this has become a positive factor, to be exploited through organized collaboration. If this is the reality, and users seem to have an advantage from this system, and if large commercial companies regularly invest in providing freely accessible discovery services harvesting a lot of scientific information, there is no reason why libraries must invest specifically in librarian-like discovery tools, striving to operate in an area where someone already works "better."

The decisions of the Utrecht University Library have been very firm: to abandon its Omega discovery tool, not replacing it with any other library discovery tool, and to focus primarily on purchasing the resources that users can discover elsewhere but would request later from the library. Initially, it was decided to keep the OPAC working only because there was not yet a valid alternative. The surveys and questionnaires carried out to test the new service practice gave positive results, thus encouraging them to continue in that direction, but taking care to support users in better conducting their research activities.

This emergence of the need to support user searches is a classic principle of the spirit of library service, along with the principle of procuring the final resources that people actually need. On this basis,

[65] About this: Cathy De Rosa [et al.], *Perceptions of libraries, 2010: context and community*. Dublin: OCLC, 2011, https://www.oclc.org/research/publications/2010/2010perceptions.html; Christine Wolff-Eisenberg [et al.], *US faculty survey 2015*. Ithaka S+R, 2016, https://sr.ithaka.org/publications/ithaka-sr-us-faculty-survey-2015/.

combining more innovative principles, such as that of collaboration also with web search engines, in Utrecht it was decided to reform the entire service of the university library, reorganizing the homepage and the guidelines on how to use library services, providing support for the choice of general and thematic network discovery services, as well as for the choice of specialized databases purchased by the University. The OPAC was also later decommissioned, and the Utrecht University Library began to use WorldCat as a means of accessing the collections, as the holdings are harvested and maintained through participation in the Dutch national catalog.

In this perspective, as it can be inferred from the type of service currently provided by the aforementioned library, the issue remains essentially a question of either implementing collaborative Web-scale search services, or those created for wider purposes than library use, rather than not using them at all. Therefore, it is a matter of getting rid of the "local" WSDS, including OPAC, which could be seen as a contradiction in terms, after all.

Even the Utrecht University Library on the one hand declared that the OPAC is "dead," on the other hand, this institution clearly stated the importance of including holdings in the national catalog and in WorldCat. Even without an own discovery tool, this library can still provide users a whole series of regularly purchased web directories and proprietary databases through which they can access to bibliographic information. Therefore, it is always necessary to participate in a discovery system, even if just as a supplier of resources and not of bibliographic information.

By not developing a local discovery tool, a library can put more energy into providing resources rather than spending time to report resources that users do not actually have access to. This principle, which does not question the need for very broad WSDS in which each institution can participate by making its content available, ends up strengthening another general principle, the one concerning the usefulness of web-scale services, if correctly implemented. It can certainly be a good choice for smaller institutions—and not just for them—and it coherently navigates in the direction in which the WSDS are an important resource for society, to

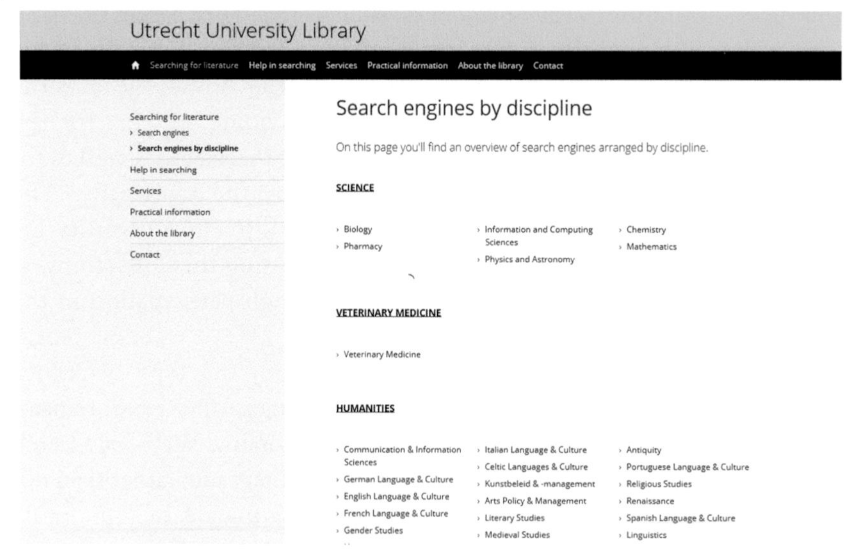

Figure 2.2 A webpage of the Utrecht University Library[66].

which every cultural institution can provide its own contribution, at their best (Fig. 2.2).

2.3 The technologies of discovery systems

The world of WSDS and discovery tools begins beyond the different types of OPACs that evolved toward the Web; beyond the federated search systems, or metasearch—which were the first to integrate the search in the catalog with that in other databases, and beyond the NGCs.[67] A characteristic of these tools is the creation of a "single index" of the data and metadata of the resources selected and made available by the library. The index is efficiently used by a single interface, with good characteristics of simplicity and friendliness, and allows the widest searches among the

[66] https://www.uu.nl/en/university-library/searching-for-literature/search-engines-by-discipline.

[67] An extensive bibliography on the subject can be found in: *Discovery tools, a bibliography*, edited by François Renaville, https://discoverytoolsbibliography.wordpress.com/.

resources of different databases to be carried out in a single solution, and, consequently a single list of results is.[68]

Regarding the debate on the key elements of discovery tools, the arguments have not changed in substance, and the expositions of a few years ago contemporary with the development of the new tools are still valid to present them[69]. In particular, an article by Judy Luther and Maureen Kelly synthesize accurately the characteristics of these systems.[70] The prerequisites are defined in a balanced way from the beginning—at least from the point of view of implementation—assuming that the goal of the renewal of the search systems is to offer the simplicity of tools such as Google, "that the user expects," to search in the library's rich digital and analog collection, "that the user needs." The new system is modeled on a "Google-style" approach, with a module for building a single index of all resources, in which to search homogeneously instead of searching each database separately. If Google builds, however, a generic index of the most diverse contents of the Web, the discovery tools constitute their own index based on the resources for which the library provides access.

In practice, this is only partially true, given that the list of databases in which the system searches is always compiled by default by the producers, and a library does not always choose to deselect all databases that have not actually been acquired. The best reason given for this nonselection is that of a "bibliographic" nature, so the discovery tool is not denied the ability to trace the metadata of resources that are not immediately accessible, which can otherwise be recovered once their existence is known. In any case, the selection made by system manufacturers is always extremely limited—for

[68] For an introduction to the innovative features and the importance—beyond the limits of "coverage"—of the single index of data present in the various databases of a library, consult: C. Bianchini, *Dagli OPAC ai library linked data* cit., p. 307—308; A. Marchitelli; G. Frigimelica, *OPAC* cit., p. 51—54.

[69] Cf., for example, the comparison of the main discovery tools in: J. Vaughan, *Web scale discovery services* cit. Cf. also: Sharon Q. Yang; Kurt Wagner, *Evaluating and comparing discovery tools: how close are we toward next generation catalog?* "Library Hi Tech," 28 (2010), no. 4, p. 690—709, https://www.emerald.com/insight/content/doi/10.1108/07378831011096312/full/html; F. William Chickering; Sharon Q. Yang, *Evaluation and comparison of discovery tools: an update*, "Information technology and libraries," 33 (2014), no. 2, p. 5—30, https://ejournals.bc.edu/index.php/ital/article/view/3471. More in-depth studies are in: *Planning and implementing resource discovery tools in academic libraries* cit.

[70] J. Luther; M. C. Kelly, *The next generation of discovery* cit.

better or for worse—compared with the unlimited scope in which generalist engines look for.

Luther and Kelly, quoting Paul Saffo,[71] recall that, with the current exponential increase in available information, the main objective of library-type search systems is even more to ensure the right balance between precision and recall. Thus, if many people use generalist search engines for their simplicity and for the large number of resources they are able to discover, they must still turn to specific systems if they want to find the information suitable to meet higher needs, hidden to Google, inaccessible even to Google Scholar, which can be considered just a "starting point" for academic research. In the library, therefore, although until recently users had to complete searches with different tools, with discovery tools they can now have a single and simple tool, with great recall capacity, but of quality validated by the institution that has selected its application space, or collaborated with the producers to this end.[72]

Therefore, the new discovery systems make available the wide potential of a unified index together with the quality of the outputs, but much of their effectiveness depends on how much commitment a library can invest to implement them, and to define their "boundaries" of application, depending on its mission and community of users.

Among the main factors to be taken into account for the proper functioning of discovery tools, there is the complex issue of content coverage. The issue of the limited coverage of the number of indexed databases opposes the issue of the size of the list of databases that the systems propose as default. Each producer indexes the data of all the licensed databases, but this list hardly coincides with that of a library that adopts the system, thus producing a positive or negative difference in the number of databases actually covered. The biggest problem occurs when databases will show up which the library has acquired but are not searchable in its discovery system.

Meanwhile, it is expected that the various publishers will be more and more willing to provide the producers of discovery tools with the license to index the contents they publish, to be included in the single index together with the data of the local contents of the library, recovered through data

[71] Paul Saffo, *It's the context, stupid*, "Wired," 2 (1994), no. 3, p. 74–75, https://www.wired.com/1994/03/context-2/.

[72] Cf. B.Thomsett-Scott; P. E. Reese, *Academic libraries and discovery tools* cit., for further discussion.

harvesting of the metadata of institutional repositories and catalog records. In the same way, however, the problem of the extent of coverage depends on the decisions of the library regarding the "expectations" that the tool itself creates: that is, whether the library offers it as a single interface, especially with a single search box, enabled to operate on what is available, or if it indicates the role of the discovery tool as limited to being a "starting" tool for a more generic search, which can then be further investigated with other specific tools reported separately in the library portal or through the discovery tool itself, also indicating what is not searchable with the single interface method.

Presenting discovery tools as "basic" tools, for launching a general or transversal exploratory research, which must then be relaunched on more specific tools or individual databases, is a fairly balanced, and fairly recent trend.[73] It is not just about defending "integralist" or traditionalist positions, and many experiences demonstrate the usefulness of not having given up on specialized databases while setting up advanced searches with these tools. Moreover, the alternative proposed by the single search interfaces is not yet equipped with tools that allow to avoid dispersion, and to calibrate the search as well as the "old" databases used to do.

With regard to the immediate welcome that discovery tools have received from people, the reason is probably that these systems generally allow the increase in the use of the resources made available by the library, both when using desktop as well as mobile devices, thus attracting again those who would tend to prefer generalist search engines.[74] Depending on their level of specialization, or the area of research, different users may prefer a wider discovery through the unified search of the various resources, or rather concentrate on specific databases, in any case with the possibility of choosing different "levels" of use of the library, including the level for "novices." The simplicity of search and navigation of the more general tool, moreover, allows librarians themselves to spend less time in the basic instruction of people to use the system, and to deepen, instead,

[73] Cf., for example: N. Fawley; N. Krysak, *Information literacy opportunities within the discovery tool environment* cit.

[74] About this: Doug Way, *The impact of web-scale discovery on the use of a library collection*, "Serials review," 36 (2010), no. 4, p. 214–220, https://www.sciencedirect.com/science/article/pii/S0098791310000882; Lucy Holman, *Millennial students' mental models of search: implications for academic librarians and database developers*, "The journal of academic librarianship," 37 (2011), no. 1, p. 19–27 https://www.sciencedirect.com/science/article/pii/S0099133310002545.

their education in the critical evaluation of the results extracted from the query, which equally applies to textual, visual, audio, and audiovisual contents.[75]

Among the various essays that discuss the need for discovery tools, some substantially anticipate and reveal how the impulse to change is the result, once again, of the pursuit of ICT developments, rather than of reasoning within the LIS—such as already happened about 70 years ago for databases: the systems are fully developed in the information technology sector and must then be "imported" and adapted into the library and information fields. The first steps, in fact, have been taken in the footsteps of innovation and simplification traced either by Google, other search engines, Internet bookshops, or various Web communication tools.[76] The primary aspect of a search service is the reflection of the retrieval capacity in which these engines excel, to which it is necessary to add the implementation of a more accurate ordering of the results and possibly analyze them with other specialized tools.[77]

In this regard, a significant view is represented by Jody Fagan's editorial, who attempts to dispel some "myths" immediately generated about discovery tools as "prodigious" tools for the discovery of the universe of information and knowledge resources.[78] Among these myths, above all, the idea that it is possible to carry out an all-encompassing query, from a single simple search box, on everything the library makes available in its various channels, has to be finally dispelled. Similarly, we must abandon the feeling that discovery tools aim to compete with Google and perhaps replace it, or chase away the belief that no instruction is required in the use of interfaces. Furthermore, the idea that these tools are useful only for general users must be refuted, as well as the opposite opinion of its uselessness for users who are

[75] Regarding this important development of information literacy, cf.: J. Condit Fagan, *Discovery tools and information literacy* cit.

[76] Cf. Ed Tallent, *iPods in the sauna or kids these days ...*, "Internet reference services quarterly," 16 (2011), no. 3, p. 83–89, https://www.tandfonline.com/doi/full/10.1080/10875301.2011.602602.

[77] Cf. Rebecca Donlan; Anna Carlin, *A sheep in wolf's clothing: discovery tools and the OPAC*, "The reference librarian," 48 (2007), no. 2, p. 67–71, https://www.tandfonline.com/doi/abs/10.1300/J120v48n02_10.

[78] Jody Condit Fagan, *Top 10 discovery tool myths*, "Journal of web librarianship," 6 (2012), no. 1, p. 1–4, https://www.tandfonline.com/doi/full/10.1080/19322909.2012.651417?scroll=top&needAccess=true.

skilled at searching in specific databases. Undoubtedly, it will be still not easy to replace the specialized databases.

Among the open questions, one still regards the "brand" problem of the single index, which can create various difficulties for the unique organization of the WSDS. The problem arises from the fact that the main discovery tools are now created and made available almost exclusively by those who produce or distribute digital publishing products, thus becoming a preferential channel for their resources. The treatment and search for "external" resources, therefore, is often made difficult to be applied to a system that is not released by the same producers as the database itself. As Luther and Kelly have also pointed out[79], it is not just about convincing unwilling publishers to include in the unified index every issued content. Also content aggregators have their role to play, by renouncing to highlight just their own products for the discovery tools and acting transparently. A trend toward openness has emerged, perhaps also due to the risk of losing databases subscriptions based on the lack of compatibility with some discovery tools. The main database producers are indeed putting every effort toward interoperability and try to produce metadata that are open to both the "second-generation" as well as "first-generation" discovery tools. This allows also comprehensive searches performed by systems produced by other subjects.

Returning to the problem of the very high number of results proposed by discovery tools, it must be emphasized that we never lose sight of the question of the "quantity" of information that these tools can retrieve after each search. In this regard, Aaron Tay reminds us that the measurement of the relationship between recall and precision must become even more decisive in the development of new systems.[80] The risk is that the WSDS will become generalist search engines, such as Google, no longer able to provide a quality indication on the information resources recovered, mixing too much information, impossible to be mastered with a relevance algorithm—already problematic in itself. It is probably useful to develop an

[79] J. Luther; M. C. Kelly, *The next generation of discovery* cit., p. 67.

[80] Aaron Tay, *Managing volume in discovery systems*. In: *Managing metadata in web-scale discovery systems* cit., p. 113–135.

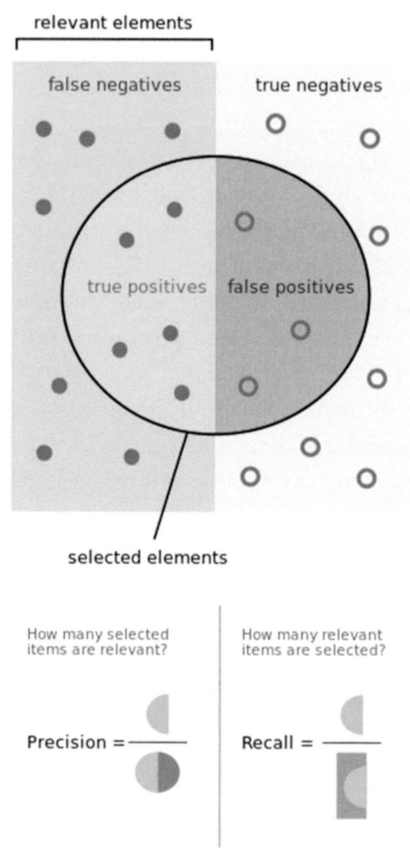

Figure 2.3 Diagram of the relationship between precision and recovery taken from Wikipedia[81].

"exclusion" criterion, to be implemented at the base of each search (Fig. 2.3).

Another issue, which opens up many discussions on the prospect of discovery tools as a possible "single point" for effective basic research on all resources mediated by a library, is the fact that a real change in the

[81] "In pattern recognition, information retrieval, and classification (machine learning), precision and recall are performance metrics that apply to data retrieved from a collection, corpus, or sample space. Precision (also called positive predictive value) is the fraction of relevant instances among the retrieved instances, while recall (also known as sensitivity) is the fraction of relevant instances that were retrieved. Both precision and recall are therefore based on relevance." Entry: *Precision and recall.* In: *Wikipedia, the free encyclopedia*, https://en.wikipedia.org/wiki/Precision_and_recall.

organization of the different databases has not yet been fully considered, to implement the discovery tools to these often closed and unrelated repositories.[82] Despite the fact that there are many debates on the topic, it is still necessary to fully regain awareness of the aims of librarianship before redesigning the tools to achieve them. The WSDS—as already mentioned—must be structured for a library that is first reorganized conceptually, with a vision toward maximal data sharing. Discovery tools can also manage a "bounded" and "secure" universe of resources within an institution, but the metadata and data that compose it must first be suitably prepared, and published in an interoperable form, to really meet to the needs of research and information, aptly revised by LIS and by society in the perspective of linked open data and the Semantic Web.

In addition to the discussions that emerged during the development of the WSDS, of course, the most recent recapitulations on the state of the art must also be analyzed, which also allow us to acknowledge which problems have remained unresolved or seem difficult to solve. In particular, the point of view, often shared over time, that discovery tools can represent an effective starting point for general or cross-sectional research, can also be questioned by studying the data on the use of library research systems. If it is easy—and acceptable—to expect that most academic users still prefer the use of specialized databases, it must be noted that searches are started more often from Google Scholar or from generalist search engines than from the discovery tool in use within any given institution.[83] Therefore, the discovery tools still have to develop their functionalities and the effects of their yield, even if only to be certainly accepted as a starting point for research that then allows users to deepen their interests just up to a certain point.[84]

Many still open issues concern the search index. The breadth and reliability of the research results depends precisely on the coverage and

[82] Cf. C. Bianchini, *Dagli OPAC ai library linked data* cit., p. 308–310.

[83] Cr. Christine Wolff-Eisenberg [et al.], *US faculty survey 2018*. Ithaka S+R, 2019, https://sr.ithaka.org/blog/new-questionnaire-for-the-us-faculty-survey-2018-now-available/.

[84] Nikesh Narayanana; Dorothy Furber Byers, *Improving web scale discovery services*, "Annals of library and information studies," 64 (2017), no. 4, p. 276–279, http://op.niscair.res.in/index.php/ALIS/article/view/19348.

quality of the metadata contained therein, and it is still not possible to have a stable and consistent index development policy today.[85] The collection of metadata produced by the manufacturers of the systems is subject to different types of agreements signed with different publishers and aggregators, for which the data are produced in different forms, with a very variable degree of accuracy and, moreover, not all content providers are reached to be involved in collaborating on the index.[86]

First of all, the timing of data supplying itself for the index is not certain or homogeneous. Those who send the metadata when ready are the content providers, and the producers of discovery tools can hardly carry out harvesting operations regularly and at regular intervals. Moreover, the same content providers are often not sure that they have updated all the data, nor they are aware of duplications, or shortcomings. Furthermore, the only indications on which databases are not included in the search index can be found by users always only through special notices created by librarians, in the form of lists of databases that are not searchable from the system interface. But these lists cannot be exhaustive and are based at most on the lists of databases to which the institution has subscribed. The issue becomes extremely complicated if you think about the impossibility of giving information on the titles of journals or books not included in the databases. In this case, only information on groups of publishers can be given.

Another issue concerns the reliability of the metadata automatically extracted from the system to enrich the index, of much lower quality than that of the metadata that populate the original databases of various publishers and aggregators. If publishers consent to the indexing of their resources, they let this happen through the automatic system and do not directly provide all the metadata they produce, through expert operators, for the services they own. Some WSDS systems have succeeded in obtaining the integration of the databases as they were originally produced,

[85] About this, cf.: Monica Moore, *But is my resource included? How to manage, develop, and think about the content in your discovery tool*, "The serials librarian," 70 (2016), no. 1–4, p. 149–157, https://www.tandfonline.com/doi/full/10.1080/0361526X.2016.1147877.

[86] Regarding the collaboration between publishers, WSDS producers, and libraries, cf.: Julie Zhu; Jalyn Kelley, *Collaborating to reduce content gaps in discovery: what publishers, discovery service providers, and libraries can do to close the gaps*, "Science & technology libraries," 34 (2015), no. 4, p. 315–328, https://www.tandfonline.com/doi/full/10.1080/0194262X.2015.1102677; Julie Zhu, *Should publishers work with library discovery technologies and what can they do?*, "Learned publishing," 30 (2017), no. 1, p. 71–80, https://onlinelibrary.wiley.com/doi/abs/10.1002/leap.1079.

provided they allow the search among the best quality metadata only to the institutions that have subscribed, separately, to each of the databases in question. In this case, we are talking about databases of which the discovery tool manages to reach 100% coverage, but in all other cases, when the original databases are not integrated, coverage can be guaranteed at around 80%–90% at the most, if the producer of the discovery tool manages to establish direct agreements with the publishers who supply the contents that populate the given database. Thus, in this case, the discussion on the homogeneity and quality of the extracted metadata does not even arise. Not to mention, finally, the extreme variety of search keys, in a set of metadata of very different origins, so "laboriously" collected.

Other "perennial" issues are related to the issue of relevance ranking.[87] In essence, each discovery system develops its own relevance algorithm, aiming to optimize the performance of its search engine as applied to its index. None of these algorithms, of course, is accessible or modifiable, and not only does it not allow to calibrate the relevance system according to the needs of certain users, but it is not clear even the criterion of the choices made by default, nor what reliability can really be given to the various proposals for "relevant" results. It may be well supposed that behind the algorithm there are balances of convenience and agreements established between resource publishers and producers of WSDS, but the fact of not knowing, or not understanding, why certain rankings of relevance are suggested can be an obstacle against the quality of searches.[88]

[87] On the general question of relevance ranking, discussed in more detail in section 3.2, cf.: Maria Teresa Biagetti, *Nuove funzionalità degli OPAC e relevance ranking*, "Bollettino AIB," 50 (2010), no. 4, p. 339–356, https://bollettino.aib.it/article/view/5340. Cf. also: Danilo Deana, *I vestiti nuovi dell'imperatore*, "Biblioteche oggi," 37 (2019), no. 1–2, p. 18–27.

[88] Many WSDS vendors, however, provide some sort of description of the general criteria adopted in designing their algorithms: Ex Libris, *Primo discovery: search, ranking, and beyond*. Ex Libris, 2015, https://files.mtstatic.com/site_11811/26778/0?Expires=1539105246&Signature=eLqOUxxUsVQ22ve5-anrQp4uzk5hdVg4kuw3h526I0I00euYi4AlgvW9LGST8ZOVbT1~IaYMaL25yiPjwyQtcXZ2-iQV-iUKYc4YLmznV31Z-EgME~S3gETfgyVCAZjQ91LjLv9nF3MAJAbFbNXbsiJbd-51Y4wT-iRC3wFRAZ4_&Key-Pair-Id=APKAJ5Y6AV4GI7A555NA; EBSCO, *Relevance ranking*, https://www.ebscohost.com/discovery/technology/relevance-ranking; Ex Libris, *Summon: relevance ranking*, https://knowledge.exlibrisgroup.com/Summon/Product_Documentation/Searching_in_The_Summon_Service/Search_Results/Summon%3A_Relevance_Ranking.

The problem of the quality of the metadata is inevitably reflected also in the ranking issues; in fact the poor or incorrect application of categories, keywords, or subjects, such as shortcomings in the abstracts, negatively affects the position in the ranking. Even the most recently published articles can create problems in defining the order of relevance if this is based too much on the amount of citations each article receives, and the first places tend to be reserved for older articles that inevitably have more citations. The same problem can arise if the relevance is also defined based on the amount of "use" of each resource, distorted by the oldest date of publication and presence in the index.

Among the long-lasting problems, there is also that of the customization of the search interface, which is the possibility, for each user, to interactively create a search environment more responsive to their needs. Search "profiles," for example, in the discovery tools that allow it, can only be created by the system administrator, who will necessarily define a thematic scope and choose which resources to insert and which filters to apply by default based on a generic vision of the user of that disciplinary sector. Furthermore, the ranking algorithm can be "calibrated" only by the institution that uses it and only within narrow limits, to give greater importance only to the resources coming from the catalog or from the institutional repositories—due to a forced intellectual honesty of the producers of WSDS? So, once an algorithm has been defined, they are not willing to accept modification suggestions from anyone.

Together with all the more or less technical issues, the question that still opens up today with greater problematicity—even if it is little dealt with, in practice or theory[89]—is that of the progressive replacement of OPACs with discovery tools tout court. It is not just a "mechanical" fact, relating to the choice of the best tool to adapt to the new technology, but to define the principles and assumptions for which the OPAC and its specific features

[89] Two very specific investigations, which at least raise the problem of "caution" in replacing catalog search tools, are: Tara J. Brigham [et al.], *Web-scale discovery service: is it right for your library? Mayo clinic libraries experience*, "Journal of hospital librarianship," 16 (2016), no. 1, p. 25–39, https://www.tandfonline.com/doi/full/10.1080/15323269.2016.1118280; Elena Azadbakht [et al.], *Everyone's invited: a website usability study involving multiple library stakeholders*, "Information technology and libraries," 36 (2017), no. 4, p. 34–45, https://ejournals.bc.edu/index.php/ital/article/view/9959.

developed to offer the best the catalog search service. We must therefore return to the question of the role of the catalog, already mentioned earlier.[90]

In this, it must be taken into account that it is one thing to talk about a single interface for all databases useful to the library, while it is another thing to define which interface should be applied to a single database. In the case of the interfaces of discovery tools, therefore, if there can be little doubt that they serve the task of allowing a single search through many databases well, various questions can be raised against the trend, which seems to have now started, which sees them as natural successors of OPACs.

For more than 5 years, the library service platforms (LSPs) have been replacing the old integrated library systems (ILS), proposing a very functional series of new management modules and a new "philosophy" that sees all types of resources on the same level, each with its own management characteristics.[91] The LSPs, however, among the modules offered do not provide any interface for the end user, therefore neither OPAC nor discovery tool. The practice and the methods offered by the producers mean that a given LSP is usually combined with the interface of the discovery tool proposed by the same vendor, and in any case, new OPAC interfaces are no longer produced. The situation, therefore, is that, although any OPAC search interface or discovery tool can be integrated into each LSP—in more or less successful integrations—in fact there are no new OPAC interfaces that have flexibility characteristics suitable for integration into the new systems.

Only the old ILS offer the related OPAC interfaces, and in various cases with updates to the new generation functions, but by adopting the LSP—especially in environments where WSDS are spreading, especially the academic ones—it is almost obliged to choose an interface of discovery as a single interface both for databases also provided with its own interface and for the catalog that remains without one. Neither the producers of LSP nor other producers seem to be developing interfaces dedicated "properly" to the catalog and only to the catalog, thus missing the possibility of offering

[90] In any case, the catalog has already taken a new face and is subject to ongoing change, so the question: "which new interface is best for the new catalog?" will take this entire book to be answered.

[91] Cf. Sara Dinotola, *I sistemi per la gestione delle risorse elettroniche*, "AIB studi," 56 (2016), no. 1, p. 59–73 (part one), http://aibstudi.aib.it/article/view/11411; 56 (2016), no. 2, p. 205–218 (part two), http://aibstudi.aib.it/article/view/11412.

users an interface of the catalog as is offered instead alternative of searching in the interface of other databases, including institutional repositories.[92]

It is also true that discovery tools are constantly being improved, and they are sensitive to the idea of replacing OPACs by inheriting their primary functions from them. The new interfaces are increasingly configurable in relation to the catalog data, allow more precise searches, and are certainly able to work on the catalog metadata separately from the other metadata in the index. It is also possible to configure search environments set by default on the characteristics of the catalog search.

The main problem, for the moment, remains the reindexing that the WSDS must still make of the catalog data to enrich the single index and also allow comprehensive searches on all available resources. Another problem, of a more technical nature, is that of the rendering of general services connected to the OPAC, from the loan to the management of the user space, which, however, some systems already solve with a certain efficiency—using the referral to the old OPAC environment via links for all cases in which the management through the discovery tool of the services is not possible.

By choosing to support the importance of tools specifically dedicated to the databases and data on which they operate, if OPACs are destined to disappear, it is necessary to focus attention on the possibilities of discovery tools to replace them. It is not wise to viscerally cling to past technologies, but new ones are to be promoted only if they are worthy of replacing older ones for the better.

Beyond the various solutions to improve the technologies of the latest generation WSDS, there are different development strategies—partly experimental, but already with fully operational applications—based on different technologies, such as that of Yewno Discover, which builds on the possibilities of artificial intelligence, text mining, and conceptual search. The developers of Yewno, launched in 2016, are faced with the problem of defining a new effective method for navigating today's ocean of information, fragmented and dispersed, following the routes of the "meaning" of the many available contents.[93]

[92] To display the catalographic data produced by LSP, a classic OPAC interface could be designed, but so far it does not appear functionally apt to solve problems, and anyway there are no endeavors toward this goal.

[93] Ruggero Gramatica; Ruth Pickering, *Yewno: an AI-driven path to a knowledge-based future*, "Insights," 30 (2017), no. 2, p. 107–111, https://insights.uksg.org/articles/10.1629/uksg.369/.

If the traditional search through terms offers excellent opportunities to achieve the desired results, it proceeds, however, in a mainly "linear" way, producing more noise the larger the information pool to which it is applied. Yewno's new "research philosophy", on the other hand, proceeds along different and more dynamic paths, assisted by visual maps and artificial intelligence technology. The system enables the discovery of "hidden" information, connecting dispersed but in some way related concepts, through the construction of semantic relationships based on "human-like" types of inferences. It does not simply search for keywords, but through the technologies of computational linguistics, neuronal networks, and data visualization, it analyzes the "meaning" of the resources to which it applies,[94] effectively allowing the exploration of concepts, the possibilities of combining them, as well as the discovery of even hidden conceptual connections.

The producers of Yewno report that, during experiments conducted in libraries, different users come to different conclusions while following the same research theme, given that each of them follows paths and connections that did not exist before the start of the research, created and varied each time interactively during the investigation paths. In this way, we can also suppose the development of a greater knowledge of the resources encountered during the research paths, since the system extracts the meanings of them and unexpected connections. The results are also proposed through a visual map, which shows a network of connections between the different concepts and their resources, allowing for visual browsing and quick movement from one concept to another. The network of connections is interactive and varies according to the position that the researcher chooses to have moment by moment; furthermore, the links of each node allow immediate access to the abstract of the resources found—and to the full text, if accessible to the institution that has the system—to allow the researcher to evaluate them directly (Fig. 2.4).

[94] A database still growing, which already includes over 120 million items: *ivi*, p. 110.

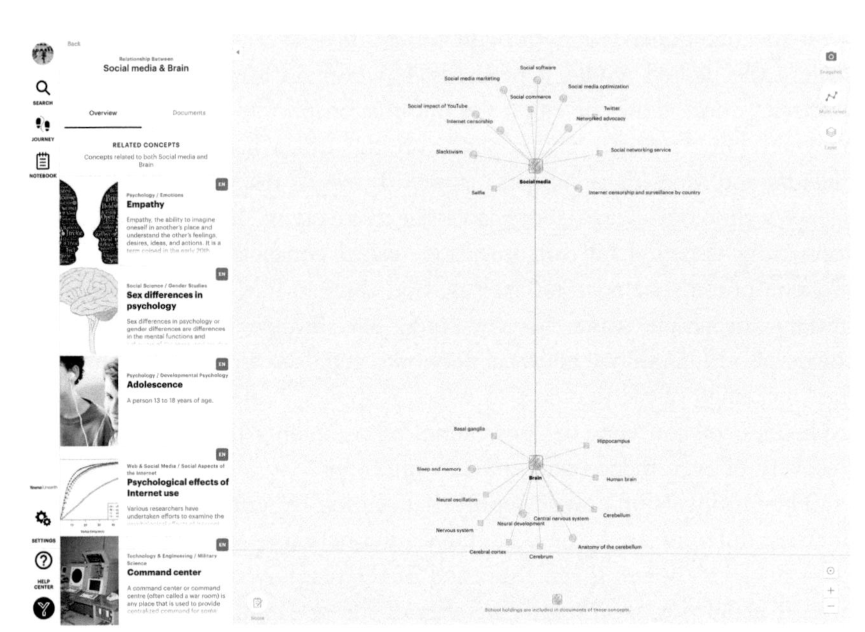

Figure 2.4 Yewno Discover demonstration screen.[95]

[95] https://www.yewno.com/discover.

CHAPTER 3

Search and discovery tools

3.1 Definition of tools and resources

To set up a general exposure of Web-scale discovery services (WSDS), Marshall Breeding's 2015 White Paper, written in the period of the first widespread diffusion of these systems, still has a good value as a recapitulative manual. Moreover, it anticipates various problems and possible developments of these services.[1]

Breeding defines the purpose of his White Paper to analyze which methods and which technologies are available to libraries to optimize and achieve the different objectives of making knowledge resources searchable and accessible to the community served. The survey concerns the tools created or acquired by libraries and also investigates the potential of those born in other environments, for a more general information search. In this context, the WSDS are the most responsive services to the research needs expressed above all in the academic field, as they are able to allow a broad and reliable investigation through the multiple resources made available by academic and research libraries. However, these tools do not "work" in isolation, but as part of the "ecosystem" made up of academic and generic publishing, abstracting and indexing (A&I) services, and the information infrastructure of the institutions that adopt them.[2]

The main component of a WSDS tool, or rather a discovery tool, is the interface presented to the end user. The first advanced discovery interfaces were certainly those called *next-generation catalogs*, which aimed to replace the OPAC interfaces connected to the various integrated library systems (ILS) used by libraries.

[1] Marshall Breeding, The future of library resource discovery: a white paper commissioned by the NISO Discovery to Delivery (D2D) Topic Committee. Baltimore: NISO, 2015, https://www.niso.org/publications/future-library-resource-discovery.

[2] Ivi, p. 2.

Web-Scale Discovery Services
ISBN 978-0-323-90298-4
https://doi.org/10.1016/B978-0-323-90298-4.00003-3

A *discovery* interface is made up of different parts, functions, and features, which can be summarized in Table 3.1.

Behind the interface, there is the central index of the system, with which the interface constantly interacts and from which it harvests the search results. The index is populated by the data and metadata of all the resources that a library deems useful to be made available for searches carried out by its users—but not only these. This index is unique, that is, it alone comprises all the data of all the resources indicated, which are extracted from the various databases, to which the WSDS system has access, and reindexed to be entered in the new "container".

Table 3.1 Parts, functions, and features of a discovery interface.

End-user screen	Accessible through the most common Web browsers. That is, a homepage able to connect the different specific screens for each function or service of the discovery tool. Some components can be integrated into the library Web pages
Query pages	Consisting of a search box in which to enter search strings for a quick basic search, and a more complete page with a series of boxes, menus, and parameters for advanced search
Results ranking pages	These pages visualize the search results and a series of options to adjust results' view, presentation, sorting, recording, and reuse
Facets navigation	This navigation is enacted by a series of selectable filters to guide the search through categories and subcategories related to topics, names, dates, characteristics of resources' content, or form. The facets are often proposed as orientation columns on the sides of the results list
Interoperability with a link resolver	Necessary to allow, from the results pages, the connection through a simple link to the accessible resources. In the case of inaccessible resources, a help screen is often offered directing the user toward services or sites that allow to request the desired content
Interaction with the library's ILS	This feature is not always effective if the discovery tool producer and the ILS producer have not established a collaboration agreement. The interaction between the systems would allow users to check the availability of resources, book them, make requests, and manage an account. If this is not possible, the discovery tool brings back the user to the interface screen connected to the ILS in use, often the OPAC
Consistency in the treatment of resources	Necessary feature to allow a certain homogeneity for the research and presentation of any type of resource: Local or remote, analog or digital, monographic or serial, and so on

Within the index are (Table 3.2):

Table 3.2 Data and metadata that populate the index of a Web-scale discovery service.

Metadata and bibliographic information	Coming from the catalog and other databases produced by an institution
Metadata and full text	Produced by various publishers
Metadata and full text	Coming from open access repositories and archives
Different contents	Produced by A&I services

The metadata produced by the publishers are available for harvesting based on specific agreements between the publishers themselves, or the aggregators, and the producers of WSDS. The same happens for A&I service products. The data and metadata from the institution implementing a discovery tool are immediately available to it, but it does not become a permanent part of the index that manufacturers continually enrich and sell to other institutions—of course, unless a specific agreement is made. The full-text resources are indexed by the systems, but if the systems themselves do not have the license to allow the use of the indexed object, they refer to the publishers' sites through the linking mechanisms.

The volume of these indices is very large and constantly growing. The different manufacturers also use different methods for "deduplication" and aggregation of the same or very similar records. Some systems choose to represent the same resource only once, by aggregating representations from different sources—catalogs, databases, A&I services—or that have identical identifying data—such as DOI, ISBN, or ISSN—at the risk of eliminating descriptions referring to different resources. Others choose to keep separate descriptions from distinct sources, accepting that the same resource is presented several times—unless the data are all perfectly coincident, making an "exact" deduplication. As a matter of fact, it is clear that these choices have a direct consequence in the composition of the list of recovered results.

Behind the interface and its interaction with the central index, there is also the integration into the single index of content from local databases. Being able to integrate data and metadata related to local resources in the best possible way is of primary importance if you want to obtain from the WSDS system a service that is well suited to the needs of an institution. To be incorporated into the central index, in fact, all the resources must be reindexed by the system, and this can create much difficulty when, for example, the database to be reindexed is that of the catalog, since the metadata are treated differently than how they were originally edited by the cataloging specialists. No less difficulties are experienced when reindexing of all the other resources coming from local repositories and databases, but the process is inevitable and presents the same issues as in any other case of reindexing and integration of data coming from databases outside the institution.

One solution would be to have a specific index available for local resources, but this is in contradiction with the very principle of the WSDS and the single index. It is not easy to even prioritize resources from local databases in the list of results.

The different types of resources managed locally by libraries, even outside the ILS, consist mainly of those mentioned in Table 3.3.

All the data of the resources reindexed by the system, whether external or internal, coexist with equal treatment in the central index. The variety of these materials, however, implies a variety of data and metadata that cannot be adequately treated in the context of the standardizing logic of reindexing. Therefore, some of the typical specifications of the detailed treatment for each type of resource are lost and, in addition, the variety of harvested data, in case they have been recorded with different forms, appear juxtaposed, next to each other.[3]

Again, due to the diversity of materials, some exceptions may also be necessary, which, nonetheless, would limit the very possibility of researching certain resources to members of a different institution.

Table 3.3 Resources managed locally by libraries.

Owned collections general catalog
Database with archive material
Database with museum material
Digital library collections
Institutional repositories
Special collections

[3] A trivial example: the same author, indicated in the catalog with "Surname, Name" and in a database with "Surname, N." will appear with two different forms in the unified list of results extracted from the index that has harvested the data from the two different sources.

However, this problem is the least urgent, since the basic trend of the WSDS is to let everyone access at least the metadata discovery tool, whenever it is not possible to freely access the resources themselves.

At the basis of the operation of the user interface and of the interaction with the index is the mechanism of the *back end* interface, which allows operators to manage all the functions of the discovery service. Some discovery tools offer greater possibilities of managing the service directly, and others require more interventions when opening tickets for assistance, which is provided by the manufacturer. Nonetheless, there are quite good possibilities of setting and customizing the service, and of taking an alternative route to bypass the typical "stiffness" that the WSDS present in either structure or policy.

As a matter of fact, it is still difficult to be fully aware of all the features that could be integrated to perfectly adapt the service to the needs of an institution and its users, given the complexity of the tools. First of all, these tools are still under development and transformation. Secondly, it is also difficult to conceive the amount of energy and skills that such an implementation requires. Nonetheless, a well-organized discovery tool management group may be able to make the most of the *back end* functions and implement the most suitable search and discovery service.

Among the main functions available in a discovery tool control interface, which is structured in different groups and pages, are those grouped in Table 3.4.

The WSDS pertaining to public libraries have different features. Clearly, public libraries are characterized by a series of specific issues that are sometimes very different from those of the academic library environment, in which Web-scale services were first felt to be necessary. Therefore, they have been "cut to size" for this context, and not for public libraries, where the WSDS have come in second place. One typical difference, which exemplifies all the others, is that academic libraries have a strong interest for scientific e-journal collections, while public libraries are commonly offering single, either general or narrative, e-books—not to mention the different proportions of these interests.

Therefore, for a public library, the scope of a discovery tool is more that of local collections of printed material, collections of multipublisher e-books, some collections of popular scientific resources, as well as some local repositories, which can represent the real "treasure" to be discovered, since they consist of materials connected to local history and culture.

Table 3.4 Main functions of a discovery tool management interface.

Options for the default setting of end users' search strategies
Options for filters, limiters, expanders, and other query conditions (available/not available to users)
Autocorrection, hint/suggestion functions, and similar ones
Alerting functions, search profiling, user recognition
List of databases included by the manufacturer with the possibility of selecting those on which to search
Options for the default setting of the results display modes
Options for results' viewing and sorting functions (available/not available to users)
User profile functions for managing references, resources, and a personal "shelf"
Management of search history functions
Management of external links and of apps to relaunch searches on specific databases or external sources
Integration with AtoZ list systems and local resource management functions
Integration with link resolving systems
Functions for reporting owned and accessible resources and functions for requesting external resources
Statistics and report production functions
Different profiles setting options
End-user interface modules for the definition of institutional branding and identity
Profile, password, and security management functions
FAQs, tutorials, pages, and forms for requesting assistance
User community mailing lists, pages, and blogs

Several specific systems have been developed for public libraries,[4] starting from the interface of the catalog for these libraries, which has evolved toward the characteristics of the WSDS, so much so that it can serve as a model. These discovery systems, although generally linked to the ILS produced by the supplier, increasingly offer, beside the ability to index local resources, faceted navigation, and the integration with WSDS of a more consolidated nature.

One of the most relevant issues, with regard to public libraries, is that of the integration between e-books searching and borrowing within the same

[4] Among the first ones, BiblioCommons: https://www.bibliocommons.com/, and AquaBrowser: https://www.proquest.com/products-services/AquaBrowser.html. Following, Encore: https://www.iii.com/products/sierra-ils/encore-discovery/, and LS2 PAC: https://tlcdelivers.com/ls2-pac/.

interface. Even in the context of academic WSDS, loan operations require that the user is directed to the publisher's or aggregator's website, where only after the creation of an account it is possible to download the desired e-book, ask for a loan extension, or return the loan before the due date. These operations clearly expropriate libraries from the function of allowing, managing, and controlling loans. Libraries are not even granted the possibility to define the loan period for each type of e-book and let alone the diversification of the loan depending on the category of user. The dialog interface of the system, chosen by the library, should be able to manage these transactions on its own, by establishing a connection between the publisher and the library service, through an application programming interface (API) or other mechanisms that are still far from being well defined, but which could allow a real dialogue between the "supplier" of the resource and the library that "acquired" it.[5]

Another important aspect, which involves the academic more than the public library environment, is the integration of the discovery service into the library Web portal, so that the latter can be the source of all the services provided, with regard to both searching through discovery tools, catalogs, single database, and repository interfaces, as well as finding general reference, place availability, information, etc. This integration can be obtained through the implementation of a series of tools and apps, such as through iframes anchored to the institution's website. At the same time, specific systems have been developed for public libraries, which, in addition to managing the search interfaces, provide a content management system (CMS) and other applications that practically organize or replace the entire website.[6]

In addition to the WSDS created for libraries and similar institutions, Breeding also refers to discovery services carried out independently by them.[7] Among them, the main one is Google Scholar,[8] and another is

[5] However, progress has been made toward the integration of e-books with library management services. Specifically, you can see the ReadersFirst initiative: http://www.readersfirst.org/.

[6] Among these products, useful both in the context of public as well as academic libraries, are Arena https://www.axiell.co.uk/arena-discovery/; BiblioWeb https://www.bibliocommons.com/products/biblioweb; Enterprise http://www.sirsidynix.com/products/enterprise.

[7] M. Breeding, The future of library resource discovery cit., p. 6–8.

[8] Google Scholar: https://scholar.google.it/.

Microsoft Academic.[9] It cannot be denied that the tendency to use general Web tools has spread increasingly among researchers as these tools have investigated, acknowledged, and satisfied the different needs expressed by the "typical" researcher. In the same way, researchers use repositories, indexes, databases, and portals not necessarily born inside the library or academic field, as well as research portals that relate very "freely" on the Web.[10] In none of these cases should we be too much surprised, and it is wrong, as well as counterproductive, to "horrify" in front of these tools, which can often favor research more than those officially meant to deliver library services. In the end, the mandate of the LIS disciplines should be studying the characteristics of Web tools, questioning the reasons for their success, the methodologies and technologies used, and understanding how to avoid a senseless "competition" and enact a productive collaboration, in which each tool can play their role. At the most, what we need to watch out for is that less attentive researchers do not give too much credibility to extemporary and imprecise tools, without knowing how to critically recognize them.

In this perspective, we can also mention Wikidata, which does not fail to spark optimism regarding its role as a tool for the discovery of information resources.[11] In fact, the Wikidata project has been devised to create a *knowledge base* in the Wikimedia "family" to support other programs, and in particular Wikicite.[12] Wikidata is being enriched through new projects aimed toward the massive upload of bibliographic information and thousands of scientific articles, which are freely accessible by everyone and which can be provided by everyone, just like the creation of a "social database."[13]

[9] Microsoft Academic: https://academic.microsoft.com/.

[10] Among them, there are also excellent tools, with their own authority, such as, to give an example that is worth all the others, arXiv: https://arxiv.org/.

[11] Wikidata: https://www.wikidata.org. On this topic: Luca Martinelli, Wikidata: la soluzione wikimediana ai linked open data, «AIB studi», 56 (2016), no. 1, p. 75–85, https://aibstudi.aib.it/article/view/11434.

[12] Wikidata: WikiProject Source MetaData: https://www.wikidata.org/wiki/Wikidata:WikiProject_Source_MetaData. Wikicite: https://meta.wikimedia.org/wiki/WikiCite.

[13] On this project, cf. Antonella Iacono, L'impatto dei linked data bibliografici nella Library catalog analysis: nuove opportunità per la valutazione scientifica. In: Maria Teresa Biagetti, Valutare la ricerca nelle scienze umane e sociali, con scritti di Antonella Iacono e Antonella Trombone. Milano: Bibliografica, 2017, p. 149–174. Cf. also, as a general reference: Wikipedia, libraries and archives, edited by Luigi Catalani, Pierluigi Feliciati, "JLIS.it," 9 (2018), no. 3, https://www.jlis.it/issue/view/789.

Finally, it should also be mentioned that these nonlibrary products represent an alternative to the "official" ones, which are, however, paid services. The main discovery tools—without detracting from their aims of scientific effectiveness—are only available to institutions that can purchase them and have the resources to fully implement them and also the databases to which they are connected. In this sense, tools such as Google Scholar represent a revolution and a valid alternative for all those users who do not easily have access to either WSDS or paid resources, and this applies both to many individuals and to all those institutions that for political, economic, and cultural reasons cannot pay the fees to granting access to discovery services. However, beyond the commercial agreements, open-source WSDS based on open indices that are enriched by open-access resources have not yet been fully launched.[14]

Another broad and still unresolved issue presented in Breeding's book is that of the "degree of independence"—and, conversely, of interoperability—between a library management system and a chosen library discovery tool.[15] The real problem is to establish whether libraries are truly free of choosing between the two products, and to what extent they are obliged, if they use a particular ILS, to use the discovery system produced by the same company. It is clear that the need of each cultural institution is to be able to freely choose different products to be applied to different services, and the necessary connection between the services must not be an obstacle against choosing the most suitable tool for each of them.[16]

In reality, especially in the case of the access function to the local contents of a library, a discovery tool cannot match the precision and efficiency of an OPAC in reporting and managing the data recorded in the ILS and in the catalog database, even if all of them are produced by the same "brand," which is obviously complicated if the manufacturer of the

[14] A discussion of these opportunities, and the NISO Open discovery initiative (ODI), is contained in M. Breeding, The future of library resource discovery cit., p. 15–21, 40–44. Cf. also: Jenny Walker, The NISO Open Discovery Initiative: promoting transparency in discovery, "Insights," 28 (2015), no. 1, p. 85–90, https://insights.uksg.org/articles/10.1629/uksg.186/.

[15] M. Breeding, The future of library resource discovery cit., p. 22–23.

[16] The general interest in the matter is documented in: Jenny S. Bossaller; Heather Moulaison Sandy, Documenting the conversation: a systematic review of library discovery layers, "College and research libraries," 78 (2017), no. 5, p. 602–619, https://crl.acrl.org/index.php/crl/article/view/16714.

discovery system and that of the ILS are different, and do not have established a cooperative relationship. The discovery tool is not a module of the ILS, as is the OPAC, and has always shown a certain ineffectiveness in processing not only the data of the ILS modules related to the availability of an object on the shelf, to the loan, to the registry of users, to the administration, but it is also less effective in viewing the catalog data, given the inevitable reindexing process.

Over time, the situation has improved with regard to the discovery systems produced by the same manufacturer as the ILS, which are able to directly process the management data of resources and users, without returning via links to the OPAC interface. A discovery tool of another brand than the library management system, on the other hand, always needs to refer to the OPAC of a given ILS to operate library services other than research, and in general, it shows poor interaction with the catalog database. Nonetheless, given the complexity of certain interaction operations also for "monobrand" systems, it may not be a fault to be completely charged at the producers' bad will.

Paradoxically, this difficulty of interaction creates the conditions for the "mandatory" maintenance of the OPAC interface of an ILS, since only this can manage the functions related, for example, to loan reservations, to the immediate communication of updates on availability, and, ultimately, even to the locations of the materials. The expectation of improvement of these WSDS functions is still partially disappointed, except in some cases in which, in fact, the discovery tool is produced by the same manufacturer as the ILS, and the data communication protocols are combined with some API specifications.[17]

This "game" of technological combinations is played on the ground of ILS producers that also create discovery tools that have a natural affinity and better operating possibilities combined with their own ILS.[18] There are open-source ILS, by nature adequate to be implemented with discovery systems of other brands, or even open ones.[19] Finally, there are WSDS

[17] Marshall Breeding, Progress on the DLF ILS discovery interface API: the Berkeley accord, "Information standards quarterly," 20 (2008), no. 3, p. 18–19, https://groups.niso.org/apps/group_public/download.php/5637/ISQv20no3.pdf.

[18] For example: the "pairs" formed by the Primo discovery tool with the Alma, Aleph, Voyager or Verde library management systems, all developed by Ex Libris, https://www.exlibrisgroup.com/; the "historic" pair Summon and Intota, by ProQuest, https://www.proquest.com/products-services/discovery-services/; or the combination of WorldCat with WorldShare, https://www.oclc.org/en/home.html.

[19] For example, Kuali OLE: https://openlibraryenvironment.org/.

producers who have not previously developed any ILS, and who have structured their discovery system for greater adaptability to management systems of other brands[20].

Today, the successors of the ILS seem to be, necessarily, the library service platforms, which are born without a specific search module for end users, therefore as naturally designed for integration with a discovery system. Therefore, if the integration issues between traditional ILS and discovery tools are inevitable, they are certainly less recurring with LSPs, because these new systems have been envisioned to managing bibliographic resources' integration.[21]

Over the past 15 years or so, although they have been adapted to adequately manage new types of resources, the ILS have first been joined by ERMS (electronic resources management systems), that is, modules created with the aim of managing the main characteristics of electronic resources in the best possible way, and are now being replaced by the LSPs, which aim at the integrated management of all types of resources.

In particular, in the past 10 years, the limits of ILS have been fully understood. ILS were created for the management of paper resources and not of resources of different types, because they lack specific fundamental functionalities that could allow to deal with electronic or digital resources. Despite an ILS can be forced to treat magnetic tapes or CDs and DVDs, which are in some way similar to the book object, the ILS cannot manage the features of an e-journal package or e-books, let alone the trial periods of databases or portals, and everything related to the management of passwords, access via IP, licenses, or statistics. Around 2008, therefore, favored by the diffusion of a series of shared practices and protocols for the treatment of electronic resources, the various producers of software for library management began to implement the first ERMS, trying to respond to the new needs developed in the management processes.[22]

[20] In this field, for example, VuFind: https://vufind.org/vufind/.

[21] For an in-depth analysis of the nature of LSPs, and of the phases of the transition from ILS, to ERMS, and LSP, see: S. Dinotola, I sistemi per la gestione delle risorse elettroniche cit.

[22] The suggestions of the DLF-ERMI program are fundamental for the start of ERMS production: Digital Library Federation, Electronic resource management: report of the DLF ERM Initiative, edited by Timothy D. Jewell [et al.]. Washington: DLF, 2004, https://old.diglib.org/pubs/dlf102; id., DLF electronic resource management initiative, phase II: final report. December 30th, 2008. Washington: DLF, 2008, http://old.diglib.org/standards/ERMI2_Final_Report_20081230.pdf.

In essence, ERMS software allows for the centralized management of the entire process of processing electronic resources, making specific functions available for new single or collective forms of resources, for the activation and control of accesses, and for the storage and administration of all data necessary for these functions. Through them, it is possible to manage with certain effectiveness the bibliographic data of the various resources, the lists of titles, the access links, the passwords and the accepted IPs, the indications on the costs and conditions of supply, the data of the suppliers, the contracts, invoicing, licenses, statistics, and everything else necessary. The novelty of the ERMS consists in that they allow to manage all this set of data and information by concentrating everything in a single interface, avoiding dispersion across a plethora of management programs to be used together with the traditional ILS.[23]

Even if they allow the ILS to be combined with a single program instead of several others—sometimes rudimentary "own" products—the ERMS, however, almost never allow true integration with the management software in use. It is true that these are much more effective software packages than Excel sheets or small databases produced by librarians to collect information on electronic resources, and make the work faster, but, similar to the latter, they do not allow you to share catalog data, or interact with the OPAC. Thus, they only serve as an additional management tool, specific for a given category of resources. In the end, the ERMS represent only a step forward toward the design of a real "single system" management—as discovery tools are a single system for research—and without spreading too much, already around 2009, they were put aside to welcome the LSP.

LSPs are developed on the principle of uniform management of all types of library resources. An LSP, in fact, has the task and functions to handle the entire workflow of all printed, electronic or digital resources, single or packaged, acquired definitively or through a time-bound, trial, or open-access subscription. In this way, the service platform operates in a "neutral" and independent way, considering each resource for what it actually is, without being set as a traditional type by default, but rather treating the traditional types from an "absolute" point of view, by reconsidering their nature and the "new" resources, as a particular form of the general resource model for the treatment of which the system itself was created.

[23] In her article, Dinotola presents the cards of various commercial and open source ERMS: S. Dinotola, I sistemi per la gestione delle risorse elettroniche cit., p. 66–69 (first section).

In practice, the LSPs are not a so exactly theorized "holistic" management model, but they have the advantage of being really able to integrate the functions of ILS and ERMS, as well as those of link resolvers, license management systems, etc., creating a single "control panel" to perform the various functions of processing paper and digital resources that were previously entrusted to very different tools. However, a typical LSP does not manage by choice the search and retrieval phase of the available resources performed by the end user: not only is an OPAC interface missing, but also any search and retrieval tool other than the structural one inside the single back end modules. This is why these service platforms are, by nature, ready for integration with a discovery tool—especially if it is the one created by the same manufacturer. Beyond that, the platforms are extremely flexible and allow integration with a number of other external modules, through an expandable architecture designed for dialog with other software.[24]

An LSP, therefore, typically presents a wide range of functions, relating to both the paper and digital processing, but not calibrated only on one of the two types: selection and acquisition, circulation, storage, license management, statistics, cataloging, metadata management, collocation, link resolving, etc. Some functions are exclusively typical of a type of resource, but shared ones are structured only afterward based on the specific type to which they apply. For example, one thing is the circulation of a paper book and another thing is the availability of access to an e-book, or, one thing is the display of a shelf mark and another is the link resolving. As a user interface for this system, therefore, it seems obvious that a discovery tool should be used, as the functionality of the "simple" OPAC would be limited in the face of the amount of different resources managed (Fig. 3.5).

An innovative example of LSP—so much so that it is still in the testing phase—is the FOLIO system, a service platform for libraries that was born as open-source software, developed in collaboration by its international community of users.[25] FOLIO is an acronym that literally means "Future Of Libraries Is Open," also in honor of the activity of the Open Library

[24] Dinotola also presents the cards of the main LSP: S. Dinotola, I sistemi per la gestione delle risorse elettroniche cit., p. 207—211 (second section).

[25] On the FOLIO project, cf.: Brandi Scardilli, Working together toward an open source future, "Information today," 33 (2016), no. 9, p. 25—27; FOLIO: https://www.folio.org/.

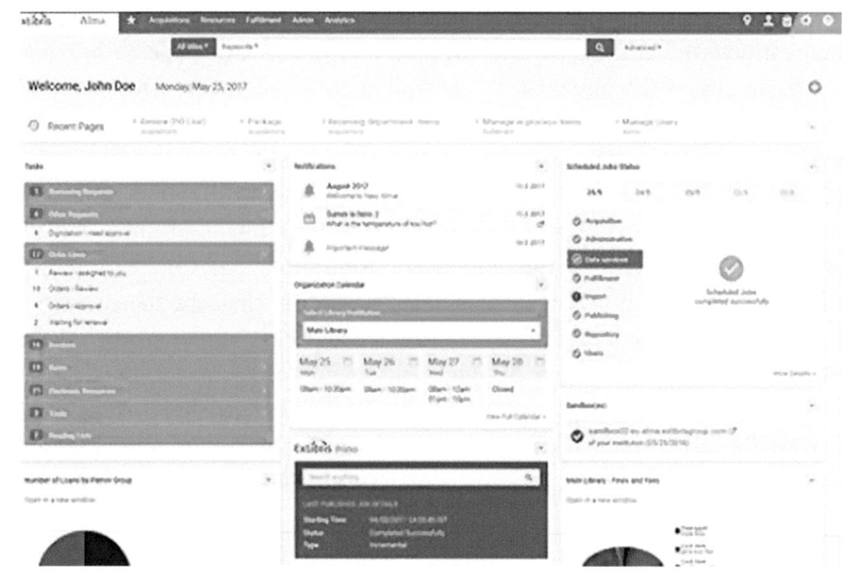

Figure 3.5 Interface of the Alma LSP.[26]

Foundation,[27] which was created with the aim of encouraging open collaboration between libraries and library systems manufacturers, and which began supporting FOLIO as its first project—also thanks to the collaboration of the EBSCO company.[28]

The project starts from the idea that an open-source LSP can first of all offer the possibility to parameterize the system according to the needs of each developer, as well as to create a series of customized modules that integrate with both FOLIO and other management systems, also contributing to the wealthy enrichment of modules and apps that are available to all members of the community. Therefore, the modular architecture of FOLIO allows the development of specific parts for data acquisition, cataloging, circulation, management, and research of each type of resource, all perfectly integrated into the general architecture of the system.

[26] The screenshots and its contents are published with permission of ProQuest LLC. Further reproduction is prohibited without permission.

[27] Open Library Foundation: http://www.openlibraryfoundation.org/.

[28] EBSCO acts as a "leader" in the first development of the system (cf.: https://www.ebsco.com/products/ebsco-folio-library-services), and its activity is accompanied by that of Index Data https://www.indexdata.com/folio/ and of OLE https://openlibraryenvironment.org/folio/, as well as those of numerous other commercial and institutional partners.

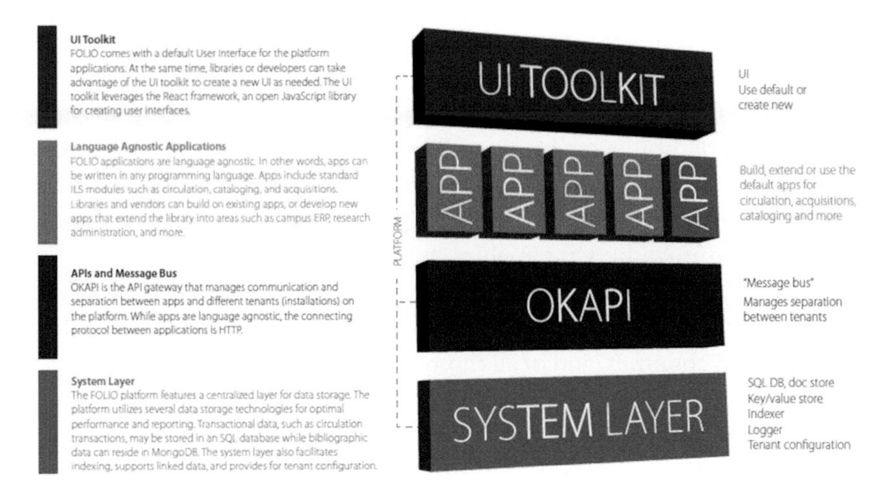

Figure 3.6 Structure of the FOLIO platform.

Furthermore, the development process of FOLIO is not "linear" and can therefore include the integration of modules for data mining, institutional repositories, learning management, and linked data at any level. The invitation to collaborate to the international community of libraries and other cultural institutions, as well as of commercial operators in the sector, is still open as today (Fig. 3.6).

In its White Paper, Breeding identifies a series of criticalities of WSDS that have not yet had definitive developments, and several situations have remained suspended. Some solutions may consist of technological developments that have yet to be achieved, while others depend on a cultural development of the context, comprising theoretical standpoints and practical aspects concurrently held by librarians, producers, and users, far from conclusion.[29]

The first of these critical issues consists in the problem of covering the relevant resources for the various research areas. Although the WSDS indices are getting bigger and bigger, the expansion is mainly due to the growth of the contents of the already owned resources, or to the acquisition of a few other data indices, but many resources still remain out of reach for a given producer. This problem is widespread among the different WSDS, and each WSDS producer tries to cope ably forging pacts and relationships with resource producers, but it is difficult to compare the different indices with each other, and none can be considered superior to the others—since

[29] Cf. M. Breeding, The future of library resource discovery cit., p. 27–32.

it is not just a quantitative problem, nor is the number of indexed resources a valid benchmark.

This does not mean that we can complain about shortcomings relating to the content produced by the main "Western" academic publishers. When there is a striking lack, it is reported by the system manufacturer himself. The first to be inclined to include the various discovery tools in the index are the publishers themselves, who see an increase in the sales in proportion to the dissemination of information on their production. More difficult is the coverage of non-English language productions, or of underdeveloped countries, and of all those publishers who are not well known at international level.

Conversely, the producers of databases of various levels, who defend—rightly or wrongly—their own search interfaces and their original indexes, demonstrate a certain resistance to inclusion. Finally, when they contract the indexing of their data, they never give up the original data, but only let the index creation service reindex such data. Given that some large database producers are at the same time producers of discovery tools, the paradox is that an index is richly endowed with the original data of a certain producer and not at all supplied with the data of the competing producer—a situation with which contractors try to cope by including directly the sources harvested by the excluded database, thus indexing an enormous amount of magazines and books from scratch.

Another considerable problem is that of the precision of advanced search, which seems to have been sacrificed to facilitate the simplification of the query path and the breadth of retrieval of results. Beyond the responsibilities of the producers of the discovery tools interfaces, a good part of responsibility can be attributed to the producers of A&I services, who have often simplified many cataloging or metadating rules born for monographs to adapt them to a faster and more effective "filing" of journal papers. On the opposite, when the metadata work of the articles is very accurate, it is based on specific metadata structures for given disciplines. As a consequence, search operations in multidisciplinary indexes become ineffective.[30]

A related problem is that of searching for "known" resources characterized by a short or common title, or for authors with a very common

[30] On the matter, Breeding returns in: Marshall Breeding [et al.], Sharing metadata across discovery systems. In: Managing metadata in web-scale discovery systems cit., p. 113–135.

surname. In these cases, due to the long list of displayed results, it is difficult to recognize the specific title or author sought, whose further identification is not known.

Therefore, in the current environment of digital resources, all these metadating options represent a problem that the indexing techniques of the WSDS cannot yet master. An example of a general solution is that of the ORCID program, which attempts to solve at least the problem of finding all the products of the same person, by assigning a unique identification number to each author, whatever form for the name is adopted[31].

One of the most relevant practical issues for discovery tool manufacturers is that of linking to resources retrieved from a performed search. Whether these are part of the subscriptions paid by the institution that has adopted the WSDS system, or whether there is no subscription for access, the system must enable the user to immediately access the resources or find a way to request the login as soon as possible. Thanks to the OpenURL standard,[32] the link resolvers connected to the discovery tools allow to direct the user to the searched resource or display an orientation page for requesting access. As it has been argued before, discovery tools tend to incorporate the link resolving system created by their own manufacturer. Thus, they are not very flexible with regard to interaction with systems from other manufacturers.[33]

The various discovery tools offer the possibility to set up the resolving system, by customizing both the button for resource access and the alternative menu if access is not available for the institution, as well as by defining a series of access possibilities, providing talking icons or written explanations, for instance, in case of direct access to resources available in the institution's databases, or through publishers' websites, or through either free or paid sources. The aim of the WSDS is to immediately present the user with a button that displays the kind of granted access to the resource, whether this is "internal" or on the publishers' sites, or is generally available on the Web—and, when the resource is not available, a button brings to a dialog page for requesting a DD, an ILL, or other information

[31] ORCID (Open Researcher and Contributor ID): https://orcid.org/.

[32] Cf. OpenURL. In: Wikipedia, the free encyclopedia: https://en.wikipedia.org/wiki/OpenURL.

[33] On the matter: Leanna Jantzi [et al.], Managing discovery and linking services, "The serials librarian," 70 (2016), no. 1–4, p. 184–197, https://www.tandfonline.com/doi/abs/10.1080/0361526X.2016.1153331.

from the library that manages the service. In the event of local availability of a nondigital resource, its convenient location is primarily displayed, instead of the access button.

The issue of relevance ranking is also well known, long-lasting, and difficult to solve. However, it can be said that WSDS producers care very much about creating algorithms for sorting results that are capable of responding optimally, because the success of the search and discovery system is connected to its ability to effectively direct users to the resources they really need. For this reason, WSDS producers invest in algorithms research to make them as objective as possible, and capable to recognize the cognitive needs of users. It is clear that interactive algorithms, which are able to "learn" from the users' preferences and to present each one the most appropriate results, would be necessary. At the moment, however, also due to economic difficulties, the aim is limited to the construction of an ordering of the results that is able to satisfy a typical search, as deduced from the terms entered in the search box.[34]

Another problem is that of multilingual search. The problem certainly grows as the primary problem of resource coverage at the international level is solved, given that entering many objects in different languages requires that starting from any language one is able to query the entire index, and retrieve relevant results regardless of the production language. Even in the current situation, however, where the coverage of non-English objects is very low, the same problem arises for the formulation of queries. The main issue is not so much that of reindexing all data and metadata in English, as that of being able to index them in their original form and then be able to carry out an independent search from this. In this regard, the development of cross-language research techniques is expected as a key technology to be acquired in the WSDS.

Among the problems to be solved is also that of covering open-access resources. A good level of coverage is still a goal to be achieved for the various WSDS, which, at the moment, have certainly managed to collect the OA contents published by publishers already included in the indexes, but are struggling to broaden the range of action toward many high-level resources published through open-access programs, which are not so readily traceable. Discovery tool producers are already indexing content from famous international archives—such as arXiv or DOAJ[35]—but the

[34] For the question of relevance ranking, see below, in paragraph 3.2.
[35] arXiv cit.; DOAJ (Directory of Open Access Journals): https://doaj.org/.

real success would be the systematic collection of OA resources carried out with the same consistency reserved for commercial resources.[36] A collaborative solution could be to cooperate with different users of the WSDS to enrich the indexes of OA resources they have produced, harvested, or discovered.

Among the various open questions, there is still that of the interoperability of the interfaces of the discovery tools with the e-learning systems used by an institution. Especially in universities, systems are increasingly used, which allow teachers to create lists of resources recommended for study and which allow interaction with students. The search interfaces can interact with these systems allowing users to report the content found directly in the e-learning modules, and the purpose of the WSDS is to allow the sending of reports in the best possible way. Some discovery tools use API for dialog with e-learning programs, others have developed their own modules that they offer in competition with those already widespread, but the criticality is to overcome the most used systems in terms of effectiveness and immediacy.[37]

Finally, another issue is that of the privacy of WSDS users and the security of their data within the system. Initially, it emerged with regard to the first large data collections created by the library management systems to register users for services, or trace the paths of loans, and it has increased with the profiling carried out for the memory of research or alerts in databases. More recently, the management of discovery tools requires more and more massive data collections on users and their behavior. Data protection technologies must always be kept up to date, not to run the risk that valuable personal information is used for purposes other than conducting cultural research.[38]

[36] For example, cf. Chris Bulock, Finding open content in the library is surprisingly hard, "Serials Review," 47 (2021), no. 2, p. 68–70, https://www.tandfonline.com/doi/full/10.1080/00987913.2021.1936416.

[37] Examples of this are Leganto by Ex Libris, https://exlibrisgroup.com/products/leganto-reading-list-management-system/, and Curriculum Builder by Ebsco, https://www.ebscohost.com/discovery/customization/curriculum-builder, which appear as an alternative to programs such as Moodle, https://moodle.org/.

[38] The topic is explored in: Marshall Breeding, Privacy and security for library systems. Chicago: ALA, 2016. (also published in: "Library technology reports," 52 (2016), no.4).

Moving from critical issues to those that Breeding identifies as development opportunities for the WSDS, the farsightedness of the prospects identified from the outset can also be measured.[39] Among these, for example, the expectation of an increase in availability and use of the various APIs that will allow different systems to interact with each other and with the discovery tools still lives today, allowing the creation of ever wider and richer WSDS of functionality.

A development possibility that the WSDS increasingly indicate as a necessity is that of making research data available. Universities and scientific institutes are increasingly convinced of the usefulness for progress of sharing the raw data that are the basis of research projects, as well as the dissemination of the final product itself.[40] In this, cross thrusts abound, both coming from the indications of the laws on research funding and from the promotion of open science. Discovery systems can be very useful if they are also set up to ensure access to research data sets, and there is no shortage of experiments to define the best practices both for preparing descriptive metadata of data sets and setting up discovery tools.

A partially "revolutionary" development toward the specific treatment of multimedia objects would be desirable. The WSDS systems, in fact, were born as pursuer of a tradition based on the textual research of resources, which, although new in form, are always intended as mainly composed of text or, in the case of visual, audio, or video resources, supported in any case from textual description and metadata. Therefore, the developed technologies and methods of archiving, research, discovery, and recovery are fundamentally based on textual representations of the different materials. The future WSDS should be able to provide research tools more suited to the multimedia nature of the different objects they deal with, and capable of investigating the different textual, visual, audio, and audiovisual features of the resources. The growing experimentation in

[39] Cf. M. Breeding, The future of library resource discovery cit., p. 33–37.

[40] On the question in general, developed in the context of digital libraries, see for example: Maria Guercio; Cecilia Carloni, The research archives in the digital environment: the Sapienza Digital Library project, "JLIS.it," Vol. 6, No. 1 (2015), p. 1–19, https://www.jlis.it/article/view/10989.

the field of multimedia technologies can provide a series of tools oriented to the multimedia treatment of resources to be integrated in the development of discovery tools.[41]

Among the features that can be expected to be more widespread, then, may be that of the social opening of the WSDS, allowing the entire community of users to enrich them with metadata and resources, sharing links, information, and objects. Whether these data are created by users or imported from different services, the main problem is how to manage it in a discovery tool. It is not functional to simply let them "coexist" with other data in the system; it would be necessary to "moderate" and integrate it as search and discovery keys.[42]

Other advancements are expected in the treatment of collections of special materials, such as archival ones, which have a precise logic of metadating and conservation that requires a different conception of the methodologies of research and discovery of the WSDS systems. Similarly, the self-analysis functions of performance need to be improved, both in terms of the absolute efficiency of the system and its effectiveness in front of people. Finally, it is necessary to follow up on greater integration with the altmetrics modules, which for some time have been supporting those of traditional metrics, shown in "icon-links" under the description of the bibliographic references.[43]

3.2 The main discovery systems

As it is certain that each library has among its objectives that of facilitating as much as possible the research and discovery of the contents it mediates and access to the available resources, in the same way the history, peculiarities, and mission of each must determine the most suitable technological system

[41] To deepen the problem of multimedia information retrieval (MIR), see: Roberto Raieli, Introducing Multimedia Information Retrieval to libraries, "JLIS.it," 7 (2016), no. 3, p. 9–42, https://www.jlis.it/article/view/11530; id., Nuovi metodi di gestione dei documenti multimediali. Milano: Bibliografica, 2010.

[42] On the topic: Louise F. Spiteri, Managing user-generated metadata in discovery systems. In: Managing metadata in web-scale discovery systems cit., p. 165–193.

[43] About alternative metrics: Altmetric: https://www.altmetric.com/; PlumX Metrics: https://plumanalytics.com/learn/about-metrics/. Cf. also: Simona Turbanti, La visibilità – e l'impatto? – nel Web ai tempi dei social: i principali strumenti di altmetrics, "AIB studi," Vol. 56, No. 1 (2016), p. 41–58, https://aibstudi.aib.it/article/view/11410.

to achieve these objectives. From the point of view of the basic principles and primary technology, the various WSDS tools seem to have similar characteristics, if not even common, but it is in the practical application and functioning that the main differences and specific characteristics of each one are visible, especially with regard to the "customization" of the service, not to mention the various policies for setting up the index or ordering the results. These aspects need further consideration.

The major discovery systems are designed and applied within academic and research libraries, but they can also be implemented effectively in the case of some large libraries, or library systems, serving a wider population. To obtain a quick catalog of the main discovery tools available today, it is useful to refer to some older schemes,[44] by adding the producers' presentations on their websites, as well as the notes of some critical articles reviewing their strengths and weaknesses.[45]

Starting from the EBSCO Discovery Service (EDS) system,[46] produced by EBSCO,[47] it can be said that, in particular, the strategy of the tool is to create the best interaction with the most widespread ILS, as well as with open-source ones. EDS, in fact, allows libraries to maintain their own knowledge bases and link resolving systems, using the API to communicate with the various producers, and aiming for better integration with the functionalities of the various OPACs. The system also allows you to specify which full-text sources must have precedence for access, if the same resource is accessible through multiple services. A set of widgets and other apps allows you to incorporate new content into the discovery tool page,

[44] In particular, we can refer to: M. Breeding, The future of library resource discovery cit., p. 2–5; Brandi Scardilli, ILS product roundup: choosing among the top discovery services, "Computers in libraries," 36 (2016), no. 2, p. 34–39, http://www.infotoday.com/cilmag/mar16/Scardilli–ILS-Product-Roundup.shtml.

[45] Some of these articles attempt a critical comparison of different systems with each other: Rosie Hanneke; Kelly K. O'Brien, Comparison of three Web-Scale Discovery Services for health sciences research, "Journal of the Medical Library Association," 104 (2016), no. 2, p. 109–117, https://www.ncbi.nlm.nih.gov/pmc/articles/PMC4816486/; Karen Ciccone; John Vickery, Summon, EBSCO Discovery Service, and Google Scholar: a comparison of search performance using user queries, «Evidence based library & information practice», 10 (2015), no. 1, p. 34–49, https://journals.library.ualberta.ca/eblip/index.php/EBLIP/article/view/23845.

[46] EBSCO Discovery Service (EDS): https://www.ebscohost.com/discovery.

[47] EBSCO Information Services: https://www.ebsco.com/.

Table 3.5 Main features of EBSCO Discovery Service.

The main specialized indexes are used, through the acquisition of metadata provided directly by the producers of the main scientific databases
Full text from databases, e-books, and e-journals of the main international publishers are used to produce the query results
A series of partnerships has been created with various ILS producers, to integrate the functions of the discovery tool with those of the catalog and make them interchangeable
The list of partnerships with content producers is very extensive, including major organizations and major publishers
The system is able to work with any type of preexisting link resolver, sharing the knowledge base
Access to the full text available for a facility is immediate, through a direct linking system to the resource on the publisher's website or in other databases

from searching on encyclopedias and dictionaries, to relaunch the query on other databases, to share results with e-learning or citations management systems.

On the manufacturer's website, the presentation of EDS is articulated by focusing on the level of service that it is expected to be able to provide. The combination of the quantity and quality of the available contents and the technology of the system that makes them available is boasted, considering all the critical elements that come into play in the research process. EDS plans to meet the different needs of each user, providing the means to effectively calibrate and conduct the query strategy, whether it is basic research conducted by students of the first years, or it is moving to the level of research specialized conducted by experienced teachers and researchers (Table 3.5).

The discovery tool makes the basic search available in a simplified and fast way through the single search box, but also this structuring of the query process is carried out in the general operating context of the system, common to the advanced search. Advanced search, in a more "explicit" way than basic search, can make use of intuitive and functional query building tools, accurate indexing based on authoritative sources, immediate access to available resources, and content provided by most international producers (Fig. 3.7).

Figure 3.7 A flier of EDS.[48]

[48] https://www.ebsco.com/sites/g/files/nabnos191/files/acquiadam-assets/EBSCO-Discovery-Service-User-Success-Infographic.pdf.

The EDS flyer boasts the offer of an excellent search capacity within the full text, as well as an excellent ability to index content.

Regarding the critical notes on the EDS system, a useful report is that relating to the installation at George Washington University, at the Himmelfarb Health Sciences Library.[49] The library already had a federated research service since 2007, and in 2011, it switched to EDS, choosing it after a comparison with WorldCat. The first problem to be addressed was the fact that, being the library one of the first in the biomedical sector to implement a WSDS, the system's default index was mainly rich in materials belonging to other sectors. Thus, the librarians, working side by side with the producer, began to select the most suitable databases for research in the health disciplines to insert their data in the index, as well as to work on defining the most suitable relevance ranking criteria for the sector.

The EDS implementation was named HI@H (Health Information @ Himmelfarb) and was assigned a central role among library services by placing the search box in the foreground on the library homepage. The initial idea of librarians, however, was that the discovery tool would be useful primarily for students of the first years, or for general and multidisciplinary searches of more experienced users. The catalog was included in HI@H, but only as a secondary access, keeping a link to the OPAC clearly visible under the system search box, since the discovery tool was unable to perform some specific functions of the OPAC itself. From the beginning, HI@H had a strong use, with constant growth from year to year, but the librarians doubted about the purposes of this use and the people who used it. In 2015, then, a specific investigation was conducted on the system, also to clarify what improvements could be adopted and whether the parallel permanence of the OPAC was still relevant.

[49] JoLinda L. Thompson [et al.], Discovery assessment and improvement at an academic health sciences library: Health Information @ Himmelfarb five years later, «Journal of electronic resources in medical libraries», 15 (2018), no. 1, p. 7–25, https://www.tandfonline.com/doi/abs/10.1080/15424065.2018.1433093.

Before presenting their survey, the Himmelfarb library working group referred to previous surveys and findings,[50] accepting some key points regarding the setting and customization of EDS:

- it is important that the name of the "source" database is displayed next to each result in the overall list;
- it is necessary to highlight the name of the link to the advanced search;
- it is important to clearly display, in a box next to the results, the search history, and the filters used to carry out the performed search; and
- it is useful to delete the EDS "custom link"—a button for direct access to available resources—so that each result shows the link resolver button in its place.

Then, the librarians of Himmelfarb conducted their own survey, using two questionnaires and a focus group, both to define who the users of HI@H were and for what purpose they used the system, as well as to establish, with the focus group, the interest, and satisfaction of the librarians themselves. The second of the two questionnaires was focused on the "awareness" of users about the discovery tool and the OPAC, on how much each was used, for what searches, with what tools, and with what final satisfaction.

The first data showed that most of the users were graduate students, looking for information for assignments related to the lessons. On the other hand, the staff used the system more often, for startup or generic searches, to produce or verify bibliographic citations, and believed that the users for whom they carry out some searches are interested in the HI@H interface. Regarding the second questionnaire, the data showed a greater interest of graduates and researchers for advanced search, but with little awareness of the characteristics of the tools used.

[50] María M. Pinkas [et al.], Selecting and implementing a discovery tool: the University of Maryland Health Sciences and Human Services Library experience, "Journal of electronic resources in medical libraries," 11 (2014), no. 1, p. 1–12, https://www.tandfonline.com/doi/full/10.1080/15424065.2013.876574. See also: Sarah Bonner; Georgia Williams, A small academic library and the power of EBSCO Discovery Service, "Serials review," 42 (2016), no. 3, p. 187–191, https://www.tandfonline.com/doi/full/10.1080/00987913.2016.1205428; Aoife Lawton, Use of ESBCO discovery tool at one university reveals increased use of electronic collections but decreased use in circulation of print collections, "Evidence based library and information practice," 10 (2015), no. 4, p. 244–246, https://journals.library.ualberta.ca/eblip/index.php/EBLIP/article/view/25473.

The working group was therefore able to discuss and make some changes to the system:

- reduction of default filters to the resources available through the library, and expansion of the search to all useful resources;
- acknowledgment that the "catalog-only" filter favors the use of the discovery tool instead of the OPAC, and that the former is also preferred for catalog searches;
- need to find a way to implement the discovery tool to perform all the functions of the OPAC;
- need to structure the interaction between the link resolver and the EDS "custom links," to allow direct access to the available full-text resources and access alternatives for the rest; and
- utility of EDS apps and widgets to better highlight and make many contents accessible (Fig. 3.8).

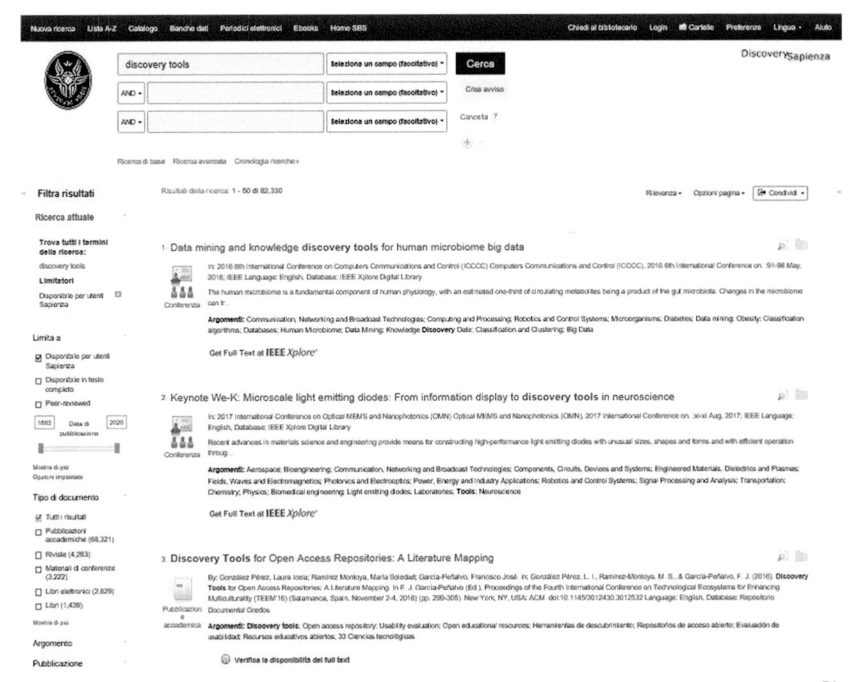

Figure 3.8 Research results of EDS implemented at Sapienza University of Rome.[51]

[51] https://eds..a.ebscohost.com/eds./search/basic?vid=0&sid=e139d77b-dae5-4a4d-9cba-2f0863510e14%40sdc-v-sessmgr03.

Table 3.6 Primo main specifications.

Access to a large amount of academic resources and to the most relevant resources of broad fields
Enhancement of the assets of a library, increase in the use of resources, promotion of their visibility, and production of operational analyses for the general evaluation of the service provided
Enhancement of library activity, by perfectioning and streamlining workflows, and allowing, through customization flexibility, to guide users' search and access processes
Connection, through a series of functions and tools, of the discovery activity with the research system, with the platforms for teaching and learning, with the apps used by students

The discovery tool Primo,[52] produced by Ex Libris[53] that acquired it in 2016 from the ProQuest group,[54] is oriented to effectively provide the different functions of the OPACs in its interface. In this way, the system aims to restrain libraries from maintaining a parallel catalog interface to which redirect certain user requests, for example, those related to the loans or the availability of paper material. The system also uses data mining functions that, referring to the search criteria of users, allow the production of lists of related results to be proposed alongside the list of main results, as well as the indication of resources widely consulted in a given field.

On the ExLibris' Primo Web page, it is immediately stated that the system can be perfectly integrated with different ILS and that the connected activity of the vast community of users allows to expand the features of the service by providing a series of suggestions for innovations, best practices, and collaborative developments.

The summary screen displaying the main features of Primo indicates those mentioned in Table 3.6.

In particular, the value of the central index of the discovery tool is presented, extended to commercial content and open access. The index is enriched through the aggregation of data from different manufacturers and carefully controlled by a team of metadata experts. The level of detail of the records includes subject terms, controlled vocabularies, original keywords,

[52] Ex Libris Primo: https://www.exlibrisgroup.com/products/primo-library-discovery/.
[53] Ex Libris Group: https://www.exlibrisgroup.com/.
[54] ProQuest: https://www.proquest.com/.

DOI, and other metadata from the main A&I services. Furthermore, the institutions that use the system can, through a special forum, propose corrections and developments of the entire service.

A particularly positive feature is also the relevance ranking system used by Primo, which aims to provide the best results list to each user. The system combines advanced analysis and ranking technologies with the options that can be set by the library based on users' profile and needs, even creating different search profiles with a sorting results criterion for each. Similarly, an institution can customize sorting criteria that enhance local collections (Fig. 3.9).

With regard to Primo's "functioning" problems, we can refer to the experience of the California State University libraries, which adopt a unified management and consequently unified discovery system.[55] The report illustrates the importance of carefully planning the acquisition of a discovery system, starting with market survey analysis. Each consequent project was tailored to suit the end user, to provide people with a simple, clear, and intuitive search interface, which is also highly customizable by the libraries that implement it.

The usability analyses about the old version of Primo found that its main weakness was the confusion generated by the search interface, also due to the too many options available, and suggested the manager to use the various customization functions to provide the user with the most convenient default environment.[56] Therefore, the working group, formed in 2016 to decide on the choice and implementation of the discovery tool, fully focused on the analysis of the search interface, to improve its customization and usability. Some model searches have been developed to be tried out across different departments of the university, being related to finding a specific book, a given film, a peer-reviewed journal article, a

[55] J. Michael DeMars, Discovering our users: a multi-campus usability study of Primo. Presentato in "IFLA WLIC 2017. Libraries. Solidarity. Society. Satellite meeting: reference and information services and information technology sections" (Wrocław, Poland, 2017), http://library.ifla.org/id/eprint/1810.

[56] Aaron F. Nichols [et al.], Kicking the tires: a usability study of the Primo discovery tool, «Journal of web librarianship», 8 (2014), no. 2, p. 172—195, https://www.tandfonline.com/doi/full/10.1080/19322909.2014.903133. See also: Clarissa Machetti, Biblioteche e discovery tool: il caso OneSearch e l'ateneo di Siena, "AIB studi," 56 (2016), no. 3, p. 391—408, http://aibstudi.aib.it/article/view/11501; Enrico Francese, Test di usabilità sul discovery tool Primo all'Università di Torino, "Biblioteche oggi," 31 (2013), no. 10, p. 10—17, http://www.bibliotecheoggi.it/rivista/article/view/342.

Figure 3.9 Primo infographic.[57]

[57] The screenshots and its contents are published with permission of ProQuest LLC. Further reproduction is prohibited without permission. https://knowledge.exlibrisgroup.com/@api/deki/files/42114/The_Top_10_Reasons_Libraries_Prefer_Primo.pdf?revision=1.

resource belonging to another library of the system and an article of newspaper. All these model searches have been proposed to different types of academic users.

First of all, many of these users have expressed appreciation for Primo's modern interface, finding it simpler and more intuitive than the various specialized database interfaces. They also have appreciated its speed, as well as features such as "error" correction. Searches for already well-defined resources have almost always produced exact results. Conversely, while performing searches for unknown materials, many users have proved confused, especially when viewing similar results within different types of resources. This has led to consider the importance of the automatic menu that appears as a suggestion in the search box, showing in which areas the terms entered can be searched: the discovery tool index, the local collection, the journals owned, and so on. Even when using facets, not all users progressed at the same pace.

The system appeared to have general weaknesses of various kinds:

- little graphic evidence of facets and other options compared to the rest of the interface; lack of clarity of the labels and names used;
- excessive number of filters presented;
- unclear differentiation between accessible and nonaccessible resources; and
- poor practice of users with the visualization according to the FRBR structure.

At the end of the test, a document was drawn up in which first of all the importance of the friendly aspect of the interface and the choice of clear and intuitive names for links, menus, and labels was appreciated. The importance of defining the primary research areas was then ascertained, eliminating the secondary areas to make the lists more targeted. Same thing for the facets, indicating the effectiveness of putting the most useful ones at the top of the list—sorting, availability, format, date, etc.—and hiding the less useful ones in a pop-up menu. Finally, to meet the needs for a local customization of the interface, it was decided to differentiate between generally available, system-level settings and single-library, local customizable settings.

A second round of testing was then carried out, using the same search models with the new functions and tricks implemented, which led to some improvement in the ability to carry out the simpler search tasks. All this indicates the importance of fully considering the need for continuous experimentation of the usability of the discovery system interface, to continuously fine-tune useful changes and updates, especially if you choose a system that can support many customizations alongside the central functions, as it should be for a consortium of libraries (Fig. 3.10).

The *discovery tool* Summon,[58] a ProQuest product for which the merger with Primo is planned, has been designed for integration with LSPs and

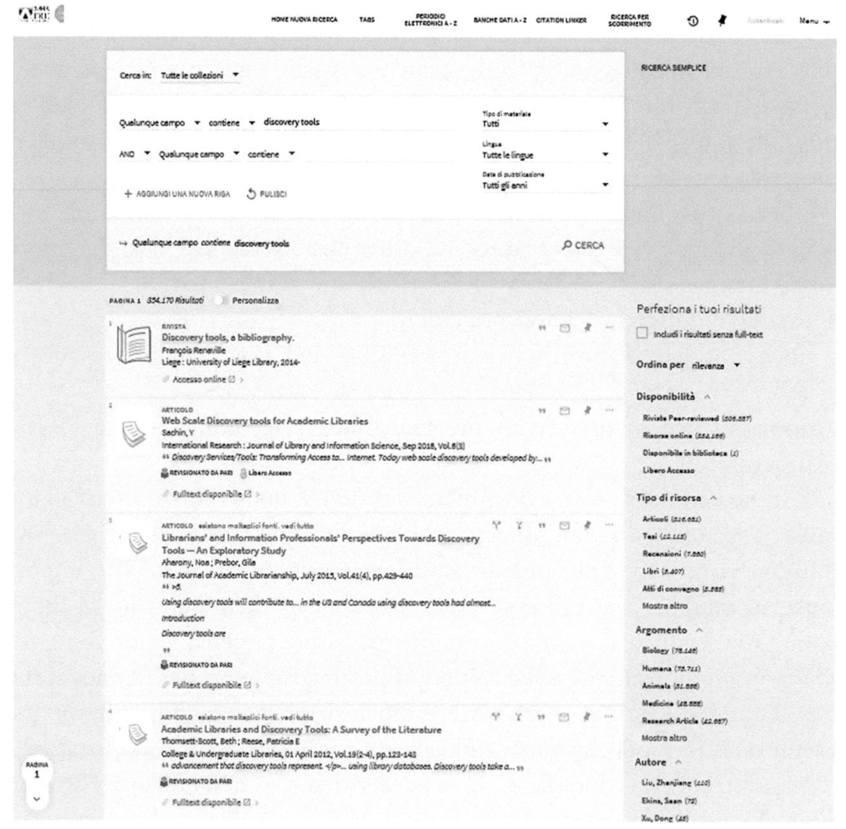

Figure 3.10 Research through Primo at the Roma Tre University.[59]

[58] The Summon service: https://www.proquest.com/products-services/the-summon-service.html. Summon's illustrative page is also on the Ex Libris website: https://www.exlibrisgroup.com/products/summon-library-discovery/.

[59] https://discovery.sba.uniroma3.it/primo-explore/search?vid=39CAB_V1&lang=it_IT.

specific search functions and access to content, to function as the search interface that is not present in these systems. For this purpose, the tool is equipped with APIs for interacting with catalogs, and linking systems to allow immediate access to resource data and full text. Other functions are the "recommendation," which allows libraries to intervene in the automated process of the system "calibrating" the suggestion criteria; exploration of the terms, which suggests the related terms and the related contents present in encyclopedias, dictionaries, and guides; and, finally, the search expansion function, which "maps" queries through controlled vocabularies to find other relevant results.

The Summon presentation page published on the ProQuest website indicates among the first qualities of the system the presence of one of the largest central indexes available, in which the various records are "optimized" for discovery and aggregate different metadata and full text from different sources to make each resource more available. The service thus returns results that are as relevant and impartial as possible, and it is precisely the matching and merging of records between different producers and publishers to provide the basis for this, preventing the "distortion" of the results in favor of any supplier.

Summon also allows users to improve their information literacy and to "connect" with librarians by presenting results' lists along with a range of tools to refine them and lead to other resources recommended by the library, such as specialists from a given field of research. Searches are always fast and simple, allowing you to enhance all the resources made available by a structure (Fig. 3.11).

Among the primary characteristics, those mentioned in Table 3.7 are higd in hlighted.

Some years ago, Anne Grigson, working at the Manchester Metropolitan University, published a study on Summon, in which she revealed the criticalities of the implementation of this system.[60] The discovery tool was launched in 2013, with the "Library search" logo, and the main purpose of the working group that dealt with its experimentation was to understand the needs of users. The tool immediately set itself as something very different from the OPAC, the databases, and the federated search system in use. It affected positively some users, less positively others, and efforts focused to make it accepted and used in the best possible way.

[60] Anna Grigson [et al.], Information without frontiers: barriers and solutions, "Insights," 28 (2015), no. 1, p. 62–72: p. 64–68, https://insights.uksg.org/articles/10.1629/uksg.176/.

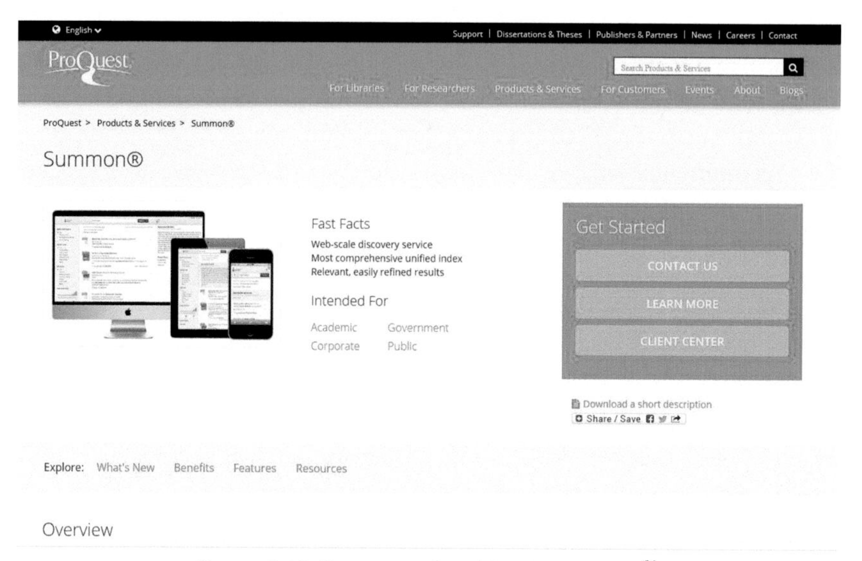

Figure 3.11 Summon-related ProQuest page.[61]

Table 3.7 Primary features of Summon.

The possibility of full customization, and the availability of APIs for dialog with external components
A truly Web-scale structure, organized on different levels to allow for system expansion
Tools for automatic query expansion, completion of strings, refinement of result lists, through filters and groupings
Tools for proposing recommendations, research guides, and reference devices
Tool for analysis and statistics, as well as for support and sharing in the user community

Simplicity, intuitiveness, and efficiency were the keywords of Summon's promotion, analyzed step by step by the working group through the use of questionnaires, behavioral observations, and focus group discussions. The questionnaires immediately captured information about users' search habits and experience. Meanwhile, direct observations monitored their actual behavior in carrying out certain assigned "tasks," and the focus group allowed to deeply dive into the participants' opinions.

The majority of participants confirmed significant data:

[61] The screenshots and its contents are published with permission of ProQuest LLC. Further reproduction is prohibited without permission. https://www.proquest.com/products-services/the-summon-service.html.

- ease of use of the search interface;
- relevance of the information found and the results of the list;
- the filter for the full text available is useful and saves time, but it can be an excessive obstacle for the discovery of information;
- search filters are not always used;
- the tools available are very intuitive;
- a comparison can be made with the immediacy of Google; and
- the results reached are still too many, considering that many do not lead to a full text available and it is not easy to understand which ones.

Consequently, the working group decided to propose an "open week" for the promotion of "awareness" in the search and use of the discovery tool, to be repeated periodically in favor of all user groups. Guides and tutorials were produced, on the basis of the investigated behavior issues. It was also decided to purchase resources as compatible as possible with the discovery system, even from the same manufacturer or its partners. Finally, a consistent plan was designed to promote information literacy and specific education on search strategies, and a critical approach to resources (Fig. 3.12).

Finally, one of the major search and discovery systems is WorldCat Discovery,[62] produced by OCLC.[63] WorldCat Discovery has privileged access to WorldCat data, which allows the system to process the data directly, returning absolutely "correct" results, such as those taken from local library catalogs. The discovery tool also integrates interlibrary loan services, the management of digital collections, and the construction of academic portals. It also allows direct access to full text or document supply services.

The WorldCat Discovery brochure highlights the system's ability to effectively provide people with all the resources they need and have identified, regardless of whether they are electronic, paper, or other media, or are available in open access when subscribing to a library, in the physical collections of a facility, on loan or by direct purchase from the producer. The OCLC service can boast a more than 45-year-long history and experience.

[62] WorldCat Discovery: https://www.oclc.org/en/worldcat-discovery.html.
[63] OCLC (Online Computer Library Center): https://www.oclc.org/.

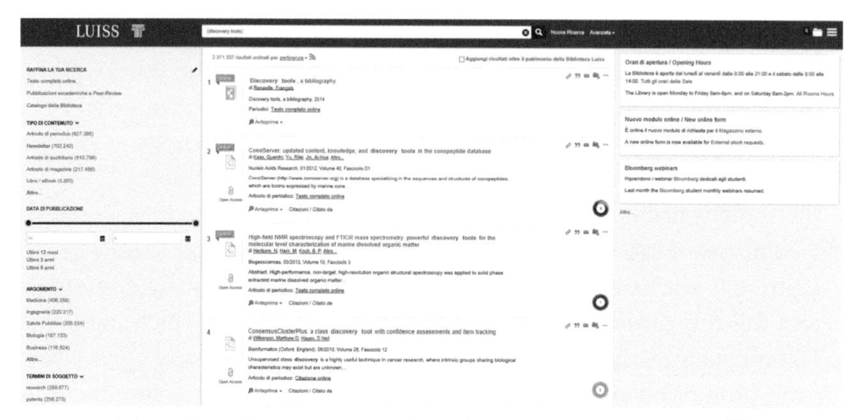

Figure 3.12 Summon research results at the LUISS University.[64]

In addition to providing rich result lists, the system allows those mentioned in Table 3.8.

The emphasis is put on the particular efficiency of the search in the unified index through a large amount of resources produced in any format, as well as on the simplicity of the query operations, favored by predefined filters. Another strong point is declared to be the large pool of publishers and producers who have made the resources available for the enrichment of

Table 3.8 Main features of WorldCat Discovery.

The use of algorithms based on user activity to define the ranking of the results, combined with further sorting options that can be defined anew each time
An environment reserved for operators that allows to fully use the functions of the OCLC catalog, to also manage interlibrary loan requests
Total adaptability of the layout and functions to the different devices owned by each user
An integrated link resolver for direct connection to subscribed resources, to those available through manufacturers and to OA resources

[64] https://biblioteca.luiss.it/risorse-elettroniche/summon.

the index and the accessibility of data, to which the broad context of open-access resources sums up (Fig. 3.13).

To learn more about WorldCat Discovery, visit oc.lc/WorldCatDiscovery.

Beyond the search. Results.

Provide a great user experience that's refined and expanded based on input from the WorldCat Discovery community. Task-based relevance algorithms and sort options work together to deliver the results you need every time.

Offer a single search box for resources in all formats instead of consulting multiple services and interfaces. WorldCat Discovery supports both novice and expert searchers. Enter keywords in the search box, or use Advanced Search options up front to refine searches, including through the use of database-specific indexes.

Empower your team with staff-specific views that include displays of OCLC numbers, OCLC symbols, and MARC records. Staff—and library users—also benefit from integrated, user-initiated interlibrary loan requests.

Make resources available wherever and whenever users want, automatically adjusting for desktops, tablets, and mobile devices. A fit-for-purpose interface delivers the experience users expect, with options to localize for your library's needs.

Connect users to the resources they need via links to full-text content you own and license through an integrated link resolver when your library's data is present in the WorldCat knowledge base. And reveal open-access collections, such as HathiTrust and JSTOR.

Get free training whenever you want it. Choose from instructor-led or self-paced classes, video tutorials, and documentation, all specific to WorldCat Discovery and available at no charge. Access this training at **oc.lc/SupportDiscovery**.

More content, less searching

WorldCat Discovery allows research to happen smarter and faster. You give users local and global resources, in all kinds of formats, at their fingertips. See how many resources by visiting **oc.lc/content-discovery** (PDF).

User needs drive enhancements

WorldCat Discovery keeps pace with your users' expectations. Strategic testing and community input guides refinements to search, relevance, and fulfillment.

"Global scale..."

"The major feature of WorldCat Discovery as a discovery tool is the global scale in which this service can help librarians. This type of tool has long been a dream of librarians."

Elisabetta Morani
Head Librarian,
John Cabot University
Rome, Italy

Figure 3.13 Excerpt from the WorldCat Discovery brochure.[65]

[65] https://www.oclc.org/content/dam/oclc/services/brochures/215405-WWAE_WorldCat-Discovery-Product-Brochure.pdf.

Regarding the features of WorldCat and their effectiveness, the experience reported in a usability report by the University of Maryland Libraries, which analyzes the two implementation phases of WorldCat Local and WorldCat Discovery, is useful.[66] WorldCat Local has been adopted as a discovery system since 2009 and, since 2012, has taken the central position on the library site, alongside the OPAC, as the main tool for finding information. Operational analyses were carried out in 2015, first of all on the Local system and, secondly, on its successor WorldCat Discovery.

Previous studies have highlighted problems to both Local and Discovery versions[67]:

- confusion regarding the ordering of the results;
- failure to maintain search strings when passing from basic to advanced search;
- loss of filters and search facets using the "back" button;
- difficulties at identifying specific resource formats;
- confusion while trying to differentiate between books and articles in the results' list; and
- difficulties at locating a resource and at the availability of the path to reach it.

Many of these problems were also found in the study carried out by the University of Maryland, which was aimed at identifying to what extent the users found the discovery tool difficult to use. The focus of the two-phase study was more to try to understand how well WorldCat Local and Discovery were able to meet users' needs, than to establish what was the ability of each user to use the systems himself/herself. The users' sample included both university faculty and the different students' cohorts.

The first thing to be noticed, in both versions of WorldCat, is the lack of flexibility of the search interface for the changes and customizations desired by libraries.[68] A certain slowness and instability of the system was

[66] Rebecca K. Goldfinger, WorldCat UMD usability final report. University of Maryland, 2017, https://drum.lib.umd.edu/handle/1903/19604?show=full.

[67] John Carlo Bertot [et al.], Assessing the usability of WorldCat Local: findings and considerations, "Library quarterly," 82 (2012), no. 2, p. 207–221, https://www.journals.uchicago.edu/doi/abs/10.1086/664588?mobileUi=0&journalCode=lq; Sarah R. Gewirtz [et al.], Evaluating the intersection between WorldCat Local and student research, «Journal of web librarianship», 8 (2014), no. 2, p. 113–124, https://www.tandfonline.com/doi/full/10.1080/19322909.2014.877312.

[68] A description of the differences between WorldCat Local and WorldCat Discovery is in: R. K. Goldfinger, WorldCat UMD usability final report cit., p. 4–8.

also noted, as well as the lack of intuitiveness of the interface. However, the two main objectives of the survey were the ease of use of the system in the search for both resources with known data and "unknown" resources to be discovered, and the ease of determining the characteristics of these resources.

With regard to the first objective, in both phases of the test and with both systems, all participants were able to easily find books and articles known and owned by the university, as well as articles not known before the search. It was more difficult to track down well-known books owned by other institutions, unknown e-books, and unknown videos. A certain difficulty was also encountered in locating journal articles not owned by the university. Findings overall confirmed the lack of clarity of the system in exposing the location and access data of the resources.

Regarding the second objective of the survey, that is, the ease for the user to identify the characteristics of the resources not previously known, in both phases, it was quite easy to identify articles and e-books, but not DVDs, despite the use of filters and limiters. In any case, the list of results presented by the discovery tool did not clearly show the format of the resource and its availability.

Based on the results of the WorldCat tests, the working group that conducted them devised various recommendations to improve usability. Some concerned the solution of technical problems—which OCLC has solved through the updates of WorldCat Discovery—others concerned the users' instruction on the use of the discovery tool and on the recognition of its functions (Fig. 3.14).

Some discovery systems have paid a greater attention to the issues of public libraries, not much involved in the needs of research and academic study, unlike the main "academic" ones, with the partial exception of WorldCat.

Arena,[69] produced by Axiell,[70] is a discovery tool created to integrate with other Axiell products distributed in libraries, archives, and museums. In essence, the system completes an LSP, which is also equipped with functions for the creation and management of the website of a cultural institution. The overall structure also allows for the integration of external content, or entered by users, relating to other resources, reviews, tags, and links, as well as linked data.

[69] Arena Discovery: https://www.axiell.co.uk/arena-discovery/.
[70] Axiell Group: https://www.axiell.com.

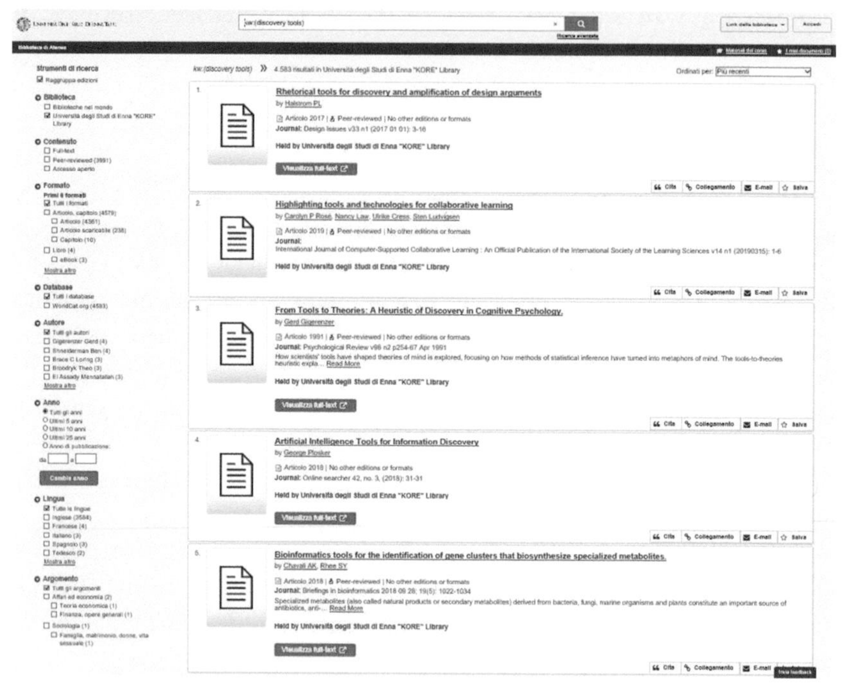

Figure 3.14 WorldCat Discovery at the University of Enna Kore.[71]

Also BiblioCore,[72] produced by BiblioCommons,[73] integrates with the other products of its own company, especially for the management of the entire website of a library. The aim of the tool is to promote and facilitate dialog between users and with the library through the catalog, favoring maximum interaction. In the social OPAC network, the system allows you to share all kinds of information and makes available a set of reviews and evaluations, but also related events and other resources, created by the library as much as by its users.

Suitable for any kind of library, Enterprise,[74] produced by SirsiDynix,[75] is a discovery tool developed to be able to use external indices as well. The system, fully customizable, searches and returns in a single interface results from the library databases, from the databases of other manufacturers, and

[71] https://unikore.on.worldcat.org/discovery.
[72] BiblioCore: https://www.bibliocommons.com/products/bibliocore/.
[73] BiblioCommons: https://www.bibliocommons.com/.
[74] SirsiDynix Enterprise: http://www.sirsidynix.com/products/enterprise.
[75] SirsiDynix: http://www.sirsidynix.com/.

from the entire Web, with which it shares linked data. It is also possible to retrieve results from databases of different publishers, by accessing the subscribed content directly.

Other tools to be aware of are open-source products. The most famous and widespread is VuFind,[76] a next-generation catalog system that can integrate with wider discovery tool systems, which represents the experience of an open tool to be developed with the help of the library community. Pioneering and exemplary is the integration between VuFind and the Summon discovery tool, originally implemented at Villanova's Falvey memorial library University.[77]

Finally, a notable project is eXtensible Catalog,[78] started in 2006 by the River Campus Libraries of the University of Rochester, which has developed a series of discovery tools that can be freely used independently or as parts of other more complex products.

3.3 Problems of system implementation and data visualization

To deal with the various issues related to the process of implementing a discovery tool, it is possible to refer to a sufficiently recent survey that presents an overview of the cases of adoption of a WSDS system in the context of academic libraries.[79]

The rich debate that took place in the past years on the usefulness and effectiveness of discovery tools seems to have died out without producing precise theoretical or practical results. At the same time, these systems have been implemented in an ever-increasing number of libraries and academic library systems. On this basis, the purpose of the authors of the survey was

[76] VuFind: https://vufind.org/vufind/.

[77] Falvey memorial library. Villanova University: https://library.villanova.edu/Find. See also: John Houser, The VuFind implementation at Villanova University, "Library Hi Tech," 27 (2009), no. 1, p. 93—105, https://www.emerald.com/insight/content/doi/10.1108/07378830910942955/full/html. Finally: Bijan Kumar Roy [et al.], Designing web-scale discovery systems using the VuFind open source software, "Library hi tech news," 35 (2018), no. 3, p. 16—22, https://www.emerald.com/insight/content/doi/10.1108/LHTN-12-2017-0088/full/html.

[78] Extensible Catalog Organization: https://www.extensiblecatalog.org/.

[79] Aaron F. Nichols [et al.], What does it take to make discovery a success? A survey of discovery tool adoption, instruction, and evaluation among academic libraries, "Journal of web librarianship," 11 (2017), no. 2, p. 85—104, https://www.tandfonline.com/toc/wjwl20/11/2?nav=tocList.

to connect the different experiences of implementation and management of discovery tools in libraries, trying to reach an overall vision of the chances of success or failure of the research and discovery tool.

An accurate literature review is the premise of the article, thanks to which the authors regret that most of the studies on WSDS have been conducted on a "small-scale" level, pertaining to a single university or institution, and often only one or a few aspects among those of systems' operation.[80] The focus of many of these studies seems to concern users' behavior, but also the attitude of librarians, and little has been studied regarding students' opinions. Much of this literature highlights the role of reference and information literacy, as well as the criticisms addressed to the tools, many of which derive from little information and prejudices. On the other hand, various reports do not clarify to which extent favorable or not favorable attitudes toward the system influence the implementation and promotion processes, and the level of integration and usefulness achieved compared with other services. Generally, there is a lack of a broad vision and perspective of an educational program regarding the new tools, for both librarians and users. Furthermore, there is a lack of data on the impact evaluation of the WSDS—above all, obviously, for the long term—but the documentation of selection and experimentation practices is extensive.

The aforementioned survey was conducted with quantitative methods, in the early months of 2016, in relation to the experiences of implementation, education, use, and evaluation of discovery systems. The sample to which the questionnaire was proposed represents the population of medium-sized public US universities, but of the 194 institutions invited, only 56 replied. Even this survey—not very recent, by the way—turns out to be partial, both geographically and numerically, but the theoretical assumptions are useful for identifying the general problem of implementation and setting up of a discovery tool.

At the time of the investigation, the Summon system was the most used, followed by Primo and EDS, and there were few installations of WorldCat or other tools. Within the institutions screened, the smaller ones showed a tendency toward Summon, the larger ones adopted Primo. However, the trend is not supported by precise differences in the adaptability of systems to the size of universities, with respect to which software is indifferent. The only hypothesis that can be formulated is that relating to the complexity of

[80] Cfr. A. Nichols [et al.], What does it take to make discovery a success? cit., p. 86—90.

the implementation and customization of each system, which requires dedicated time, personnel, and resources.

It is clear that a small- to medium-sized institution, which gains a quantitatively limited benefit from the adoption of a WSDS, tends not to invest much in implementation, retaining the default options and delegating the definition of a useful profile to the manufacturer. Any subsequent work to enrich and customize the system must be motivated by a clear users' request for development of the service and be connected to user experience evaluation, and involves the purchase of modules, apps, and maintenance, as well as electronic resources to be included among the accessible ones. All this needs dedicated staff to follow the entire growth process.

The first questions of the questionnaire concerned software configuration and technical support, i.e., the choice of the discovery tool, the organization and responsibilities of the dedicated staff, the need to delegate some functions outside, and the definition of a working group for monitoring and maintenance tasks.[81] Most libraries have established a semi-permanent group engaged in the development of the system. In some cases, this group is composed by staff volunteers who take roles in turn; few libraries have appointed a "full-time" discovery librarian. Outsourcing is, in any case, very limited, or at most delegated to the system manufacturer himself. Some of the working groups have closely followed the various operations of choosing and implementing the system, but not always continued to follow the operation after entering the "go-live" phase.

The issue of having a dedicated working group to the discovery system implementation is in many ways linked to that of the criteria for choosing a given product. If the institution is unable to dedicate time and resources to the discovery tool—or is not interested in it—the staff who deal with this process will also be either reduced or totally lacking. A permanently

[81] The discovery tools literature has produced a number of guides for the early stages of this process, such as selection and initial configuration, but there is a lack of specific guidance on staff organization, advanced configuration, maintenance, and evaluation—for which, with the exception of organizing the staff, one can resort to the guides and extensive assistance that producers offer. Among these guides: Planning and implementing resource discovery tools in academic libraries cit.; Marshall Breeding, Library resource discovery products: context, library perspectives, and vendor positions, "Library technology reports," 50 (2014), no. 1, p. 5—58.

constituted group for maintenance and development is, of course, essential to the success of a WSDS, but a number of specialized, full-time members must be part of it. Given the cloud management of the software, for technical problems, it is always possible to refer to the manufacturer, but staff members with IT skills are needed for a series of related issues, such as connections, proxy services, Web pages hosting the services, and data management. Librarians who deal with databases, e-journals, and e-books must also interact constantly with the system, to monitor the searchability and accessibility of resources, to update metadata, etc. Same thing for librarians who deal with catalog services and other institutional databases, but also reference services, evaluation, and user education, not to mention resources promotion and funding.

Therefore, the management of a WSDS must be extended to the entire library and be integrated with all its functions. The staff who is constantly following the system implementation must be knowledgeable on a set of skills that are to be shared with other librarians, and, despite the assistance of producers that is generally always provided in relation to each of these aspects, many decisions and activities remain of "political" nature and cannot be effectively supported by an outside party. In addition, creating a working group is always positive in the light of the expenditures for a WSDS and the outcomes that are expected from its implementation. Deciding not creating it at all and entrusting the system to the producer's assistance might prove to be an undemanding but highly risky solution.

The questionnaire then asked what were the strategies for presenting discovery tools in training programs, which parts of the academic population were reached, and if librarians were directly involved in training. The results state that librarians were not usually required to teach the discovery system, but when they did, they turned right to the first-year students—who from the results of the questionnaire always seem to be more interested than the rest of the academic population. For students, the aim is almost always to explain how to start a search on very broad or general topics.

The issue of educating to the use of searching tools is a very broad and delicate one, but fortunately there are a number of studies and guides on the subject, even if discovery tools are not at the center of information literacy programs.[82] Although the relative ease of use of the tools allows them to focus more on preliminary issues, such as education in the critical evaluation of the results and the tools themselves, most librarians who dedicate themselves to explaining discovery tools tend to instruct users on the management of long lists of results and filters to allow them to discern which are more centered on the search theme.

The answers to the question relating to the presence of discovery tools on the library's Web pages confirmed the general trend, which is also clear outside the surveyed population.[83] Discovery systems tend to have a central position on the home pages of libraries and library systems, often through an *iframe*[84] that shows the main box for the basic search and a few links for the advanced search and information on the WSDS, as well as for any subsections of the system. This positioning is often due, rather than for promotional reasons of the discovery tool itself, to the attempt to "attract" users to the pages of the library by showing a Google-like tool. Furthermore, the discovery tool is easily accessible from many other pages related to electronic resources, the catalog, e-learning systems, and services users' guides.

The OPAC, in fact, must often adapt to a secondary position, in few cases equal to that of the discovery tool. Many institutions, however, almost no longer see the reason to maintain the OPAC as such, and often it becomes a search option of the discovery system, called local collection or similar.

[82] This question is dealt with more fully later in Chapter 4. The bibliographic indications relating to information literacy on discovery tools are mainly concentrated in the chapter, but also present in various points of the entire discussion. Regarding this point, see: Stefanie Buck; Christina Steffy, Promising practices in instruction of discovery tools, "Communications in Information Literacy," 7 (2013), no. 1, p. 66–80, https://pdxscholar.library.pdx.edu/comminfolit/vol7/iss1/6/.

[83] On this topic: Julia Gross; Lutie Sheridan, Web-scale discovery: the user experience, "New library world," 112 (2011), no. 5–6, p. 236–247, https://www.emerald.com/insight/content/doi/10.1108/03074801111136275/full/html.

[84] "An inline frame places another HTML document in a frame. Unlike an <object/> element, an <iframe> can be the 'target' frame for links defined by other elements, and it can be selected by the user agent as the focus for printing, viewing its source, and so on. The content of the element is used as alternative text to be displayed if the browser does not support inline frames." See: Iframe. In: Wikipedia, the free Encyclopedia, https://en.wikipedia.org/wiki/HTML_element#Frames.

Another question in the survey investigated the system evaluation practices and the measurements obtained. The largest percentage of responses stated only "informal" feedback criteria, derived from opinions gathered during routine meetings with students, researchers, professors, and other librarians. Few libraries referred to employ usability tests or usage statistics, available, beside other things, among the functions of the discovery tool in use. Very few mentioned to have brought about real evaluation studies, while others did not bother at all to test the system's effectiveness.

Yet the evaluation of the discovery system should represent a priority before to decide about either the maintenance or the development of the service and to establish the changes to be made to it to improve its usefulness to the community served. In this regard, there are plenty of studies carried out by various institutions, and published for the benefit of all,[85] but other institutions' surveys cannot and should not be the guide for one's own operational strategies—they can, however, serve as a model for producing one's own strategy and evaluation tools. Each evaluation and subsequent correction activity must be tailored to the exact size of the instrument being managed and must lead to a subsequent promotion and reevaluation cycle of the implemented changes.

The final question of the survey investigated what success rate was believed to have been achieved with the implementation of the new research and discovery system. The acquisition of a discovery tool is often considered a success, even if it is not immediate, but conquered after a series of improvements and promotions. Few have considered it a failure, but some others do not quite know how to see it. In any case, all failures seem to be due to weak implementation policies, little investments, and almost no involvement of the manufacturer in the early stages of setup.

Regarding the general comments to the questionnaire, it can be noted that many librarians believed in the usefulness of discovery tools and in the need to learn about them and use and promote them, but the number of

[85] Take for example: David J. Comeaux, Usability testing of a Web-scale discovery system at an academic library, "College & undergraduate libraries," 19 (2012), no. 2–4, p. 189–206, https://www.tandfonline.com/doi/full/10.1080/10691316.2012.695671; Jody Condit Fagan [et al.], Usability test results for a discovery tool in an academic library, "Information technology and libraries," 31 (2012), no. 1, p. 83–112, https://ejournals.bc.edu/index.php/ital/article/view/1855; A. F. Nichols [et al.], Kicking the tires cit.

those who resist them is still high, perhaps biased by prejudice due to lack of retraining, or concern about one's own inadequacy to understand the new tool—often emerging through unmotivated criticism and irony, which generically recall the quality of traditional tools and the tradition that produced them. Conversely, some resistances may depend on an initial disappointment in the face of technical inefficiencies of the tool, such as the imprecise harvesting of the catalog data, or the incorrect reporting of inaccessible resources. Despite being grounded as dependent on real problems, the willingness to solve the technical problems would overcome these failures.

In any case, following the first process of implementation and verification of the functioning of the discovery tools, it is still possible to change the tool or the manufacturer, to change or replace the implementation staff, and to reorganize the resources used by the system or other related services. The implementation plan can be varied or strengthened, and evaluation and reevaluation can strongly intersect with promotion. Things can change, and the effectiveness of the service can grow to the point of making it indispensable. In all this, obviously, it is necessary to always maintain a critical but proactive viewpoint toward the aforenamed tool, to avoid easy disappointments but also equally easy optimistic illusions.

Reading research and specialized literature can be a great help to assist in the development of the WSDS. Especially useful are studies about the implementation of a WSDS as a process that must concern the entire library environment and related cultural factors—anthropological, social, intellectual, technological, etc. Nonetheless, libraries essentially need to be in contact with their users and understand and guide them, taking care to carrying out the implementation and development process while balancing among the necessary time, personnel, and money resources. We should not be afraid of the difficulties and the confused and infinite world that discovery tools seem, at first sight, to evoke. The necessary political, administrative, and technological changes, as well as more general "mentality" changes, must be faced with patience and confidence in the "investment."

Without prejudice to a critical stance and a constant attention, the new tools can be welcomed with optimism, because they will not destroy the achievements of the librarianship tradition. We can also trust some advice from the producers, however, interested in the functioning of the system and the benefit of the community using these tools.

At the conclusion of each implementation practice of the WSDS, at the end of each operating procedure, the goal of each process is always the display of the retrieved data, which takes place through a graphical user interface (GUI) designed for the final user. The whole problem can be seen from the perspective of the "communicative process," through which a library communicates to users about the entire process of research and discovery of information, the nature, quality and specificity of the information retrieved, and the possibility of accessing the contents.

Regarding this communication process, Antonella Trombone considers the application of cataloging methodologies in view of the final visualization of the data on the Web, considering the cataloging itself as a communicative activity, deeply connected to the final form of data visualization.[86] In fact, in a short span of years, catalogs have revolutionized their communication system, from a "local" communication based on the paper format of resources to a Web-scale one possible with the OPAC, since they have always evolved following the updated trends of society in general and the needs of its users.

Card catalogs are now considered only for their historical value, so much so that in some cases the old catalogs have been digitized like ancient books, and are often only used for historical reconstructions—except in some cases, when card catalogs or copies thereof are still necessary to explore collections that are not electronically cataloged. The type of communication that these catalogs allowed was rather "direct"; it took place between cataloger and user through what was reported on the card, without data or metadata internal to the system and basically not displayed, and without the mediation of a visualization software or a code that structured the data itself. The order of the cards was fixed for the users, whereas it could be changed by the catalog staff for updates of different types, and consequently the procedures for scrolling and searching for information were fixed.

This clearly entailed no possibility of visualizing the data according to patterns and combinations redefined from time to time according to the needs of a search, and, even worse, the user had no possibility of

[86] Antonella Trombone, New displaying models of bibliographic data and resources: cataloguing/resource description and search results, "JLIS.it," 5 (2014), no. 2, p. 19–32, https://www.jlis.it/article/view/10063. The topic is extensively detailed in Antonella Trombone, Principi di catalogazione e rappresentazione delle entità bibliografiche. Roma: AIB, 2018 (in particular, cf. p. 149–240).

"manipulating" the data through query strategies useful to satisfy specific information needs. A "flat" and static data production and search system was reflected in a consistent display criterion, without any possibility of dynamics and interaction to reproduce the following search, and consequently, the first display of the results.

This system has been deconstructed and rebuilt following the technological innovations of the communication systems. Since the early 1970s, Trombone continues, the ISBD model has also appeared as a model for the communication of bibliographic data, not only for the description, precisely because it allows the identification of the elements and their function, regardless of the language in which they are described, as such being independent from the linguistic understanding itself. The ISBD structure, in fact, can be considered a "knowledge model," so much so that today it is "compatible" with the structures of the Semantic Web, given that the syntactic relationships provided by the model itself express the meaning of the elements contained in it.

In any case, the communication format of ISBD—after being used for the latest paper files and for the first digital records—has been replaced by other less rigorous communication models, which are easier to understand for nonexpert users, based on descriptors and tags that explain the function of the reported elements. For example, the visualization model called "flag" in OPACs and discovery tools is certainly clearer for anyone, but it is less strong in structure than the expressive punctuation of ISBD, since it is not based on a stable coding of defined symbols, and the elements are variable and understandable according to the language in which they are produced.

In the 1970s, with the advent of the Web and the publication of OPACs in HTML, the way of preparing cataloging data changed again, also due to the new display destination. This innovation and the structure of the cataloging software have shaken the ISBD model, given the development of dynamic record visualization schemes composed of tags that include the description of the function of following data, aside of the possibility to still display the record in ISBD format, anyway. These display models, however, were associated to HTML links capable of ensuring navigation through the data and interaction with the search system, allowing not only customized views of the search results and the records themselves but also to relaunch the search starting from one of the data shown.

In subsequent generations of catalogs, the communicative relationship between cataloger and user is definitively mediated by the ILS software and the MARC format—which also entails the necessary hiding of some catalog production data that are useful only for catalogers and for the management of the catalog and related services. The MARC format also brings a degree of elaboration of the knowledge model that is now compatible even with the extreme granularity of the data required by the Semantic Web, but which would make the direct reading of the results even more incomprehensible to the end user.

This entails a series of advantages in the communication schemes of OPACs from the "second generation" onward and in the first discovery tools, which have become even more "discursive," but the overall universality of the information structuring scheme is lost, with all its rigidity but also efficiency. It is the IT mediation system that fully assumes the task of allowing the user to take advantage of the dynamic features of the display and search interface, leaving the system itself to solve issues such as those related to the language of communication—which at best can be changed at least at the level of descriptive tags.

Trombone then discusses the next-generation catalogs, which present a communication interface suitable for the Google era. According to the "classic" definition, these are not really catalogs, but rather systems capable of proposing a single list of results and services for accessing them, possibly relating to open resources.[87] In fact, these search systems are comfortable to users in that they offer simplified searching methods, such as the single search box, but use result ranking algorithms capable of displaying reliable selections of resources.

This is an important step forward in data communication and visualization methods, which brings librarians' perception of the functionality of the catalog closer to that of users. In fact, people prefer a communication environment whose characteristics resemble those of the Web, and where they are facilitated thanks to the enrichment of the catalog through links to content indexes, images, reviews, libraries, and all "additions" that maintain the quality of the set of data shown, while improving their visualization.

It has already been said how appropriate are search options through facets, or access links to full text, which together with new display options relaunch the possibility of searching and discovering useful results, and this leads more and more toward the communication system of the WSDS. Titles and authors almost become "secondary options," in the middle of the list presented in order of relevance, and knowing or not knowing names and titles does not hinder the achievement of a cognitive objective. Even

[87] Cfr. E. L. Morgan, Next generation library catalog cit.

more, however, as Trombone writes, this means that the order of the cataloging records cannot be arranged by librarians but is entirely mediated by the software and its relevance criteria, and the data on which the search takes place, the use of filters and sorting are not all set by librarians, but many are imported while the entire records metadata are harvested.

The possibilities of researching, recombining, and refining the results are endless, and this is something good, but the risk of this communication and visualization system through algorithmic relevance is to leave too much power to the mediation of the software, often mistaken for "disintermediation," and to forget that librarians improve the quality of data entered, as well as that they can facilitate searching paths.

In 1998, the publication of the FRBR model opened up new perspectives for the development of data visualization criteria, allowing some forms of record grouping with "near" data, as well as suggesting new possibilities for data navigation. The experimentation of the visualization anticipated by FRBR has been carried out for some time by a couple of discovery tools.[88] By showing the results related to the search for well-known works, which are present in multiple editions, versions, and formats, they also display a list of groups of similar records enclosed in boxes. Each box is expandable and leads to each individual manifestation, each of which has been included in the group mainly because it has a uniform title that identifies it as a version of a specific work.

This type of communication is effective in showing a sorting criterion of the results that is certainly alternative—and also parallel—to that of the automatic ranking, but technically it does not yet lead to the possibility of a new navigation system. As a consequence, the opportunity to structure a method of grouping the results that does not trespass this level without allowing further navigation still needs to be evaluated. Conversely, the conceptual vision of FRBR leads to a sort of navigation tree, which always allows to view the structure and hierarchy of the data among which you are navigating, and also to disclose each single node by clicking on it. This structure, which allows a real data visualization map, should be the most useful criterion for the development of new visualization models. All this, of course, can be relaunched in consideration of the current IFLA LRM model.

Coming to today's stage of the WSDS, Trombone recalls that it is a new type of research tools that cannot theoretically be linked to catalogs. In fact,

[88] Trombone suggests WorldCat and Primo, cf. p. 25.

they query an index of data collected "also" from catalogs, together with a series of other data from local and external databases with respect to a specific library. Also in this case, the communication and display criteria of the data traced in a search is strongly mediated by the ranking algorithm used by the system. In fact, in some systems, users can influence this algorithm, with their continuous searching and selection of results, but also through some tools created specifically to achieve this interaction.

The most evident outcome of these possibilities for the user to interact with the results is the availability of tools that allow to sort and reorder result lists each time according to different filters or facets, to the point that in some systems new relevance criteria are created. Moreover, some system producers can agree with the structures that acquire the discovery tool about a basic setting of the relevance criterion, for example, by favoring the results coming from the catalog. In addition, there are examples of tools that allow users to express their opinion about the adequacy of the results. Finally, the possibility of intervening on the sorting and display of the results is based on the use of the exclusion or inclusion filters, or on included or excluded data categories.

Regarding the effort to establish a good way of communicating with users, the latest discovery systems have certainly overcome the rigidity of the more than 200-year-old card catalog. However, we need to ask ourselves to what extent the extreme dynamism of discovery tools must be left free to develop, and to what extent it must be controlled to reach a compromise among librarians, users, and system producers. It is necessary to mind how much the cumbersome mediation of libraries is being replaced by an even more cumbersome mediation of software, which is dangerously hidden and disguised as disintermediation.

It is not possible to say that the WSDS, and the communicative mediation entrusted to them, are entirely guided by librarianship principles, nor can it be said that they are designed entirely for the needs of the users.[89] The first disillusionment, Trombone says, is created by the large amount of results recovered, the lack of a clear order, and the impossibility of reaching many contents beyond descriptive data. On the other hand, the first impression is that the rules, especially those for choosing and displaying the results, are dictated by the manufacturers of the systems, despite the possibility of customizing both systems and searches.

[89] On these critical elements, Trombone also returns in: Antonella Trombone, Formare e gestire collezioni con i discovery tools, "Biblioteche oggi," 37 (2019), no. 3, p. 11–19.

An undisputable point is the need to preserve library knowledge in every phase of the creation, structuring, archiving, research, and visualization of data. Only in this way, libraries will correctly manage and clearly define the principles of each part of the process of creation, collection, and communication of the raw material that is at the basis of every search for information and knowledge, thus allowing people to navigate among reliable, consistently processed, and effectively displayed data.

PART TWO

CHAPTER 4

Principles and theories

4.1 The linked data methodology and the Semantic Web project

In his White Paper, Breeding indicates the current discovery service model as the most suitable one to develop and endure from now on, both because it is a Web-scale model, and, precisely for this reason, it is ready to open up to the linked data system. Therefore, discovery systems can still improve and become more powerful, as they increasingly integrate into the general and widely shared ecosystem represented by the new Semantic Web, giving birth to systems based entirely on linked data rather than on descriptive and citational metadata.[1]

Despite the persistent reluctance in the activities of exposing academic, research, and bibliographic data in general, some ideas make us soon hope for the availability of a critical mass of open and connected data such as to make the new search and discovery system operate successfully, well beyond the commercial implementations that preside the field of discovery services today.[2]

In this sense, the innovation of information and knowledge management methods and systems must aim not only at the transformation of research and discovery systems, as well as the related database query

[1] Cf. M. Breeding, *The future of library resource discovery* cit., p. 24–26. See also: *Managing metadata in Web-scale discovery systems*, edited by Louise F. Spiteri. London: Facet, 2016.

[2] About the main international programs and projects for the dissemination of Linked Data, see: *Progressi dell'informazione e progresso delle conoscenze* cit. (in particular, see following papers: Mauro Guerrini and Carlotta Vivacqua, p. 139–160; Klaus Kempf, p. 161–172; Loredana Cerrone and Patrizia De Martino, p. 237–254); Tiziana Possemato; Roberto Delle Donne, *SHARE Catalogue: un'esperienza di cooperazione*, "Biblioteche oggi," 35 (2017), no. 1, p. 21–29; Raphaëlle Lapôtre, *Library Metadata on the Web: the example of data.bnf.fr*, "JLIS.it," 8 (2017), no. 3, p. 58–70, https://www.jlis.it/article/view/12402; Valeria Lo Castro, *Linked Data nelle biblioteche digitali e di ricerca*, "Biblioteche oggi," 33 (2015), no. 1, p. 36–44, http://www.bibliotecheoggi.it/rivista/article/view/5.

Web-Scale Discovery Services
ISBN 978-0-323-90298-4
https://doi.org/10.1016/B978-0-323-90298-4.00004-5

interfaces, but also at a new way to think, create, and organize the data in the same bases. Only in this way can the development of theories and methodologies reach the point of proposing a true "paradigm shift" in the definition of new lines of thought and action.[3]

A new organization of catalog data and other databases means above all "opening" the data, creating them in granular and interoperable format, beyond the classic rules and schemes of cataloging records and metadata formats.[4] Each data must have an "atomic" form, be autonomous, defined through widely shared models, prepared to be exposed on the Web, disseminated, reused, and must be such as to allow the integration and reaggregation of individual data in dynamic combinations, according to the needs and the point of view of the diverse end users. In this direction, catalogs must be restructured to provide the user with a systematic presentation of the bibliographic and nonbibliographic universe, relating to all forms of information registration, by effectively and dynamically organizing knowledge, assembling, and summarizing the granular data referring to the different entities related to a resource. All this is what the first FRBR model already suggested, which is reiterated in IFLA LRM, and which we try to implement through the implementation of schemes such as RDA.[5]

[3] In this regard, it is useful to reflect on essais that embrace some considerations on the current digital revolution in the library field: Sridevi S. [et al.] *Investigation on Blockchain technology for Web service composition: a case study*, "International Journal of Web Services Research." 18 (2021), no. 1, p. 1–23, https://www.igi-global.com/article/investigation-on-blockchain-technology-for-web-service-composition/261592; Rossana Morriello, *Blockchain, intelligenza artificiale e internet delle cose in biblioteca*, "AIB studi," 59 (2019), no. 1–2, p. 45–68, https://aibstudi.aib.it/article/view/11927.

[4] Regarding the first comments on the nonrelevance of rules and schemes such as AACR or MARC, see for example: Tom Delsey, *Modelling the logic of AACR*. In: *The principles and future of AACR: proceedings of the International conference on principles and future of AACR*, edited by Jean Weihs. Ottawa: Canadian Library Association, 1998, p. 1–16. See also: R. Tennant, *MARC must die* cit.

[5] Cf. Carlo Bianchini, *Futuri scenari: RDA, REICAT e la granularità dei cataloghi*, "Bollettino AIB," 50 (2010), no. 3, p. 219–238: p. 224–238, https://bollettino.aib.it/article/view/5319.

The openness and accessibility of data do not only depend on the methods of creation in a granular and interoperable format, but also on the philosophy underlying the methodologies of metadating, and on the reasons of creating open data, and linked open data (LOD), which dialog with the outside world, society, and the Web. Against various kinds of restrictions on the circulation and reuse of data[6] that limit the development of knowledge and the progress of society, it is necessary to agree on at which level to achieve the interconnection between open science and open government. This level can be represented by open bibliographic data, and substantiated by OPAC, databases, open archives, institutional archives, knowledge organization systems (KOS), and all the renewed bibliographic library system, really open to today's world.[7]

Data structures described through models applicable and usable in an interoperable way, metadata that can be shared between different information systems, and open and connected data are nothing new speaking of integration projects between libraries, archives, and museums (GLAM). In this regard, Alfredo Serrai recalls that ancient civilizations considered all these institutes as the "home of the Muses," and had almost the same name, diversifying over time and then carrying out different functions. Museums displayed unique specimens, libraries, and archives preserved and disseminated bibliographic resources and "legal" documents.[8] Therefore, and not only conceptually, it is necessary to propose a return to integration.

The linked data methodology and the Semantic Web focus on and simplify these integration objectives,[9] because in the basic logic of the RDF

[6] In this regard, the commitment of initiatives and projects such as: Open Knowledge Foundation: https://okfn.org; Open data commons: http://opendatacommons.org; Open library project: https://openlibrary.org. In addition, it is necessary to refer at least to: Public Knowledge Project: https://pkp.sfu.ca/; African Open Science platform: http://africanopenscience.org.za/; AmeLICA: http://www.amelica.org/en/; OpenAIRE: https://www.openaire.eu; cOAlition S: https://www.coalition-s.org/; OA2020: https://oa2020.org/; SciELO: https://www.scielo.org/.

[7] On this topic: Antonella De Robbio, *Forme e gradi di apertura dei dati: i nuovi alfabeti dell'Open Biblio tra scienza e società*, "Biblioteche oggi," 30 (2012), no. 6, p. 11–24; Mauro Guerrini, *La filosofia open: paradigma del servizio contemporaneo*, "Biblioteche oggi," 35 (2017), no. 4, p. 12–21; Bernard Rentier, *Open Science: the challenge of transparency*. Bruxelles: Académie Royale de Belgique, 2019.

[8] Alfredo Serrai, *Biblioteche, archivi, musei*, "Bibliothecae.it," 6 (2017), no. 1, p. 361–369, https://bibliothecae.unibo.it/article/view/7041.

[9] See: Ed Summers; Dorothea Salo, *Linking things on the Web: a pragmatic examination of Linked Data for libraries, archives and museums*, 2013, http://arxiv.org/abs/1302.4591.

scheme, which structures the new Web, integration is pushed far beyond the institutions of culture and memory,[10] and each data producer has a basic "grammar" and some specific "vocabularies" available to write their data in XML-RDF strings that can be widely shared.[11] Obviously, there are critical issues related to the various licenses for the reuse of data and, above all, to the distance between the original "semantic context" of aggregation and interpretation and that of any reaggregation and reinterpretation, which could only be covered through complex agreements between communities that by their nature create different data sets influenced by different ontologies.[12]

With regard to the universe of information, considered "also" from the perspective of libraries, the philosophy of the open data world converges toward various initiatives aiming at a conscious reevaluation of the principles of bibliographic processing. The tendency is to promote, instead of the traditional "linear" structure of description of a data set, "reticular" structures to open individually taken data, which can give a broader idea of the context of which a single resource is part of. Thanks to the RDA, BIBFRAME, or IFLA LRM models, libraries are increasingly looking at

[10] Examples of broad integration are represented by the SNAC project (Social networks and archival context): http://socialarchive.iath.virginia.edu, and, obviously, by Europeana: http://www.europeana.eu (see also: http://labs.europeana.eu/api/linked-open-data/introduction).

[11] See: Eric J. Miller, *An introduction to the Resource Description Framework*, "Journal of library administration," 34 (2001), no. 3/4, p. 245–255, https://www.tandfonline.com/doi/abs/10.1300/J111v34n03_04. Furthermore, cf. *RDF schema 1.1*, edited by Dan Brickley, Ramanathan V. Guha. W3C, 2014, http://www.w3.org/TR/rdf-schema.

[12] For a first survey on the problem of MAB integration through Linked Data, cf. Salvatore Vassallo, *L'integrazione tra archivi e biblioteche alla prova del Web semantico*. In: *Biblioteche in cerca di alleati. Oltre la cooperazione, verso nuove strategie di condivisione*. Milano: Bibliografica, 2013, p. 430–454. *To evaluate the problem from the point of view of discovery systems*, cf. T. Louise; M. Kidder, *Exploring discovery @ Rosenberg Library: what happens when a library, a museum, and an archive get together to share a single discovery tool?* In: *Exploring discovery: the front door to your library's licensed and digitized content*, edited by Kenneth J. Varnum. Chicago: ALA, 2016, p. 35–43.

the possibility of creating data, or of linking existing data, according to a new method based on maximum interoperability, and of managing such data with new means of treatment and research, which will really meet people's needs, providing more powerful and semantically organized tools.[13]

The emphasis is on the need to truly bring the focus of the catalogs back to the people who should use them, a decisive step to hinder their preference to other less reliable but apparently helpful tools. In this sense, the publication of FRBR in 1998 already represents a real fundamental turning point for catalogs. In fact, the report presents a new logical model to modify bibliographic and cataloging concepts in depth, and was at the basis both of the logic reorganization of the ICPs in 2009, strengthened in the 2016 edition, as well as for the revision of IFLA international standards such as ISBD,[14] and for the development of cataloging codes such as REICAT[15] and RDA. Regarding all the applications of what has been called the FRBR family,[16] now consolidated in IFLA LRM, the impulses for change deriving from FRBR presuppose not only the transformation of the catalog data structure, but also of the bibliographic formats and of the cataloging software. Therefore, the object is no more the "monolithic" record in itself, but the entities as related one to another, thus allowing a broader and more global approach to resources, also interpreting them as sets of connected data, to be processed, disseminated, and shared. The traditional perspective of the bibliographic "record" is replaced by that of the "data set," consisting of the connection of autonomous data, once again underlining the growing importance of a granular conception of data organization (Fig. 4.15).

[13] For an analysis of information processes that can serve as a model for new systems, cf. Antonella Iacono, *Verso un nuovo modello di OPAC. Dal recupero dell'informazione alla creazione di conoscenza*, «JLIS.it», 4 (2013), no. 2, p. 85–107: p. 92–102, https://www.jlis.it/article/view/8903. Concerning the possibilities of interoperability between the different bibliographic conceptual models, cf. Sofia Zapounidou [et al.], *Representing and integrating bibliographic information into the Semantic Web: a comparison of four conceptual models*, "Journal of information science," 43 (2017), no. 4, p. 525–553, https://journals.sagepub.com/doi/full/10.1177/0165551516650410.

[14] In particular the 2011 edition.

[15] REICAT are the *REgole Italiane di CATalogazione*, inspired by FRBR, and published in 2009.

[16] The family is composed of *Functional requirements for bibliographic records* (FRBR), *Functional requirements for authority data* (FRAD) and *Functional requirements for subject authority data* (FRSAD): cf. Functional requirements: the FRBR family of models. 2014, http://www.ifla.org/node/2016.

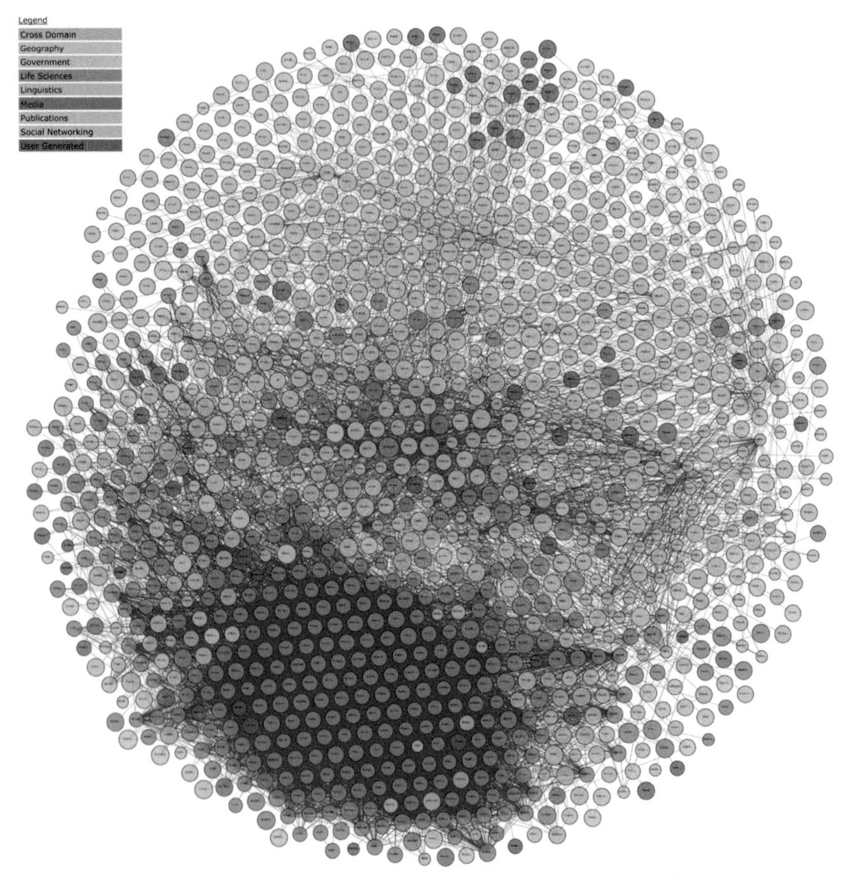

Figure 4.15 *Linked Open Data cloud* in May 2020.[17]

Starting from different assumptions, even the world of the Web must face a similar revolution, which can lead it to transform itself from the Web of monolithic documents to the Semantic Web of atomic and interconnected data.[18] As a consequence, far more than just a convergence

[17] John P. McCrae, *The Linked Open Data cloud*. 2020, http://lod-cloud.net/.

[18] In general, cf.: Tim Berners-Lee, *Semantic Web road map*. 1998, http://www.w3.org/DesignIssues/Semantic.html; Tim Berners-Lee [et al.], *The Semantic Web: a new form of Web content that is meaningful to computers will unleash a revolution of new possibilities*, "Scientific American," 284 (2001), no. 5, p. 34–43, https://www.scientificamerican.com/article/the-semantic-Web/; Tim Berners-Lee, *Linked Data*. 2006, http://www.w3.org/DesignIssues/LinkedData.html; Tom Heath; Christian Bizer, *Linked Data: evolving the Web into a global data space*. New York: Morgan & Claypool, 2011.

between libraries and the Web is achieved, both because the principles set by Tim Berners-Lee for Linked Data, as foundations for the Semantic Web, can be transferred into the new logic of creation and publication of bibliographic descriptions, and furthermore because the highly reliable data disseminated by institutions such as libraries are, in fact, highly regarded for the functioning of the Semantic Web itself.[19]

Technological interoperability has always been recognized as the basis for achieving these innovations aimed at maximum openness and sharing of data, which would be impossible without tools that enable to enrich large unified databases or to connect databases scattered around the planet one to another. Interoperability is based on shared models for structuring data relating to resources, on agreement about languages and vocabularies for analysis and description, on authority control of the uniqueness and reliability of access data, on open protocols for the circulation of data itself, and on a series of technological but also political choices and decisions regarding the possibility and right of reuse of data and resources, and regarding the creation and property rights.[20]

From a technical point of view, the wide sharing of each resource immediately seemed to be a problem mainly in the light of two factors: the data description scheme and the identification of each data. The interoperability of a descriptive scheme is the basic achievement to be developed through a format capable of meeting the needs of different cultural

[19] This is also in: W3C. Library Linked Data incubator group, *Library Linked Data incubator group final report* cit. The convergence between libraries and the Semantic Web, it has been said, has been the subject of conferences and subsequent LIS publications, in particular: "Global interoperability and Linked Data in libraries" cit.; *Global interoperability and Linked Data in libraries* cit.; "Convegno AIB CILW 2016" cit.; *Progressi dell'informazione e progresso delle conoscenze* cit.; *L'universo delle risorse culturali* cit.

[20] Cf. Junzhi Jia, *From data to knowledge: the relationships between vocabularies, linked data and knowledge graphs*, "Journal of Documentation," 77 (2021), no. 1, p. 93–105, https://www.emerald.com/insight/content/doi/10.1108/JD-03-2020-0036/full/html?skipTracking=true. Regarding the experience of a portal that aggregates cultural assets of very different types: Paul Gabriele Weston [et al.], *Authority data and cross-domain intersection within aggregation portals: the case of BeWeb,* "JLIS.it," 8 (2017), no. 1, p. 139–154, https://www.jlis.it/article/view/12127.

communities that deal with diverse resources[21]; the reliability of an identifier can be obtained by developing a permanent system for pointing to a resource.[22]

In this sense, the identifier is reliable if the "agent" who proposes, manages, and maintains it is a priori faithful and reliable, recognized by all as undoubtedly able to define by authority the identified object, its code, and address.[23] Similarly, the descriptive scheme truly encompasses everyone's needs if the issuing organism is composed of various components of the communities to which it is addressed and with which they can identify.[24]

In this context of mutual trust and collaboration, also considering the current technology, it is possible to introduce the linked data mechanism and the Semantic Web project, as already proposed in 1999 by the inventor of the "traditional" Web, Tim Berners-Lee.[25] Linked data and Semantic Web develop, in fact, not as a top down, but as a bottom up system, to be implemented by a multiplicity of subjects on the Web as we now know it, in the sense in which they leverage a given sharing disposition between individuals who, each on their own path, come together on a great common road to build together.[26]

The fundamental even if simple rules to implement this revolution, which involves the entire Web, were set by Berners-Lee himself, who proposed them to achieve the evolution of the "Web of documents" toward the "Web of data"[27]:

- Use URIs as names for things.

[21] The first reference model is undoubtedly the Dublin Core Metadata Initiative (DCMI): http://dublincore.org/.

[22] In this regard, a lot of work has been done on the development of URLs (Uniform Resource Locators) in URN (Uniform Resource Name), PURL (Persistent Uniform Resource Locator) or URI (Uniform Resource Identifier). See: *Uniform Resource Identifier*. In: *Wikipedia, the free encyclopedia*, https://en.wikipedia.org/wiki/Uniform_Resource_Identifier (a compendium, for the LIS sector: Alberto Salarelli; Anna Maria Tammaro, *La biblioteca digitale*. Milano: Bibliografica, 2006, p. 108–111).

[23] VIAF was born on the basis of the recognition of the authority in identifying people of national bibliographic agencies (Virtual International Authority File): https://viaf.org/.

[24] Thus, the DCMI scheme, and the more recent EDM, arise from the agreement of a multiple group. For EDM (Europeana Data Model), see: http://pro.europeana.eu/page/edm-documentation.

[25] Tim Berners-Lee; Mark Fischetti, *Weaving the Web: the original design and ultimate destiny of the World Wide Web by its inventor*. San Francisco: Harper Collins, 1999.

[26] Cf. Antonella Iacono, *Linked Data*. Roma: AIB, 2014, p. 12–13.

[27] T. Berners-Lee, *Linked Data* cit.

- Use HTTP URIs so that people can look up those names.
- When someone looks up a URI, provide useful information, using the standards (RDF*, SPARQL).
- Include links to other URIs, so that they can discover more things.

Through these rules, and by sharing the practices and protocols of the World Wide Web Consortium (W3C),[28] linked data can be written and their relationships represented, which in the form of a "triple" populate the space of the Semantic Web allow inferences to "intelligent" search engines and allow semantic browsers to navigate the Web through new paths.[29]

In this way, a semantic network is built for the organization of resources, which can also be "interpreted" by machines, made up of triple connections of entities and relationships, between various resources described according to the model RDF[30] and identified by URI,[31] with an XML syntax composed of terms and markers.[32] Appropriate tools, with the same characteristics of generality and shareability, allow to structure the system in its entirety: OWL, for the structuring of formal ontologies, each aimed at representing the different domains of knowledge[33]; SKOS, for the coding and interoperability of thesauri with the aim of formally defining the relationships between concepts and terms of different fields[34]; SPARQL, for querying the data produced in RDF[35] (Figs. 4.16–4.18).

[28] World Wide Web Consortium (W3C): http://www.w3.org/.

[29] To enter the world of Linked Data: T. Berners-Lee [et al.], *The Semantic Web* cit.; T. Heath; C. Bizer, *Linked Data* cit.; W3C. Library Linked Data incubator group, *Library Linked Data incubator group final report* cit.; M. Guerrini; T. Possemato, *Linked Data* cit.; A. Iacono, *Linked Data* cit.; *Linked Data for cultural heritage*, edited by Ed Jones, Michele Seikel. ALA, 2016.

[30] RDF (Resource Description Framework): http://www.w3.org/RDF.

[31] *Uniform Resource Identifier* cit.

[32] The Semantic Web technology—he repeats—is based on the use of URIs, uniquely assigned to an object, which identify it exactly, distinguishing it from all the others, and which allow its localization. The new Web, through the linked data network, is structured by dynamically organizing different connection relationships in the form of a "triple"— primary semantic structure, also very simple: subject–predicate–object— among the data identified by such URI. The linked data strings are written in XML language, to be fully interoperable. For an example, see also: M. Guerrini; T. Possemato, *Linked Data* cit.

[33] OWL (Web Ontology Language): https://www.w3.org/OWL/.

[34] SKOS (Simple Knowledge Organization System): http://www.w3.org/2004/02/skos/.

[35] SPARQL Protocol And RDF Query Language: http://www.w3.org/TR/sparql11-overview/.

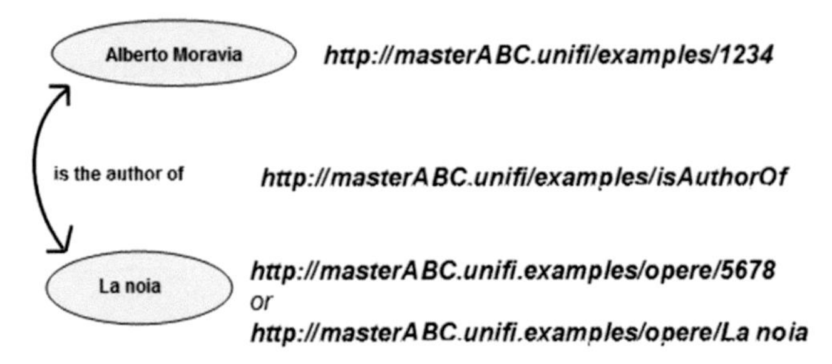

Figure 4.16 Representation of a triple (nodes and arcs) in RDF.

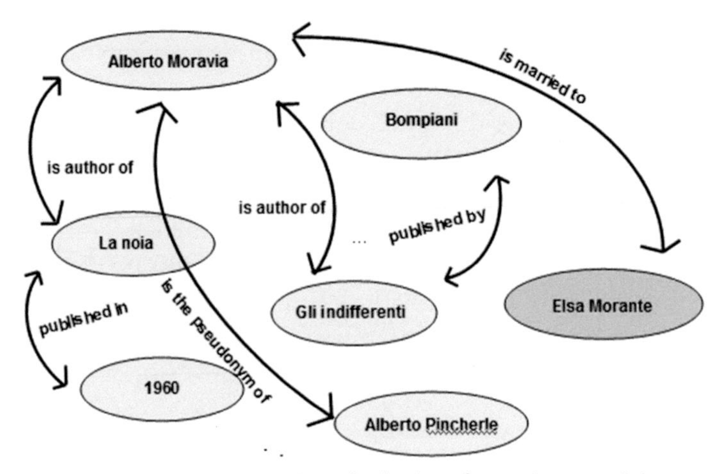

Figure 4.17 Representation of a lattice of assertions or triples.

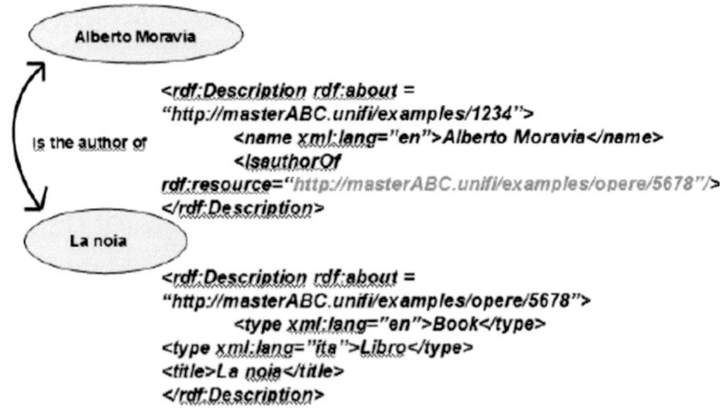

Figure 4.18 Representation of a triple in RDF/XML.[36]

[36] The three explanatory images are taken from M. Guerrini; T. Possemato, *Linked Data* cit., p. 81–82.

On the whole, this new technology, which is rapidly growing because it is simple, neutral, and open,[37] could be the right solution to achieve a true and wide exploitation of also open[38] data produced and disseminated by cultural organizations.[39] Improving the conditions of interoperability of resources would become the constitutive basis of their dissemination, to the point that it is no longer even necessary to talk about "data interoperability," but simply to indicate linked open data, or LODs.

The LODs are maximally granular and atomic, they are not enclosed in any predefined card, they are by nature interoperable, they are in principle shareable and reusable, they can be summed up and incrementally increased, they do not bind an institution to any language or culture, they are composed of neutral labels that are not directly related to concepts, and they refer to authority definitions identified by reliable URIs. Therefore, the Semantic Web is, as a result of their application, an unlimited set of connections, created by all and accessible to all while being owned by no one, under the responsibility of everyone, without predefined concepts or schematizations but capable of reaching valid concepts and models universally recognized.

Precisely because we are talking about a technology that must meet the needs of all the communities concerned, including those less "equipped" with IT or semantic tools—such as the generic community of "simple" Web users—some critical issues must be faced, also illustrated by some of the main communities involved in the project, such as libraries, archives, and museums.

The granularity of information is the main prerequisite of the revolution that ushers from the monolithic bibliographic record to a set of data, not necessarily of bibliographic nature, which is expandable, interconnectable, and reusable "also" in the bibliographic field.[40] The data in its own right,

[37] Based on the RDF scheme, truly all-encompassing because it is simple and basically neutral.

[38] Open data are published in an easily traceable way on the Web, in standard and widespread formats, according to rules of sharing and nonownership that are increasingly accepted at a technical and political level. About it, cf.: A. De Robbio, *Forme e gradi di apertura dei dati* cit.; M. Guerrini, *La filosofia open* cit.

[39] To make the point of the situation, cf. Thimmaiah Padmavathi; Madaiah Krishnamurthy, *Semantic Web tools and techniques for Knowledge Organization: an overview*, "Knowledge Organization," 44 (2017), no. 4, p. 273–290.

[40] An overview of this development in: C. Bianchini, *Dagli OPAC ai library Linked Data* cit.

understood in its individual and absolute value—"agnostic" with respect to processing languages and cultures—as the informational atom identified by a URI, is the foundation of the XML-RDF string system that can be interconnected. However, this "isolated" information can belong to all possible contexts, which is equivalent to admit it and does not belong to any context. This condition can lead, as already mentioned, to the risk of dispersion of the original belonging context of a resource, which is represented in various occurrences by the single data. The need for contextualization is strongly felt in the archival community,[41] but no less in the library field,[42] and it can certainly generate perplexity also in other areas, whenever several data diverge too far from the aggregation that, in a certain sector, can better represent an organic resource, to be variously combined and interpreted in other kinds of sets.

As a matter of fact, the architecture of the Semantic Web still implies an organizational choice of raw data, and consequently a specific information choice, however neutral or agnostic, it can be from a cognitive point of view. Granularity is therefore a way of seeing the information world, a paradigm for knowledge. This affects the subsequent visions of information data through the technological system of linked data that originates from this base, despite the general tendency to consider LOD one of the most neutral and general solution, in any case.[43]

As a consequence, the act of sharing remains of high value, for the many reasons mentioned above, but—like the connected culture of "convergence"—it must not damage the recognizability of the resource itself, which is shared together with its "own" data. The LOD paradigm provides the basis for bibliographic, archival, and museum communities, together with many other more or less strictly cultural communities. But, to effectively achieve the result of sharing heritage and culture, each of the communities involved must play its role, and promote its own authority, to achieve a

[41] In addition to the historical discussion of the importance of the context of each archival document, more recent examples of the problem in the digital environment are in: Giovanni Michetti, *Linked Data nel dominio archivistico: rischi e opportunità*. In: *Progressi dell'informazione e progresso delle conoscenze* cit., p. 255–277; M. Guercio; C. Carloni, *The research archives in the digital environment* cit.

[42] Alberto Salarelli, *Sul perché, anche nel mondo dei Linked Data, non possiamo rinunciare al concetto di documento*, "AIB studi," 54 (2014), no. 2/3, p. 279–293, https://aibstudi.aib.it/article/view/10128.

[43] On this topic: Giovanni Michetti, *Ma è poi tanto pacifico che l'albero rispecchi l'archivio?*, "Archivi & Computer," 19 (2009), no. 1, p. 85–95.

convergence that shall not be perceived as homologation, flattening, or dispersion. Each context must be identifiable and reliable, precisely defined, and able to relate and contextualize the various information data that constitute it inside and outside its community. Even if renouncing to the closure of specialization and the "branding" on the data are elements of sincere desire to share among the different bodies, one must not give up identity, the presence of the "character" with which a resource can be distinguished, the "narrative," emotional, and all the other dimensions of cultural resources.

We cannot also be silent about the difficulties in effectively representing resources from a semantic point of view, especially when we are talking about cultural resources, which are even conceptually very complex. Moreover, they can be interpreted differently by diverse groups of people. Thus, the difficulty of developing ontologies appropriate for each context and that relate to different contexts is certainly a challenge for the development of the Semantic Web.

Apart from OWL and SKOS technologies, the conceptual fine-tuning of an ontology is a complex issue already within a given domain. Since it is a question of forcing content and concepts that are often very dynamic and "alive" within rigorous schemes, the agreement inside a community is the only solution to start finding the structures and terms capable of representing resources. Behind the simplicity of the LODs, there is certainly the complexity of defining the data with which to then compose the strings, and this complexity obviously increases when one points to the connection of different domains and data sets.

Also in this case, therefore, it is always essential to be able to reach a free international and intercultural agreement between the communities that produce and disseminate knowledge, at least within the various areas. Besides an intellectual agreement, then, it is also necessary to consider which society can benefit from this knowledge, while aiming for solutions that are not fumbled, but within the reach of all people, regardless of any educational and cultural level.

In this sense, a further criticality is related to the query language of the RDF systems. Using SPARQL is not easy, and it is necessary to know both the language and the ontology to which it applies to generate and perform a query. In this case, technology can help, if we aim at the creation of mediation tools that can create the relationship between common users and the questioned source. Thus, we always return to a discussion and commitment that is not only generally social, but, to develop tools and languages for the processing and dissemination of information and knowledge, one must always aim at all walks of life, and not to a small number of users.

It is a duty of current technology to produce tools that are not reserved for a few skilled users, and to prepare systems that can really be used by all people. It is always the task of the final dialog interfaces with the user to make the task of research and access simple and effective, transforming the operating structures of the machines into structures that anyone can intuitively use, so that cultural heritage is truly available to all mankind.[44]

The tools used first to navigate the Semantic Web, or Semantic Web browsers, are still being tested. A semantic browser, in essence, is a type of search engine that can navigate data and semantic connections. These tools can have an autonomous structure, or be structured as extensions of normal Web browsers.[45]

Semantic browsers were born following the W3C standards for the production of linked data and are, precisely, the machines capable of interpreting connections, of giving semantic value to connections, of creating new connections, and of finally allowing the sharing and reuse of data found between different applications. Therefore, the system allows each person to browse the Web of data and its interconnections in the same way as a traditional search engine allows you to visit the Web of documents, and its "static" sites, through the link mechanism. Obviously, instead of the HTML standard, semantic browsers refer to the RDF standard, which is able to formalize the semantics relating to the links between the navigated data. The machine "notes" the Web resources, associates them into categories, structures the links on the principle of entities, and presents users with a "meaningful" map of the resources found.

The need for these tools has obviously been increasingly required alongside the development of Semantic Web technologies, given the growing amount of semantic data published and the need to facilitate their navigation and make it simple for anyone. The user can, therefore, have a sort of direct access to data and information, not bound by the way in which

[44] On the "social" role of interfaces, see: Paola Castellucci, *George Boole: il pensiero dietro la maschera*. In: *L'organizzazione del sapere: studi in onore di Alfredo Serrai*, a cura di Maria Teresa Biagetti. Milano: Bonnard, 2004, p. 55–69. As a concrete example, you can see the semantic map of Google Knowledge Graph: https://www.google.it/intl/it/insidesearch/features/search/knowledge.html.

[45] The best known semantic browsers are Elda, Facet, LodLive, LodView, Marbles, Oh Yeah Chrome, Ripple, SView, Zitgist. A guide to these browsers is available at the URL: https://www.w3.org/2001/sw/wiki/Category:Semantic_Web_Browser.

they have been entered on a traditional Website, but referring directly to the data taken in itself, published according to RDF. The browser takes care, "democratically," of all the most complex processing and "interpretations," allowing the user a simple and intuitive view of the nodes and links.[46]

In this social and democratic perspective, the idea of the Semantic Web was soon rooted in the founder Berners-Lee and soon became a concrete project for the effective and democratic sharing of ideas, resources, and "things."[47] Linked data, in fact since 2009, are proposed as the simple and "open" technology for the structuring of the Semantic Web, as best practices to be followed even if only to conceive the principle of sharing atomic data, their interoperability, and granular constitution inside the new information network.[48]

Thus the Web of documents will be able to evolve into the Web of data, and the Semantic Web will be able to connect—cooperatively—data and information to which a meaning is attributed that can be interpreted by machines, even belonging to different domains. Moreover, these data can be interconnected through the ontologies that structure them.[49] The strings of the linked data represent a simple language, fully interoperable in XML-RDF format, far from the schemes defined within a specific area, but at the same time able to represent and display on the Web every type of data that the different sectors produce, handle, and must continue to treat and produce with the same dedication and specialization developed over time, thanks to their acknowledged authoritativeness, while publishing and sharing them with the new method.[50]

[46] On this topic, cf. Alper Aksac [et al.], *A novel Semantic Web browser for user centric information retrieval: PERSON*, "Expert systems with applications," 39 (2012), no. 15, p. 12,001–12,013, https://www.sciencedirect.com/science/article/pii/S0957417412005799?via%3Dihub. Among the first projects of *Semantic Web browser*, cf. Dennis Quan; David R. Karger, *How to make a Semantic Web browser*. In: *WWW '04. Proceedings of the 13th international conference on World Wide Web*. New York: ACM, 2004, p. 255–265.

[47] T. Berners-Lee, *Semantic Web road map* cit.; T. Berners-Lee; M. Fischetti, *Weaving the Web* cit.

[48] T. Berners-Lee, *Linked Data* cit.; *id.*, *The next Web*. 2009, https://www.ted.com/talks/tim_berners_lee_on_the_next_Web.

[49] T. Berners-Lee [et al.], *The Semantic Web* cit.

[50] A survey of Berners-Lee's long project and his collaborators is in: Luís Miguel Oliveira Machado [et al.], *Semantic Web or Web of data? A diachronic study (1999 to 2017) of the publications of Tim Berners-Lee and the World Wide Web Consortium*, "Journal of the Association for Information Science & Technology," 70 (2019), no. 7, p. 701–714, https://asistdl.onlinelibrary.wiley.com/doi/abs/10.1002/asi.24111.

The Semantic Web, in the course of its design and experimentation, has had two stages of development and has found its own application path, based on the mechanisms of complete collaboration, only after the first attempts of a less participatory and less community nature have been abandoned.[51] The first phase—which can be framed between the first ideas (1999) and the year of the launch of linked data (around 2006)—proposed a top-down approach and involved the development, by an international and interdisciplinary group of experts, of a sort of "universal knowledge" model, based on a network of diverse domain-related models, to express the concepts and relationships concerning each field of knowledge. On the basis of this model, the various knowledge resources would be classified and tagged, some "intelligent agents" would then navigate and interpret the Web assisting people in their search. The program—also defined as "foundational ontology"—soon came to a halt in the face of the impossibility of performing the task, which, however vast it was, did not have the greatest obstacle in its breadth, but rather in the impossibility of reaching an universally recognizable ontological level, due to the fact that not everyone would be able to contribute to its foundation. In practice, this model would be defined a priori and imposed "from above."

Therefore, the second phase stems from the "return" to the original idea of the Web itself, understood as a dynamic, participatory, shared environment capable of hosting very different resources and ideas, conceived in the most diverse cultural and social environments, as enriched by the experience gained in the Web 2.0 phase. Starting from 2006, with the launch of linked data, a bottom-up approach has been adopted. The aim is to take advantage of everyone's contribution, providing everyone with a simple and independent language that allows them to define, publish, and share data without first having to accept external, predefined, rigid formal structures.[52] The same ontologies, adequate and useful in every sector, can be developed collaboratively, and in the same way also the connection systems between data sets created with a specific ontology and those created

[51] Cf. A. Iacono, *Linked Data* cit., p. 5–20.

[52] Nigel Shadbolt [et al.], *The Semantic Web revised*, "IEEE intelligent systems," 21 (2006), no. 3, p. 96–101, https://ieeexplore.ieee.org/document/1637364; Christian Bizer [et al.], *Linked Data: the story so far*, "International journal on Semantic Web and information systems," 5 (2009), no. 3, p. 1–22, https://www.igi-global.com/article/linked-data-story-far/37496.

with another ontology in a nearby or similar area can be developed in a collaborative way.

The whole project of the Semantic Web is therefore enriched with instances of sharing within specific communities and then among diverse communities, creating together a tool for the human community in general. After all, the road "from above" had almost led to the failure of the program. The "language" of linked data does not actually belong to anyone, is not developed for any specific sector, is fully adaptable to any need, and remains as neutral as possible in structuring the tiniest form of data. Nevertheless, the data can be subsequently reaggregated according to whatever model or scheme the diverse communities may use within them, allowing a posteriori the definition of a precise cultural communicative scheme, and not losing its advantages in terms of the final structuring of knowledge proposed in each field.

Precisely being aware, together with the advantages just indicated, of the great risks of producing and publishing knowledge in a "widespread" and open-to-all way, Berners-Lee equips the Semantic Web with some criteria of self-protection and control, which are still in phase of study and experimentation. Already in 2000, the architecture of the Semantic Web contemplates such development criteria as constitutive levels, illustrated in the context of the general graphic representation then defined as *Semantic Web stack.*[53] This architecture places among the lowest levels those of the fundamental technologies on which the Web is built, first HTTP, URI, then XML, above RDF, at the center OWL, and SPARQL. The three highest levels are those of "unifying logic," "proof," and "trust," the spaces of "unifying logic," "demonstration," and "credibility," which would complete the architecture of the Semantic Web with essential structures to give reliability, certainty, accuracy to the data, and knowledge disseminated by it.

The unifying logic, therefore, will ensure the compatibility and harmony of the work of different software agents alongside people, and the demonstration will be the mechanism to guarantee the validity of the inferences and "deductions" made by the machines. Finally, the level of trust will be at the top of the system, the search for the credibility and authority of the sources of production, and entry of data on the Web, which will ensure, together with the tools of cryptography and digital signatures, that

[53] Cf. Tim Berners-Lee, *Semantic Web — XML2000.* 2000, http://www.w3.org/2000/Talks/1206-xml2k-tbl. See also: A. Iacono, *Linked Data* cit., p. 10—11.

the operations of the machines will be based on verified and safe sources. Finally, the user interfaces and the various applications for the real use of the Semantic Web will allow its real usefulness for all, its effectiveness, and the development of its intrinsic value.

The work of the community would therefore be saved from errors, misunderstandings and "boycotts,"[54] and the Semantic Web would allow everyone, according to their abilities, to contribute to the enrichment of collective knowledge. Conversely, everyone, according to their needs, would be allowed to draw on this inexhaustible and dynamic source of knowledge.

In this way, by converting the data produced by the various cultural institutions into LODs, the Web is enriched with an enormous and growing quantity of atomic data fully available for any use, for any cultural enrichment, social production, or political—economic development, without having to recognize anything to those who have produced such wealth and enrichment tool, if not the merit of freely serving knowledge and progress. Furthermore, this amount of data helps the "producers" themselves to increase their knowledge, by allowing that around each object links, connections, and additions, or even unpredictable inferences developed directly by the machines are created, and also by allowing anyone else the widest navigation among the information, with the sole need of a map not to get lost, a tool that can be "easily" integrated in every area of use of linked data.

The most democratic effect of all this would be that any person, from any part of the world and any level of society, could access any resource starting from any data they have available. Even minimal information, not supported by education or means of study, in whatever language it is expressed, allows to begin the journey toward the richest knowledge, regardless of who and how it has produced it, just by following the roads of the LODs up to arrive at a bibliographic file, a digital image of a museum,

[54] With regard to fears of boycotts, even for their own sake, just think of the current problem of fake news and similar episodes of "poisoning" of information sources. For example, see: Gino Roncaglia, *Fake news: bibliotecario neutrale o bibliotecario attivo?*, "AIB studi," vol. 58 (2018) no. 1, p. 83—93, https://aibstudi.aib.it/article/view/11772; Riccardo Ridi, *Livelli di verità: post-verità, fake news e neutralità intellettuale in biblioteca*, "AIB studi," vol. 58 (2018) no. 3, p. 455—477, https://aibstudi.aib.it/article/view/11833; Karolina Andersdotter, *Fatti alternativi e fake news: la verificabilità nella società dell'informazione*, "AIB studi," vol. 57 (2017) no. 1, p. 5—6, https://aibstudi.aib.it/article/view/11618; Sapna Maheshwari, *How fake news goes viral: a case study*, "The New York Times," 20 November 2016, https://www.nytimes.com/2016/11/20/business/media/how-fake-news-spreads.html.

and a project digitized by the holder of the rights. In support of all this, Berners-Lee always returns and supports his projects through specific acts, such as the proposal of a Magna Carta *for the Web* directed to all the governments of the world,[55] accompanied by a series of other informative documents and writings.[56]

Despite all this, the lack of a computer or a connection to the network, almost impossible realities in some places even in civilized society, are still essential obstacles, which must not, however, block the attempt to make a PC and a Wi-Fi connection available, in any place, to people who do not have them. The real problem is "what can be found" via the PC and the connection once activated. Thus, it is the world of the Web which can help build knowledge sharing, what must not be overseen, or improvised, because the Web is "for everyone" and created "by everyone."

In this vision of the new Web, linked data methodologies can be the tool that unifies the data produced by cataloging activities, within a well-regulated bibliographic "domain," with those produced by resources' analytic and descriptive activities, created by other Web actors who develop different data sets. In this, the system allows to express the semantics of the connections made between stable and guaranteed "absolute value" data, and also to "infer" implicit connections and semantics in an already declared network of connections. The new network of "assertions," moreover, is "interpretable" both by the human operator and by machines, so much so

[55] The Magna Carta for the Web was expected to be published by the World Wide Web Foundation in 2019. In this regard, a 2014 TED talk by Berners-Lee: https://www.ted.com/talks/tim_berners_lee_a_magna_carta_for_the_Web/reading-list?curator=MediaREDEF; as well as a 2018 Telegraph article: Laurence Dodds, *Sir Tim Berners-Lee launches '*Magna Carta *for the Web' to save internet from abuse*, "The telegraph," 5 November 2018, https://www.telegraph.co.uk/technology/2018/11/05/sir-tim-berners-lee-launches-magna-carta-Web-save-internet-abuse/.

[56] About Berners-Lee's democratic idea of the Web, cf.: Tim Berners-Lee, *Long live the Web: a call for continued open standards and neutrality*, "Scientific American," 303 (2010), no. 6, p. 80–85, https://www.scientificamerican.com/article/long-live-the-Web/; *id.*, *The many meanings of Open*. 2013, http://en.blogthinkbig.com/2013/10/09/tim-berners-lee-telefonica-open-agenda/ (available also at the URL: http://www.w3.org/DesignIssues/Open.html); *id.*, *The year open data went world wide*. 2010, https://www.ted.com/talks/tim_berners_lee_the_year_open_data_went_worldwide; *id.*, *Three challenges for the Web, according to its inventor*, "Web foundation," 12 marzo 2017, http://Webfoundation.org/2017/03/Web-turns-28-letter/. See also the World Wide Web Foundation Website: http://Webfoundation.org/. A recap of the discourse is in: Roberto Raieli, *La comunità della conoscenza: senso e possibilità del progetto LOD-Semantic Web*. In: *Progressi dell'informazione e progresso delle conoscenze* cit., p. 37–76.

that it is possible to indicate the difference between MARC and the new XML-RDF systems for defining bibliographic "machine-readable forms" to "machine-understandable formats."[57] It is therefore important that libraries structure the creation and dissemination of bibliographic data according to these new principles, integrating them into the Web, and allowing to search and recover resources owned or mediated by the library "system" even from the Web.[58]

The forms of records currently widespread, however, despite a certain evolution according to FRBR principles and RDA standards, do not always have the optimal degree of definition and richness of the data models developed to meet the needs of the Semantic Web, based on the RDF model. The traditionally conceived record is structured as a set of indivisible data, even if of a different type, collected to describe a resource. What the Web "asks" is that all data, prepared following library standards, are ultimately granular, atomized, and independent. The data must reside on the Web and be independently accessible through diverse paths, search systems, and generic semantic browsers of different personal and portable devices. The convergence of the different data toward the identification of a specific bibliographic resource must not be a preset fact and limited to the library technique, but it must dynamically derive from the discovery of various relationships along a research path.[59]

Therefore, an effective reconceptualization of the bibliographic description model is necessary, meaning it in the perspective of granularity and interoperability, which leads to a transformation of the cataloging activity, truly opening the development of the catalog to the current progress of information and knowledge, thus allowing uses and reuses not only in the library field.[60]

In this context, the Library of Congress project called Bibliographic framework initiative, or BIBFRAME, has been promoted since 2011, with

[57] A. Marchitelli; G. Frigimelica, *OPAC* cit., p. 23.

[58] For an in-depth study of the relationship between the linked data methodology and libraries, see: Erik T. Mitchell, *Library Linked Data: early activity and development*. Chicago: ALA, 2016; Mauro Guerrini; Tiziana Possemato, *Linked Data per biblioteche, archivi e musei*. Milano: Bibliografica, 2015; Seth van Hooland; Ruben Verborgh, *Linked Data for libraries, archives and museums: how to clean, link and publish your metadata*. London: Facet, 2014; Antonella Iacono, *Linked Data* cit.

[59] In this regard, cf. Karen Coyle, *Library Linked Data* cit.

[60] Take a look at the following reports: Library of Congress working group on the future of bibliographic control, *On the record*. Washington: Library of Congress, 2008, http://www.loc.gov/bibliographic-future/news/lcwg-ontherecord-jan08-final.pdf; W3C. Library Linked Data incubator group, *Library Linked Data incubator group final report* cit.

the aim of launching the future bibliographic universe, consisting of common work and exchange of data, in which not only libraries will be involved.[61] The BIBFRAME program, which has already reached a 2.0 version, defines that "the new model is more than a simple replacement of the current model represented by MARC. It is the foundation for the future of bibliographic description, as part of the Web and the networked world we live in."[62]

BIBFRAME is a theoretical–practical model that is oriented toward all category of individuals and that defines bibliographic descriptions in a "lighter" way, thus allowing them to be more easily displayed and disseminated on the Web. These descriptions are made of curated data that they are universally reusable through the methodology of linked data and the RDF model. Various content description rules and different metadata models—including RDA—can be accepted in the BIBFRAME environment, in which the diverse rules that actually coexist in different communities and between different periods are acknowledged and balanced. In addition, BIBFRAME can work also for Web environments lacking specific rules or showing different "points of view" on objects. This flexibility, among other things, allows the model to respond, through specific implementation technologies, to particular and contingent needs, such as those related to the location of resources or practical management.[63]

[61] Among the many writings concerning BIBFRAME starting from the date of its launch, the following are worth mentioning: Amanda Xu [et al.], *From MARC to BIBFRAME 2.0: crosswalks*, "Cataloging & Classification Quarterly," 56 (2018), no. 2–3, p. 224–250, https://www.tandfonline.com/doi/full/10.1080/01639374.2017.1388326; Sally McCallum, *BIBFRAME Development*, "JLIS.it," 8 (2017), no. 3, p. 71–85, https://www.jlis.it/article/view/12415; Thomas Meehan, *BibFrame*, "Catalogue & index," 2014, no. 174, p. 43–52, https://archive.cilip.org.uk/sites/default/files/documents/Catalogue%20and%20Index%20issue%20174%2C%20March%202014.pdf; Angela Kroeger, *The road to BIBFRAME: the evolution of the idea of bibliographic transition into a post-MARC future*, "Cataloging & classification quarterly," 51 (2013), no. 8, p. 873–890, https://www.tandfonline.com/doi/full/10.1080/01639374.2013.823584.

[62] Library of Congress, *Bibliographic framework as a Web of data* cit., p. 3.

[63] To learn more about the model, see: Shoichi Taniguchi, *Is BIBFRAME 2.0 a suitable schema for exchanging and sharing diverse descriptive metadata about bibliographic resources?*, "Cataloging & Classification Quarterly," 56 (2018), no. 1, p. 40–61, https://www.tandfonline.com/doi/full/10.1080/01639374.2017.1382643; Antonella Trombone, *Il progetto BIBFRAME della Library of Congress: come stanno cambiando i modelli strutturali e comunicativi dei dati bibliografici*, "AIB studi," 55 (2015), no. 2, p. 215–226, https://aibstudi.aib.it/article/view/11100; Mauro Guerrini, *BIBFRAME. Un'ipotesi di ambiente bibliografico nell'era del Web*. In: *Il libro al centro. Percorsi fra le discipline del libro in onore di Marco Santoro*. Napoli: Liguori, 2014, p. 103–115.

The foundation of BIBFRAME is a new two-level model of relationships between entities, which is reached with the awareness that it is reasonable to define FRBR concepts through a greater or lesser number of levels.[64] It is essentially based on the relationships of four entities or resources: Work, Instance, Authority, and Annotation. The main relationship between Work and Instance is structured in such a way as to clearly distinguish and relate a conceptual essence and its concrete manifestation. The Authority entity identifies a concept or thing associated with a Work or Instance, and the Annotation allows to expand the description of the Work, Instance, or Authority.[65]

In a bibliographic environment, as reorganized through a new paradigm regarding data and their opening and exposure to the Web, the search systems could function in a much more responsive way to meet the needs and expectations of all end users, also in the sense of building an adequate "context" during the information process.[66] Furthermore, once linked data will be effectively used, many problems could be solved, and not only from the technical point of view or the design of a single system for the search in the various databases that a library makes available.[67]

Let us try, then, to imagine that if all the data were really shared, and the linked data relating to the various resources populated both the Web and the bibliographic databases, it would be possible to indicate both the Web as the space in which search engines carry out their "boundless" search, as well as libraries as such spaces in which discovery tools develop a search within boundaries that can be "defined" by a given institution. Library spaces would therefore really be a more "secure" partition—qualitatively and semantically—for contextualization and orientation between information and knowledge resources, in a potentially limitless "docuverse" or universe of resources.

[64] The program documentation is published on the site: http://bibframe.org/documentation.

[65] The site of the BIBFRAME program is at the URL: http://www.loc.gov/bibframe.

[66] Regarding the context of the information processes relating to the new OPACs, cf. Antonella Iacono, *Dal record al dato. Linked Data e ricerca dell'informazione nell'OPAC*, "JLIS.it," 5 (2014), no. 1, p. 77–102, https://www.jlis.it/article/view/9095.

[67] Among the papers on this topic, cf. Axel Kaschte, *Linked Open Data on its way into next generation library management and discovery solutions*, "JLIS.it," 4 (2013), no. 1, p. 313–323, https://www.jlis.it/article/view/5492.

4.2 Possibilities and criticalities of the new methods

Before considering with sincere but immediate optimism the relationship between the "docuverse," as extended to every resource of the new Web, and the library methodologies and theories, it is necessary to contrast the most favorable and enthusiastic opinions examined so far with other opinions that invite to pay the utmost attention to the pillars of library science and tend to evaluate in a more cautious and exhaustive way any paradigm revolutions.

An "old" contribution by Alberto Petrucciani counts among the first writings that disclose an awareness of the need to prepare a true theoretical acceptance for new methods and tools in library science, by critically rediscussing its basic paradigms.[68] Beyond the clichés and passively accepted "fashionable" practices, the author warns from being subjected to the information revolution produced on the Web, inviting readers to steer it instead and acknowledging that the discussion was inspired by Thomas Mann's response[69] to the famous report written for the Library of Congress by Karen Calhoun.[70] The clichés on the need to change the nature of the catalog, on the unavoidability of adapting it to the technological advances of the Web, on the importance of considering the new needs of Web users, are "continually repeated and almost never critically examined." This leads to self-evidence, without understanding the actual reasons for change, which should instead be analyzed with lucidity, aside from dangerous prejudices, as harmful as unconcerned appreciation.

In the wake of catalog simplification and "unloading," many of the decisions taken by "decisive" bodies, such as the Library of Congress itself, can be worrying from the point of view of library professionalism, as they can lead to the cancellation of a distinctive library identity. On the contrary, this identity must always be clearly recognized from that of other bibliographic data aggregation, management, and dissemination systems, because it qualifies for paying specific attention to data evaluation, verification, correctness, disambiguation of dubious information, and in general the construction of a

[68] Alberto Petrucciani, *La catalogazione, il mercato e la fiera dei luoghi comuni*, «Bollettino AIB», 46 (2006), no. 3, p. 177–185, https://bollettino.aib.it/article/view/5153.

[69] Thomas Mann, *Il catalogo e gli altri strumenti di ricerca: un punto di vista dalla Library of Congress*, "Bollettino AIB," 46 (2006), no. 3, p. 186–206, https://bollettino.aib.it/article/view/5154.

[70] K. Calhoun, *The changing nature of the catalog and its integration with other discovery tools* cit.

clear, "honest" bibliographic universe that preserves the identity and nature of the cultural objects it represents, and that is "dedicated" to the end user.

As Petrucciani emphasizes, the "business model," often inappropriately applied to library issues, is among the main targets of Mann's criticism. The risk is the creation of a "self-sufficient" management model, which imitates the economic model and is forcefully applied despite being far from the reality of the library itself. From this widespread application, commonplaces arise such as the concern for the little interest that the catalog receives on the "information market," thus forgetting that the catalog as such has never wanted or needed to be a "successful commodity," but rather a tool for organization, mediation, research, and knowledge that could be more or less difficult to use, but perceived by people as such and not as a simplistic application. The interface of an OPAC or a discovery tool must certainly be rich and friendly, but it does not necessarily need to "mimic" Google, Amazon, or other book presentation interfaces that have been created precisely with the concern of defending market shares to the companies they represent. Libraries do not aim for a profit with their services; therefore, they must not overcome real competitors. They only need to enhance a precise cultural identity, paying attention, therefore, not to disappear behind commercial services, without compromising on quality and reliability of their activities.

Furthermore, information provision is neither the only nor the main quality service provided by libraries, as reading and study services are also a priority. In this regard, then, the problem is not the remote use of a work residing on a library or another website, but rather the orientation and assistance role that libraries can have in choosing information, and consequently in the construction and the organization of collections, both owned and not owned. Mann also notes that, in the most common cases, the use of the most popular Web tools is sufficient for searching and retrieving the resources useful to meet the simplest needs. Libraries, then, without fearing to lose users performing this kind of searches, must not just try to do the same things as commercial services, but rather prepare their own tools for the most complex needs, for which specific and reliable guidance services are really necessary. The typical qualities of library services, such as precision and diligence, must never be abandoned in the name of speed and simplification, which are denying library principles, just because required by a more "marketable" vision of the information world and knowledge resources.[71]

[71] Cf. A. Petrucciani, *La catalogazione, il mercato e la fiera dei luoghi comuni* cit., p. 180–184.

While searching for new library methodologies, which can be more appropriate to contemporary times, one must not fall into the clichés connected to the spirit of the current market; in the same way, one must also critically look at the technological and social models of our times. This is also underlined in an essay by Fabio Metitieri, who already some years ago warned against clichés emerging from the spirit of the so-called Web 2.0.[72] Libraries, in fact, enthralled by the spirit of the "Google generation," sometimes aim to reproduce Google-like models or those of social networks to reorganize their OPACs in a friendly and social way, without critically addressing the problem of contents of these operations. Even if we can think of a "collaborative" OPAC model, this project must be carefully planned and evaluated in its implications against the principles of cataloging.

Metitieri points at the simplistic misunderstandings of visions such as those of David Lankes and David Weinberger. According to both authors, users could orient themselves in the Web 2.0 using accurate tools and "conversing" with one another,[73] or by tagging and reviewing the various resources "bottom up."[74] In this way, all the library work of collecting, preserving resources, cataloging, and classification, as well as bibliographic information curation, appears needless. In reality, however, it is only a matter of deeply discovering the new value of the identification activities of the qualified action of libraries, in the light of the many changes toward the digital and networking world that are transforming information and knowledge.

First of all, it must be emphasized that the Internet generation itself does not have adequate knowledge of the network, the Web, and the possibilities of the tools and resources available.[75] However, as Metitieri comments, it seems that libraries are not responding, as one should expect, by enhancing their information literacy activities, but by trying to equal and

[72] Fabio Metitieri, *L'OPAC collaborativo, tra folksonomia e socialità*, «Biblioteche oggi», 27 (2009), no. 2, p. 7–12, http://www.bibliotecheoggi.it/2009/20090200701.pdf.

[73] See R. D. Lankes [et al.], *Participatory networks* cit.

[74] Cf. David Weinberger, *Crunching the metadata. What Google print really tells us about the future of books*, "The Boston globe," 13 November 2005, http://www.boston.com/ae/books/articles/2005/11/13/crunching_the_metadata.

[75] On this topic, Metitieri cites the following report: University college London, *Information behaviour of the researcher of the future*. London: University college, 2008, http://www.jisc.ac.uk/media/documents/programmes/reppres/gg_final_keynote_11012008.pdf.

perhaps overcome the means of the Web, rather than deepen and define specific and qualifying differences for themselves and for users, with the result of even more confusing people's ideas and losing themselves in the universe of the Web. Considering the Facebook model, for example, it is immediately clear that "it is not a space where users love to dialog with librarians": social networks were born, and are used, for personal reasons disconnected from library services that people expect to be organized with other criteria.

In this sense, even the "folksonomy catalog," and social cataloging, cannot be more than a "legend." Folksonomies and people's comments have developed for other than bibliographic and cataloging reasons. Tags can be wrong, confusing, and mismatched, and reviews can be dull or biased. Despite being useful whenever bibliographic data are not available, information created by users can, if anything, accompany the "products" of cataloging and classification without claiming to replace them. Moreover, people lack any interest in "conversing" with one another about OPAC documents.

Therefore, the new OPACs and the new information search and discovery systems must always remain faithful to the experience and theory that produced classic catalogs and services. Nonetheless, they must be connected to new technologies and new people's needs. In this direction, the "Googleian" example is useful to simplify the basic search screen or the first access to the OPAC, as much as the Facebook model can be useful to connect any user opinions and display them at the bottom of the catalog sheet. In addition, a reasoned innovation of the interfaces can better enhance some characteristics of the catalogs, for example, by integrating the search functions with seamless suggestions or error correction systems. Besides, the usefulness of the search refinement guide columns allows to group the results by author, format, language, or by tag cloud, "clouds" of labels built on the basis of subject headings, thesauri, or other KOS. These "faceted" columns can be important qualifiers of the library search interface, despite being hidden from the general user's skills and implying some critical issues.[76]

Despite what the market and technology favor as an effective solution also in the field of librarianship, which should not be uncritically accepted, an issue that it is necessary to scrutinize is that of the ordering of search results. This issue is not new and, in the logic of the development of new

[76] Cf. F. Metitieri, *L'OPAC collaborativo, tra folksonomia e socialità* cit., p. 10.

search systems, gains a central place.[77] In fact, the interfaces of the new OPACs and discovery tools normally show a single and simple list of all the results collected around the research theme, which are presented in a single list, almost without distinction, if not at graphic level, which includes the type of resource, its local or remote origin, the database to which it belongs, or the Web link. In any case, an order must be supplied to the often long and "decontextualized" Google-like list, and when it is not a material order by date, author or title, all that remains is that of "relevance."[78] The gathering of different resources in the same list, rather than simplifying the search for the less or the more experienced, can confound users, and a reliable relevance ranking system can be the right solution even for information professionals.

The possibility and reliability of sorting methods that take care of the arrangement of search results on the basis of a "presumed relevance" considering the user are discussed in an essay by Maria Teresa Biagetti, who, first of all, notes that the techniques based on the frequency of terms, used by search engines and online bookstores, are applied too simplistically to OPACs.[79] The relevance ranking, that is, the presentation of the results according to a presumed relevance ranking, and the relevance feedback, that is, the semiautomatic reformulation of the query based on explicit indications of relevance provided by the user, are based on full-text document processing techniques developed in the scope of IR, and connected to the relationships between the frequency of the terms in the full text of each document and the "inverse" frequency of the terms in the entire database that contains them.[80] The application of these techniques to

[77] See the specifications in: H. Yu; M. Young, *The impact of Web search engines on subject searching in OPAC* cit.; California digital library, *The Melvyl recommender project final report*. 2006, http://www.cdlib.org/services/publishing/tools/xtf/melvyl_recommender/report_docs/Mellon_final.pdf; K. Calhoun, *The changing nature of the catalog and its integration with other discovery tools* cit.

[78] Regarding the techniques most consistent with the needs of the first OPACs, and the simple alphabetical ordering of the results, cf. Jeffrey Beall, *The value of alphabetically-sorted browser displays in information discovery*, "Library collections, acquisitions & technical services," 31 (2007), no. 3/4, p. 184–194, https://www.tandfonline.com/doi/full/10.1080/14649055.2007.10766164.

[79] M. T. Biagetti, *Nuove funzionalità degli OPAC e relevance ranking* cit.

[80] For the clarification of measurement techniques, cf. *ivi*, p. 342–345. See also: Karen Spärck Jones, *A statistical interpretation of term specificity and its application in retrieval*, "Journal of documentation," 28 (1972), no. 1, p. 11–21, https://www.emerald.com/insight/content/doi/10.1108/eb026526/full/html.

the OPAC is in fact less effective, given that the fields of the records contain only a few terms, however essential, and, in any case, techniques of this type never manage to take into account semantic relationships between terms and meaningful relationships, because they are treated as stand-alone elements.

Relevance rankings, calculated on the basis of the frequency or even the proximity analysis of the terms, cannot really satisfy the needs of individuals who are also interested in the conceptual context of information, and who are looking for topics with a precise meaning and specific aspects. For this reason, Biagetti emphasizes that after a critical analysis of relevance ranking, it is necessary to develop a theoretical analysis of the concepts of relevance and appropriateness, as they are linked to the "state of knowledge" of individuals. In this way, it will be possible to define new semantic search functions based on indexing strategies that capture the variety, richness, and complexity of in-depth analysis of the topics, so that results truly consistent with the need to know will emerge.[81] In this perspective, it is impossible not to be fascinated by the projects of merging bibliographic data into the Semantic Web, which would allow semantic research in OPACs in line with the linked data model. However, it is necessary to take some precautions, reflecting on which "level" of semantic data may already be available to the user, and designing a new level of indexing better suited to the characteristics of a multidimensional, subjective, and dynamic "rediscovered" relevance.[82]

Returning to a fundamental point, such as that of the sorting criteria of high quantities of search results, something else needs to be explored, that is, the hypothesis of an open relevance ranking algorithm. This algorithm

[81] Biagetti explains the value and 'relativity' of relevance and relevance referring mainly to the theories of Tefko Saracevic and Birger Hjørland: cf. M. T. Biagetti, *Nuove funzionalità degli OPAC e relevance ranking* cit., p. 349–353.

[82] Regarding studies for the establishment of "semantic" digital libraries through the creation of semantically enriched metadata, cf. Maria Teresa Biagetti, *Sviluppi e trasformazioni delle biblioteche digitali: dai repositories di testi alle semantic digital libraries*, "AIB studi," 54 (2014), no. 1, p. 11–34, https://aibstudi.aib.it/article/view/9955. Other updated analyses relating to digital libraries are in: Shriram Pandey; Sidhartha Sahoo, *Research collaboration and authorship pattern in the field of semantic digital libraries*, "DESIDOC Journal of Library & Information Technology," 40 (2020), no. 6, p. 375–381, https://publications.drdo.gov.in/ojs/index.php/djlit/article/view/15680; Maria Teresa Biagetti, *Le biblioteche digitali: tipologie, funzionalità e modelli di sviluppo*, con scritti di Roberto Raieli, Antonella Iacono, Antonella Trombone, Simona Turbanti. Milano: Angeli, 2019.

could be open source and built by the international community; therefore, it could be "transparent," standardized, and applicable to databases of all kinds. Such a tool could settle a whole series of issues related to the exclusivity of the producers of given interfaces, but above all issues of "trust" in the ordering of the proposed results, and could also be tailored to the need to have or not specific suggestions. But, without a specific discussion, all this could end up in other utopias discussed so far.[83]

It is important, with regard to the type and usefulness of the interaction that users can establish with the catalog and its "related" tools, at least to mention the assumptions on which a revision of the cataloging paradigms, and of the OPAC interfaces, can be based. This especially when aiming at a reform of how the catalog can communicate with the user, and better understanding in which direction to lead it, whether toward a simplification for everyone's benefit or the maintenance of a didactic professional aspect. On this, a clear discussion is provided in an essay by Agnese Galeffi, which proposes the application of the analysis criteria generally used in communication to "cataloging communication."[84]

In the user-catalog interaction, Galeffi explains, there is a regular exchange of information, both aware and unconscious, which takes place throughout the entire search. The typical triangulation in this exchange process, that is, the sender—message—receiver connection, is "translated" into the triad "libraries/librarians—systems—users," and this allows us to propose and discuss five axioms of cataloging communication: it is impossible for a research system to not communicate; systems also establish metacommunication; there is a "punctuation" that marks the catalog—user communication; there is a "digital" communication, which is the data, and an "analog" communication, which is the information relating to the catalog; cataloging communication can be symmetrical or complementary.

Based on these assumptions, since the catalog is a precise communication tool, it can be analyzed, studied, modified, tested, and reorganized, according to precise lines of action, and according to the clearest principles and objectives of improvement that can be set in the sincere intentions for reform. Therefore, if one really intends to improve the interaction between

[83] For the discussions on this hypothesis, I thank Mattia Vallania, of the Sapienza Library System, hoping that he will soon begin to concretely investigate this possibility.

[84] Agnese Galeffi, *Se il catalogo parlasse, lo capiremmo? Cinque assiomi della comunicazione catalografica*, «AIB studi», 57 (2017), no. 2, p. 239—252, https://aibstudi.aib.it/article/view/11648.

catalogs and users—always remaining in the field of librarianship and catalog communication—there is no shortage of means, all you need is an action plan. The same, of course, can be said for the "heirs" of the catalog such as discovery tools, which can become the best new bibliographic communication tools without having to "move" to areas that are no longer relevant.

Again, to add discussion points to the comparison between the catalog and the discovery tools and between established methodologies and new perspectives, an essay built as a collection of interviews on the subject is worth mentioning.[85] The essay consists of interviews with personalities belonging to the LIS area, carried out by asking three questions to five internationally recognized experts, and proposing a careful evaluation of both "classic" and "innovative" theories and principles. In this sense, the essay represents an account of the evolution of the activities about description and organization of information and resources, to open up discussions and comparisons with other disciplines close to LIS.

The questions aim to draw the attention to some key issues in this regard. First of all, it would be useful to clarify the ideas on the role that the catalog can still have, in libraries and for society: whether it will continue to be a central tool for research activities, or whether its position will continue to sink hierarchically until it will align or take a lower position compared with the other current tools of information search and discovery. The catalog, in fact, is faced with the Semantic Web, the linked data methodology, and the need to open up to other communities, to be the users' preferred tool.

In addition, the ineffectiveness of catalogs in the search for information is often due to the transformations of the objects of the research itself, that is, the resources for knowledge: it is therefore necessary to ask ourselves what definition shall the new object of the catalog take, which actually are the current resources of knowledge, and which tools are best suited to deal with them.[86] Today, the useful resources for knowledge are very different from each other and from what has been understood as a "document" so far. Their main quality is the interest that users have for them. They fit into multiple networks of meaning and belong to multiple contexts.

[85] *Old wine, new bottle? Principi e metodi per una reale innovazione nelle prospettive LIS. Il parere di Marshall Breeding, Mauro Guerrini, David Weinberger, Paul Gabriele Weston, Maja Žumer,* a cura di Roberto Raieli [et al.], "AIB studi," vol. 55 (2015), no. 3, p. 385–403, https://aibstudi.aib.it/article/view/11384.

[86] We return to this topic later, in paragraph 3.3.

Finally, regardless of the technological tools most suited to the needs of society, it is necessary to clarify the desirable policies and methodologies for the treatment of resources, information, and data, which remain the primary object of every knowledge organization and management tool: the importance attributed to data correctness and reliability is growing, and this need grows as much as their freedom of expansion and dissemination. Descriptions must be decentralized, the contribution of others trusted, and the integration into the Semantic Web favored, all this without sacrificing data "credibility."

In view of the answers provided to these questions, it is always essential to maintain the right balance between "conservation" and "revolution." Considered from different perspectives, the basic, more or less classic, principles can be reconsidered at a theoretical level, in terms of strengths or weaknesses, to set up a project that can be viewed as truly innovative from a theoretical and methodological point of view. True progress and true innovation are achieved not only by "overcoming" the principles and practices that are really obsolete or aligned with realities that are no longer current, but also by developing and "reunderstanding" those well-grounded principles, which are not time-bound, which always remain valid for the maintenance and development of library science disciplines and LIS. If the basic principles are not adequate, updated, and at the same time durable, a new container, whether technological or conceptual, is of no use to try to propose them as a true methodological innovation.

4.3 Toward a new definition of resource

As it is convenient to be cautious in the face of commonplaces about innovations of search criteria and interfaces, one must also be wary of the various proposals to go "beyond" the document—understood in the most classical, bibliographic sense. Many of these proposals, in fact, either refer to a general idea of resource that has not yet been fully defined or start from the hypothesis of a possible "disaggregation" and "reaggregation" of resources that is almost unconditional and oriented to very different purposes.[87]

[87] A lot of space would require a reflection on the very concept of "information," whether or not conveyed by the "information resources" whose status and identity are being sought. Here one can at least refer to a recently published essay that traces the principles and nature of the "information pyramid": Riccardo Ridi, *La piramide dell'informazione: una introduzione*, "AIB studi," 59 (2019), no. 1–2, p. 69–96. See also: Alberto Salarelli, *Introduzione alla scienza dell'informazione*. Milano: Bibliografica, 2012.

With regard to the concepts of identity and value of the document, be it identifiable or not in new types of more or less "broad" information, equally or more "variable" resources, some reflections by Paola Castellucci should be considered.[88] The observation from which the discussion begins is that in many advanced programs for the dissemination of information on the Net, such as that of open access, the idea of "document-centered" research methodologies, based on the very idea of a document, may seem a legacy of the past, contrary to the progress of knowledge. In fact, an increasingly central position is taken by the concept of "data," which can be extracted not only from "canonical" documents, but from a whole series of other resources that are of growing importance, and must be the subject of research.

For example, in the Open Annotation project by Herbert Van de Sompel,[89] the focus is on "nanodocuments," or "nanopublications," such as annotations, comments, posts, and tweets, which may contain valuable information, many of which have always been in use in the practice of scientific communication, but marginalized compared with the main documents in print, and therefore at high risk of disappearance. Printing technology has favored documents having a given "mass," not considering annotations and comments: in this logic, it may even be the fault of the press "to privilege the authorial sign rather than the trace of reading paths." New digital and network technologies, on the other hand, can restore this relationship. In all this, it is a fact that a plethora of information, contained in either annotations, posts, tweets, or in other nanodocuments, continually grows in importance, giving authority to new authorial forms, which are expressed by publishing new resources such as lines of research, projects, reflections, images, films, and data of all kinds. The single data can be extracted from each of these resources, however "nano" it may be, and shared in scientific research. Furthermore, a similar argument can be made for "megadocuments," or "enhanced" documents, that is, resources enhanced as "hub" in an integrated system of data and services.

Obviously, as Castellucci writes, the possible question of what the mass of a resource must be to be considered valid—like the "traditional" document—does not concern quantitative aspects, but exclusively qualitative ones. For example, not every list of aggregated bibliographic data can

[88] Paola Castellucci, *Tempo e massa: una nuova energia nella comunicazione scientifica*, "Bollettino AIB," 51 (2011), no. 3, p. 237—244, https://bollettino.aib.it/article/view/5428.

[89] Open annotation collaboration: http://www.openannotation.org.

be a bibliography; what characterizes a bibliography as a resource of scientific value is its structure or its index.[90] In any case, a discourse relating to the mass to validate a resource must involve a total rethinking of typologies: the ways of production, validation, and dissemination of information and knowledge must be redefined. In the system of scientific production, the involvement of creators and products of creation not previously considered must be well evaluated.

Beyond this, a thoughtful view of the issue of validation, as well as conservation, calls for another physical category beyond the mass: time. In this sense, Van de Sompel's other project, Memento,[91] aims to solve the problem of resource volatility. By adding a timestamp even to simple segments of online resources, the system makes it possible to trace their successive versions over time, to verify the primogeniture of citations in a search results list, as well as recontextualize the nanodocuments in their original places. In this way, the possibility of having a scientific dignity can also be offered to volatile resources, such as many Web pages that are continuously updated.

Therefore, Castellucci concludes that beyond an easy enthusiasm for free and democratic online communication, accepting the role of a given quantity of new resources means implementing a real cultural revolution, which scholars of the LIS area must take on, deepening and "renegotiating" all the concepts connected to the traditional idea of document, connected to the processes of production, preservation, evaluation, and dissemination of research, and also to the possibility of relationships between authors and readers, and to the reuse of data[92] (Fig. 4.19).

In addition to the conception of new types of information resources, the "classic" concept of a document must also be carefully reviewed, as the center of all discussions on the systems of treatment, dissemination, and research of information and knowledge. Just as we can evaluate different,

[90] Regarding the possibility of "expanding" the concept of bibliography and its structure, cf. David G. Hendry [et al.], *Collaborative bibliography*, "Information processing & management," 42 (2006), no. 3, p. 805–825, https://www.sciencedirect.com/science/article/pii/S0306457305000683?via%3Dihub.

[91] Memento project: http://mementoWeb.org/about/.

[92] Regarding this cultural revolution, Castellucci also cites the considerations of George Landow: cf. George P. Landow, *Hypertext 3.0: critical theory and new media in an era of globalization*. Baltimore: The Johns Hopkins University, 2006. For a general consideration of the "quality" problem of this revolution, cf. Pierluigi Feliciati, *La qualità dell'universo documentario digitale: dai contenuti al servizio*, "AIB studi," 58 (2018), no. 1, p. 53–63, https://aibstudi.aib.it/article/view/11740.

Figure 4.19 The time travel tool of the Memento project.[93]

however optimistic, visions, even though more cautious and thoughtful, regarding the structuring and use of new research systems and new resources, in the same way, referring to the essential conditions of integrity and authority of any type of documents, which are in libraries and on the Web, an analysis by Alberto Salarelli concerning linked data and the Semantic Web can be taken into account.[94]

If the adoption of the RDF scheme to identify the nature and attributes of the elements that make up a resource, to allow the creation of semantic links between the data of different resources, may imply, through the granularization of its data, the "destructuring" of the original resource, the risk is that the evolution of the concept of document leads to understand it as something too different from how it was constituted in centuries of reflection on its principles. The users of the contents of the resource referred to by the granularized data could begin to see the original "coherent" documents, born digital or not, almost only as "containers" of data to be disaggregated, to create around these semantic paths that are often not "sound," to freely reaggregate new containers each time, without proper consideration of the semantic constraints that govern the contents originally created prior to this logic of reuse, or "resignification," created on the basis of other schemes of structuring the meaning. In this case, the attention would be placed only on

[93] Time travel: http://timetravel.mementoWeb.org/.

[94] Alberto Salarelli, *Sul perché, anche nel mondo dei Linked Data, non possiamo rinunciare al concetto di documento*, "AIB studi," 54 (2014), no. 2/3, p. 279–293, https://aibstudi.aib.it/article/view/10128.

"information" understood in general and in absolute terms, and not on the "sources" of knowledge, on the network of connections, and not on related contents, on data and not on their interpretation, on the "collective intelligence" and not on the intellectual work of the individual.

In any case, as Salarelli points out, linked data represent a "profitable" form of treatment of the various resources. Precisely because by allowing the contents stored in different archives to be correlated, they permit the creation of new information tools, even if at the moment it is difficult to "try to name with terminologies borrowed from the past" new types of resources still to be "evaluated" in depth.[95]

It is therefore difficult to continue to use the term "document" to fully understand the new information resources, which can be distinguished, perhaps, only on the basis of the "information value" of the content conveyed in increasingly variable and dynamic containers. Beyond the problem of objectively evaluating the reliability or scientificity of the resource, therefore, there is the problem of the "trust" granted by the author himself to the integrity of his own creation: that is, whether, in his own intentions, the creator has structured it to maintain a "non-deconstructible" identity, within and with the "rules" of a specific area of use, or has designed it from the start for the deconstruction and reuse of content, in any area, with the risk of a certain weakness in its primary semantics.

In this perspective of sharing information and knowledge assets, any cultural organization responsible for a given sector must not lose the role and the task of verifying these assets. The various cultural organizations will have to "change mentality and procedures to operate in an open sense" to allow different people the free but conscious reuse of open data through the LODs, ensuring that the context and the original meaning of each resource, the context and the sense of the irreplaceable "documentary substrate," of data, of metadata, favoring valid and "sensible" new aggregations, to appear in new contexts.[96]

[95] Cf. *ivi*, p. 280.

[96] Cf. *ivi*, p. 280–283. Regarding the role of "responsible organizations," Salarelli cites the "contrast" between top-down and bottom-up positions linked to the discussions on the transition from MARC to BIBFRAME: cf. Kim Tallerås, *From many records to one graph: heterogeneity conflicts in the Linked Data restructuring cycle*, «Information research», 18 (2013), no. 3, http://InformationR.net/ir/18-3/colis/paperC18.html. Regarding the relationship between the "substratum" of coherent and autonomously meaningful documents and the "layer" of the related connections added by Linked Data, Salarelli cites: C. Bizer [et al.], *Linked Data: the story so far* cit.

Continuing the analysis, Salarelli discusses the critical elements of linked data with respect to the general theory of the document, in consideration of the importance of establishing different degrees of authority and stability of resources, a question of epistemological and ontological orientation whose relaunch has become essential in the current reality of network communication. Specifically, the aspect on which attention is paid is the logic of the organization of data referring to the contents of a resource based on the purpose of its creation. The more the ends are "declarative," the more determined is the role of the authority that structured the contents and expressed "declarations," in discursive form as well as in the form of a triple RDF, thus also expressing an idea of the value of the contents and of the form of expression. The identification of the creator's authority is not a problem in "traditional" documents that are built following rules and architectures that guarantee their evaluability. The question arises with respect to the freer logic of constitution of new types of resources, which, obviously, cannot reach the deconstruction of the starting resources, which maintain their own degree of integrity and coherence, but can deconstruct them in the "perception," disaggregating the contents through the atomized data that refer to them and reaggregating them into a new whole that has an undefined coherence, achievable by "anyone" even without specific characteristics of authority. Often the identity of the creator is therefore a problem, both for those who define the ontologies and those who use the schemes, whose authority on the net seems to dissolve too much with respect to any scientific system, however open it might be.

Other critical elements are the "provenance" and "granularity" of the data. The problem of the origin, and identifiability, of the data depends on the possibility of defining the responsibility for their creation: "where, when, and why they were created."[97] The problem of the granularity, and of the interpretability, of the data concerns the limit level of atomization to which a resource can be subjected through the atomization of its description without losing its sense and its meaning: a limit that resides in the "concept of 'RDF molecule,' an intermediate entity between the original document and the single triples." Without the solution of the problematic points, the linked data system risks being of limited reliability, both in the

[97] Although the third rule of linked data—recommending "When someone looks up a URI, provide useful information, using the standards (RDF *, SPARQL)"—tends to prevent the dissemination of data that is not qualified with the necessary specifications: cf. T. Berners-Lee, *Linked Data* cit.

attempt to establish articulated relationships between the resources based on the data extracted from them and between such data and the resources of origin, and, even more, in an attempt to build new resources such as dossiers or "agglomerations" of content and data extrapolated from other resources and related in various ways.[98]

In conclusion, even in the new systems of the network and digital resources, a search for solutions must be deployed to guarantee that data and the related constructs acquire a validation in respect of its authority, dating, integrity, and semantic coherence, according to principles related to the world of "classic" documents. The need is to contain the "liquidity of information," its decontextualization, and perpetual reinterpretability, through systems provided with the reliability characteristic of the methodologies of the bibliographic tradition. Social reality itself is based on the reliability of certain documents—in the "strict" and archival sense—such as laws, pacts, treaties, and nevertheless those of knowledge. For the possible categorizations of resources, of "old" or "new" type, the principle does not change: the validity is linked to the possibility of transforming the volatility of information into "sufficiently stable data aggregations," useful as knowledge bases for intellectual and social progress.[99]

Obviously, the issue linked to the prospect of a new necessary definition of resource immediately arises around the necessity of collecting these resources, since it invests the very meaning and possibility of collecting digital resources as recently defined. In this line of investigation, an essay by Maurizio Vivarelli can be illuminating, and useful for defining what the current space of action of a library can be[100]—even if "bounded" and "safe."

First of all, Vivarelli reiterates that the theme of collections is increasingly "residual," given the effective weakening of the role and concept of

[98] Cf. Alberto Salarelli, *Sul perché, anche nel mondo dei Linked Data, non possiamo rinunciare al concetto di documento* cit., p. 286—288. On the concept of RDF *molecule*, cf. Li Ding [et al.], *Tracking RDF graph provenance using RDF molecules (Technical report TR-CS-05-06, Computer science and electrical engineering, University of Maryland, Baltimore County, 30 April 2005).* 2005, ftp://www.ksl.stanford.edu/local/pub/KSL_Reports/KSL-05-06.pdf.

[99] For a further examination of the issue of fragmentation and complexity of the current information universe, cf. Gino Roncaglia, *L'età della frammentazione: cultura del libro e scuola digitale*. Roma: Laterza, 2018.

[100] Maurizio Vivarelli, *C'è bisogno di collezioni? Teorie, modelli, pratiche per l'organizzazione di spazi documentari connessi e condivisi*, «Biblioteche oggi Trends», 1 (2015), no. 1, p. 18—29, http://www.bibliotecheoggi.it/trends/article/view/38.

the "book" and of all the other traditional information objects. The concept of collection, however, can no longer be "confined within the limits of pure physicality." In fact, the concepts most linked to the physical entity of the collections are decaying: space, location, availability, renewal, ownership, etc. For a long time now, the digital collection has been "intertwined" with the physical collection, which at times overlaps, replaces, and at best interacts with the former. Finally, the concept of the ordering of a physical collection intersects with the new concept of the order of collections, which is more dynamic, complex, shared, and open to infinity.

David Lankes[101] is also cited, to declare that "value should not be sought in the collections, or in the physical spaces, or in the organization of the library," but must be found in the "actions." In this sense, therefore, it can be said that, instead of collections, it is more appropriate to speak of the "space of action" of the library, or of a cultural entity, which acts in a physical and nonphysical, defined and indefinite context, making available some resources and "indicating" the availability of others. Overall, the library, even as a simple "index," mediates its physical collection together with a virtual collection, assuming in both cases a precise cultural responsibility and identity. Mediation, or even the Lankesian "conversation," rather than disappearing in that sort of disintermediation implied by the new research tools, is more than ever present in the very actions that the user carries out through the means indicated by the library tools, or other search engines.

Resuming his introductory speech, Vivarelli discusses a series of elements of economic, social, and sociological nature that are mentioned in relation to the so-called supply chain of the book, and which concern various aspects, from reading practices, ways of consuming information, up to content reception "styles." It is precisely in this context that one of the roles of the library and its collections assumes high value, that of granting a wide possibility of access to information and knowledge that is fair, democratic, available to all, and that the virtual state of the collections facilitates beyond measure.[102] The asset of the library collections, then, represents a brake on the advancement of commercial interests, which influences both

[101] R. David Lankes, *The atlas of new librarianship*. Cambridge: MIT, 2011.

[102] Vivarelli cites both IFLA/UNESCO *Public Library Manifesto* (1994, available at the URL: https://www.ifla.org/publications/iflaunesco-public-library-manifesto-1994), and the *Lyon declaration* cit., as political and programmatic orientation documents.

the diffusion and the choice of a series of works rather than others, of a typology of writings or studies, favoring instead a "bibliodiversity."[103] To this, a further role of guiding users into the information and knowledge space can be added, since the development policy of the collections and its wisdom are entrusted either to expert librarians, to a group of experts, or to a scientific council of academic or "popular" composition.

The scholar, therefore, wants to discuss the configuration of this library space, the strategies for organizing it in a "sociotechnocognitive" context, characterized by the development of digital resources, which can and must remain bound to the "history" of each library. After all, this problem should no longer have been discussed for at least 10 years: a well-developed collection is always a collection of contents, regardless of the content carriers and the systems for organizing them, which can always be those best suited to the respective times for action.

From the mid-18th century, it has been possible to witness the progressive abstraction of the bibliographic space of the library from the "visual fabric" in which it was inscribed, since its representation was increasingly delegated to cataloging tools, and the library was no longer totally "a view" based on the composition of its shelves. Since the 1960s, the bibliographic space has been conceived as an uninterrupted whole and, as the space of resources becomes increasingly large and indefinite, the role of the tools and people who steer it becomes increasingly important. Furthermore, the collection, in addition to its "synchronic" value and meaning, increasingly acquires a "diachronic" sense as a heritage intentionally accumulated for cultural transfer from past to future generations through the people of the present time. Finally, in more recent years, after the phase that gravitated around management linked to the "success" of the cultural asset, the specialized literature does not yet seem to have well identified a precise conceptual model, which could move between instances of managerial, as much as technological and social type. In any case, the principle of access has definitively affirmed its reasons in the face of the old model of—restricted—ownership, and digital objects can "worthily" be part of the area of action, or indication, of a library, in that they are checked and validated. The most suitable model, today, could be represented by a library

[103] Cf. Gilles Colleu, *Editori indipendenti & bibliodiversità*. Torino: Fidare-Federazione italiana editori indipendenti, 2011.

collection, or space, being open to development in both a reticular, or rhizomatic, and a social or democratic sense.[104]

In the end, Vivarelli argues that, regardless of the possibility of choosing a "better" model, the library can abandon the anxiety of interpreting the space of the collections—material or digital—in an "aseptic and chilly technocratic" sense, aimed at achieving an imperturbable "mediation neutrality," to grasp all the advantages of building one's own "identity profile," aware of its own history and open to the territory and to novelties. The library would therefore become a "very human" institutional guide, educated and conscious, to guide people in the space in which it acts according to their "point of view," but also beyond this reliable space, providing the basic means toward independent sailing.

As a matter of fact, there is always a "need for collections"—a collection "space," not necessarily a physical one—with a clear communicative identity, which can "give life to a vibrant, dynamic bibliographic, and informative space, producing meaning and significance for people who decide to use it."[105] However, the "visible form" of the collections—the bounded and safe material "space"—is no longer traceable in the fragmentation, and often decontextualization, of the digital content. The substance of a space in which the identity of the library acts—the bounded and safe "space" of action—is revived, however, in "new information architectures," made up of dynamic forms, new exchange interfaces, and new unitary structures. It is always the critical thinking and cultural capacity of those who conceive, organize, and manage new libraries, the resource on which to rely to keep the library rooted in the reality that surrounds it, modifying the perspectives that it is necessary to move, to create "complex information spaces," but in any case "able to communicate," for the benefit of the community and human progress.[106]

[104] For an accurate examination of this progress of the collections, cf. M. Vivarelli, *C'è bisogno di collezioni?* cit., p. 20–23.
[105] *Ivi*, p. 27.
[106] Cf. *ivi*, p. 28–29.

CHAPTER 5

Information discovery and information literacy

5.1 Information retrieval and discovery

Notably, the systems based on linked data, the hypotheses of next-generation library management, the various discovery solutions, and the most advanced discovery tool systems are not as "rigorous" in information retrieval as databases, OPACs, and other instruments of recognized reliability which we have been accustomed to. The discovery tools can be defined as "basic," starting-up search tools. On the other hand, the proprietary database interfaces appear as the most suitable tool with which to perform specialist research, by using metadata and precisely defined record fields, and especially specific indexing languages. Depending on users' needs, information discovery systems, although capable of producing reliable search results, cannot be considered sources of information as such and apt to replace the diverse, topically specialized databases.[1]

If discovery tools lose many advanced query functions, and thus "homogenize" the search path at the lowest level, the best solution is not to reject the new tools, thus remaining bounded to specialized interfaces for the higher search levels. It is a matter of reflecting on the actual value of the tools in relation both to the people who need to use them and to the contents to which they apply. Always depending on users' needs, in fact, there are also valid reasons opposed to those that approve information retrieval systems, which, in the light of their complexity, support the value of more agile information discovery systems that are more easily capable of

[1] On the topic, see: Elizabeth Ketterman; Megan E. Inman, *Discovery tool vs. PubMed: a health sciences literature comparison analysis*, "Journal of electronic resources in medical libraries," 11 (2014), 3, pp. 115–123, https://www.tandfonline.com/doi/full/10.1080/15424065.2014.938999.

Web-Scale Discovery Services
ISBN 978-0-323-90298-4
https://doi.org/10.1016/B978-0-323-90298-4.20002-5

handling many other "nontraditional" resources and pieces of information on the Web.[2]

If we talk about information "discovery," we refer in general to a set of attitudes, practices, and tools that aim at an "exploratory" type of research, in which the subject of the research is not well defined, and often the specific language, keywords, or indexing terms, if any, are unclear. In this case, the help of a noncomplex system fully equipped with guiding functions is important to help a person, who, in fact, discovers undreamed-of data, information, and resources, or even type of data, that one did not deem important. On the other hand, in the context of "conscious" research, there is a clear objective of information, or better a precise resource to be "found," as well as a certain mastery of the tools, terms, and languages of research. What is needed, then, is an advanced and precise system, which allows the development and growth of what one already knows or owns.[3]

In all this, of course, the role of the human assistant who can guide the user by interacting with the system is always recommended. Furthermore, categories of users and search behaviors cannot be clearly defined, because each time the needs, mastery of themes, and contents differ widely.[4] In addition, a person who may initially be in a "category" less prepared for research and who uses information discovery systems can soon acquire

[2] See, for example: Stephen E. Arnold, *Real-time search: where retrieval and discovery collide*, "Online," 33 (2009), no. 6, p. 40–41.

[3] Cf. Mike Sweet, *There's nothing wrong with discovery services that can't be fixed by the reference layer.* In: *The Fiesole collection development retreat, April 12, 2012.* 2012, http://www.casalini.it/retreat/2012_docs/sweet.pdf. Furthermore, for a discussion of the comparison between the different systems of retrieval and discovery, cf. Roberto Raieli, *Oltre i termini dell'information retrieval: information discovery e multimedia information retrieval*, "Bibliothecae.it," 6 (2017), no. 1, p. 178–232, https://bibliothecae.unibo.it/article/view/7028. See also: Rachael A. Cohen; Angie Thorpe Pusnik, *Measuring query complexity in web-scale discovery: a comparison between two academic libraries*, «Reference & user services quarterly», 57 (2018), no. 4, p. 274–284, https://journals.ala.org/index.php/rusq/article/view/6705; Todd Enoch, *Tracking down the problem: the development of a web-scale discovery troubleshooting workflow*, "Serials librarian," 74 (2018), no. 1–4, p. 234–239, https://www.tandfonline.com/doi/full/10.1080/0361526X.2018.1427984; Donald O. Case; Lisa M. Given, *Looking for information: a survey of research on information Cf.king, needs, and behavior* (fourth edition). Bingley: Emerald, 2016.

[4] On the topic, cf. Boram Lee; EunKyung Chung, *An analysis of Web-Scale Discovery Services from the perspective of user's relevance judgment*, "The journal of academic librarianship," 42 (2016), no. 5, p. 529–534, https://www.sciencedirect.com/science/article/pii/S0099133316301021.

mastery and information such as to enter the higher "level" where he needs specific IR tools.[5]

Therefore, various considerations on the limits and capabilities of information discovery are possible: a definition that can be attributed, more specifically than it has been until now, to the wide scope of application of the Web-scale discovery services (WSDS), in which generally the advantages are highlighted more than the disadvantages. Compared with the solid tradition of information retrieval,[6] the field of information discovery is more elusive and more complex to be defined in its variety and vagueness, but the research around Web-scale discovery systems is undergoing continuous development, especially in the past decade, and the debate includes not just applications.[7]

In short, with regard to information retrieval, the specific research tradition starts from classification and indexing studies, which in the 1950s and 1960s joined up with the technologies to develop the first computerized systems for information treatment and retrieval, based on statistical processing algorithms of the distribution of terms in documents, their

[5] Not to mention the opposite path, where those who are or become experts in one field find themselves at the initial stage in another field. Therefore, the person who moves up a "level," the scholar who is a "novice" in another field, and the scholar himself in his own field can benefit from friendly tools. For example, cf. Tod A. Olson, *Utility of a faceted catalog for scholarly research*, "Library hi tech," 25 (2007), no. 4, p. 550–561, https://www.emerald.com/insight/content/doi/10.1108/07378830710840509/full/html.

[6] Among the various treatises, see: Wolfgang G. Stock; Mechtild Stock. *Handbook of information science*. Berlin: De Gruyter Saur, 2013; Christopher D. Manning [et al.], *Introduction to Information Retrieval*. Cambridge: Cambridge University press, 2008; Frederick W. Lancaster, *Indexing and abstracting in theory and practice*. Urbana Champaign: University of Illinois. Graduate school of LIS, 2003; Ricardo Baeza-Yates; Berthier Ribeiro-Neto, *Modern Information Retrieval*. New York: Longman, 2000; Lauren Doyle; Joseph Becker, *Information Retrieval and processing*. Los Angeles: Melville, 1975.

[7] On the topic, see: Tamar Sadeh, *From search to discovery*, "Bibliothek," 39 (2015), no. 2, p. 212–224, https://www.degruyter.com/view/j/bfup.2015.39.issue-2/bfp-2015-0028/bfp-2015-0028.xml?format=INT; H. A. H. Richardson, *Revelations from the literature* cit.; Priscilla Caplan, *On discovery tools, OPACs and the motion of library language*, "Library hi tech," 30 (2012), no. 1, p. 108–115, https://www.emerald.com/insight/content/doi/10.1108/07378831211213247/full/html; *Planning and implementing resource discovery tools in academic libraries* cit.; Henderik A. Proper; Peter D. Bruza, *What is information discovery about?* "Journal of the American society for information science," 50 (1999), no. 9, p. 737–750, https://asistdl.onlinelibrary.wiley.com/doi/10.1002/%28SICI%291097-4571%281999%2950%3A9%3C737%3A%3AAID-ASI2%3E3.0.CO%3B2-C.

descriptors, and the databases containing them.[8] Since then, the developments of ICT have always guided the developments of IR, both applied to databases and to systems that address the entire Web. In the course of this evolution, however, various theoretical and applicative trends have been developed with regard to systems, from those based on natural language processing to user-oriented and cognitive ones, from multilingual to multimedia ones, expanding the field of research also toward semantics or psychology.[9]

In this evolution, systems have often moved away from the original perspective of the "exact match" to be reached between search terms and descriptive terms to find a resource considered useful, moving toward more dynamic and updated "best-match" perspectives. Following a looser line of research and discovery, given the large amount of information available even at Web-scale level, the new IR systems tend not to "clean up" the search results too radically, to present a wider range of resources arranged by "relevance,"[10] which can suggest new research paths, albeit to the loss of the "precision" of the results list. Undoubtedly, this new logic of discovery tends to indicate more than one point of connection between specialized information retrieval systems, applied to specific fields, and those that can more broadly be defined as information discovery systems, which, in addition to resources more easily schematized in description or indexing systems, can be applied to every kind of resource more widely available, ready to perform better clearcut searches in the organized space of the Semantic Web.[11]

Alongside the terminologies used in many studies on information retrieval methodologies, the generic expression information discovery—when it does not commonly also indicate IR—is increasingly used to indicate the idea of new possibilities for the discovery of information and knowledge related to WSDS, although the terminology relating to the new

[8] For a summary of the technological issues of information retrieval, cf. A. Marchitelli; G. Frigimelica, *OPAC* cit., p. 5—12. A broad survey of the history and 'meaning' of databases, on the other hand, can be found in: Paola Castellucci, *Carte del nuovo mondo: banche dati e open access*. Bologna: il Mulino, 2017.

[9] Cf. Kalervo Järvelin, *Information Retrieval (IR)*. In: *International encyclopedia of information and library science*, edited by John Feather, Paul Sturges. London: Routledge, 2003, p. 293—295.

[10] Regarding the criticalities of the sorting systems based on the "presumed relevance" for the user, cf. M. T. Biagetti, *Nuove funzionalità degli OPAC e relevance ranking* cit.

[11] On this aspect, cf. A. Salarelli, *Introduzione alla scienza dell'informazione* cit., p. 101—117.

tools and the transformations they brought is still being defined. Given the tangible growth of research around Web-scale systems, however, a proper terminology must be developed, to allow for a stability of the specific area.[12]

While discussing a series of issues from a variety of standpoints, ranging between application and programmatic perspectives, with some voice for more theoretical openness, the literature has already investigated the limits and effectiveness of information discovery for some years. In general, from the beginning of the discussions, the points on which various scholars converge concern above all the fact that discovery services, in addition to expanding the space of discovery, are able to "add value" to research thanks to the ease of use, the one-stop shop criterion,[13] the filters and facets, and the wealth of related information retrieved. Similarly, some typical early perplexities are confirmed, such as the excess of proposed results, the lack of relevance of many of them, the loss of useful results, and the lack of specificity and functionality typical of catalogs and databases.[14]

If, therefore, people need to have access to an infinitely expanded space of discovery, and libraries can no longer limit themselves to marking their boundaries within the space identified by their proper collections, the implementation of the WSDS can represent the point of convergence between the different needs that manifest themselves in the information discovery methods, first of all the breadth of the recall and the guarantee of precision. Thus, the library "collection" can be composed of any resource identified as useful for satisfying the information needs of its community, conceptualizing it as the information discovery space in which it guarantees and enables mediation through appropriate tools and methods.[15] Besides confirming the validity of this much more than only logical and theoretical expansion of the library collections toward the Web, there are the opposite, much longer-felt needs, to define which information discovery tools are

[12] As can also be seen in the essays contained in: *Planning and implementing resource discovery tools in academic libraries* cit.

[13] Nicholas Joint, *The one-stop shop search engine: a transformational library technology?* "Library review," 59 (2010), no. 4, p. 241–248, https://www.emerald.com/insight/content/doi/10.1108/00242531011038550/full/html.

[14] Cf. B. Thomsett-Scott; P. E. Reese, *Academic libraries and discovery tools* cit.

[15] On this topic, see: Michael Levine-Clark, *Access to everything: building the future academic library collection*, "portal," 14 (2014), no. 3, p. 425–437, https://muse.jhu.edu/article/549201.

suitable for treating the Web, possibly with the same accuracy with which library collections are treated.[16]

In fact, a clear boundary for studies and theorizations around information discovery has not been identified yet, on the contrary, the system is not even coherently defined as such, except at times in the various surveys concerning Internet and Web searches as generally understood. In any case, some attempts to theorize information discovery principles and methodology are represented by essays such as the one written by Henderik Proper and Peter Bruza, among the first to indicate the core of the question.[17]

The two authors immediately point out the constantly growing number of "information carriers" of any kind and type available on the Internet. Each of these resources has a specific informative value, and the overall value of the network is based precisely on the quantity and diversity, as well as on the accessibility, of the entire dynamic complex of information carriers: Web pages, newsgroups, mailing lists, databases, archives, portals, etc., along with more traditional documents. Every need for information and every information source can always meet online, but they need valid tools and valid methodological paradigms that make possible the most "useful" encounter among the infinite possibilities and are, therefore, enormously time-consuming. Regarding this issue, at the end of the nineties, Proper and Bruza commented that there was still no theory, and they intended to frame information discovery in its relationship with the information retrieval tradition.

The main difference between the two systems lies in the scope of application, since IR focuses on the "search for relevant documents within established collections: typically textual" ones. It is also necessary that users have a good awareness of their information needs, and a precise knowledge of the languages and tools for indexing and research. Information discovery, on the other hand, is aimed at an open and shared space; the set of resources is constantly developing and is not just represented by textual sources. Thus, information discovery is composed of a set of activities ranging from the simple localization of a well-known digital object, to the development of an entire search strategy aimed at identifying a partition of the universe of potentially useful resources, to their organization and ordering, to the

[16] Vedere, per esempio: Michael T. Frame, *Information discovery and retrieval tools*, "Information services & use," 24 (2004), n. 4, p. 187—193, https://content.iospress.com/articles/information-services-and-use/isu445.

[17] H. A. Proper; P. D. Bruza, *What is information discovery about?* cit.

choice of the desired ones, and to the repetition of this entire strategy starting from these discoveries.[18]

Proper and Bruza disclose then their formal model of the information discovery process, conceptualizing it as an iterative relationship of search and retrieval, request and supply, of "information particles," or information data, whose relevance is defined as a variable linked to the more or less satisfactory compliance with the requests expressed in the process phases. The logical approach to the correspondence process between need and satisfaction is based on the concept of "aboutness," which established that people should not be forced to specifically define the object of the information need and can instead easily express degrees of "preference" for the correspondence of some pieces of information rather than others compared to one's general idea. In all this, the entire model of the information discovery process will differ from similar, but generally more linear, approaches of IR, in that it will be fully "user centered," and articulated in a reticular way, as well as based on the unpredictable randomness of the discovery process of information.[19]

Variations in the use of LIS terminology reveal how the idea of information discovery has become clearer only in recent times, and only when related to the applications of WSDS and discovery tools. The expression discovery tool itself acquires a given meaning only around 2009, as we ascertain by informally verifying its use both on websites and topic-related blogs as well as in articles and specific publications. Previously, the expression did not have a shared meaning, and the terms "discovery" and "tool" rarely appeared together, while rather expressions such as "discovery environment" or "discovery service" were used.[20] The string WSDS, indeed, has been used in a complete and meaningful way in even more recent years, and only in some specific essays.[21] Finally, the expression information discovery is used in different types of contributions, to widely understand systems and methodologies ranging from information retrieval to generic Internet browsing. This more or less general expression,

[18] The authors cite: Clifford A. Lynch, *Networked information resource discovery: an overview of current issues*, "IEEE journal on selected areas of communications," 13 (1995), no. 8, p. 1505–1522, https://ieeexplore.ieee.org/document/464719.

[19] Cf. H. A. Proper; P. D. Bruza, *What is information discovery about?* cit., p. 740–749.

[20] For a complete overview of the use of this terminology, cf. P. Caplan, *On discovery tools, OPACs and the motion of library language* cit.

[21] See, for example: N. P. Ellero, *Integration or disintegration* cit.; H. A. H. Richardson, *Revelations from the literature* cit.

however, is now clearly used to indicate the idea of the new possibilities of discovering information and knowledge connected to the new Web-scale services, even if other terminology relating to the new tools and their transformations is still being defined.

In any case, the theorization of information discovery does not aim at creating an opposition to information retrieval and other traditional library methodologies and tools, but rather at giving everyone their own role back, as underlined, for example, in a very short article with an exemplary title: *Open Web V the library*.[22] The paper highlights the widespread use of the Web even in areas such as scientific research and libraries at its service. This use, however, must be weighed within specific services provided by libraries, adapted from time to time to initial or in-depth knowledge needs, always considering the Web as an important starting point but not a goal of the research path, while exploring the many valid resources made accessible through generalist search engines. The "open" Web, in conclusion, is really useful given its breadth and richness as a "complement" to the priceless heritage of libraries which consists of catalogs, databases, repositories, and "local" collections.

Notwithstanding that the process of discovering useful information concerns complex combinations of relationships among researcher, research tools, and resources sought, the effectiveness of discovery services must be thoroughly tested, in addition to and independently of the "common praise" of their ease of use. Information discovery is "an exploration in continuous development," and an iterative process, which precedes and prepares access to resources or information useful to the individual who enters this path without a clear idea of one's needs. Moreover, it is precisely from this process that both ordinary people and scholars can acquire further knowledge relating to their research topic, whether general or specific, familiar or new it might be. For this reason, all WSDS must be effective and satisfactory for each type of individually parameterized search, offering sophisticated tools alongside simple ones, faceted filters alongside large central indexes.[23]

A trend shared by both scholars and professionals, therefore, is to always seek a solution of "collaboration" between new and already implemented library tools in the field of librarianship, and the general tools offered by the

[22] Richard Levy, *Open Web V the library*, «inCite», 35 (2014), no. 10, p. 19.
[23] N. P. Ellero, *Integration or disintegration* cit. In the essay, many conclusions are drawn from a thorough review of the literature on *Web-Scale Discovery Services*.

Web, which always belong to that ICT area that has more than one productive relationship with LIS. The need to include and redefine tools that have not been entirely designed in libraries following the purest librarianship principles, however, is often also dictated by some pragmatic evidence, which can generate positive impulses toward a methodological reorganization, if the right direction is taken. A lot of professional literature expressed a positive acceptance of discovery tools and the consequent logic of information discovery, which can be summarized within the period of greatest debate in Hillary Richardson's reflections.[24]

The author begins by stating that given the fact that discovery tools have the potential to easily attract people through their characteristics of ease of use and richness of discovery, it becomes important to fully understand their value and explain, also through activities of information literacy, the advantage of using such library tools rather than those offered by the Web. Referring to Jody Fagan,[25] Richardson confirms that the WSDS developed for libraries do not compete with Web search engines, but rather aim to transform services while maintaining their quality and specificity. If even the discovery tools have learned "some important lessons" from the Web industry, they still have different purposes and a different mission, corresponding to that of the library in which they are applied. The most important aspect of the new systems is the ability to replicate the "discoverability" of generalist search engines, that is, the ability to also discover resources that were not explicitly sought, but which meet the implicit needs for knowledge.[26] Discovery tools, therefore, always confirm their basic value, not just as a starting point, for the discovery of richer resources and contents than those made accessible by traditional search systems.

According to Marshall Breeding,[27] Richardson then explains the sense of the Web-scale structure of the discovery tools, understood as revolutionary as they allow to manage access to all the resources made available by the library through a unified index, which permits researching through a single interface, a single path, and a unique set of tools to guide and refine the single list of results. Beyond the critical issues presented by this unified index and the single list of results, this is an important achievement of library technologies, exactly because the discovery tools thus developed are

[24] H. A. H. Richardson, *Revelations from the literature* cit.

[25] J. C. Fagan, *Top 10 discovery tool myths* cit.

[26] Richardson cites: A. Carlin; R. Donlan, *A sheep in wolf's clothing* cit.

[27] In particular: M. Breeding, *The state of the art in library discovery 2010* cit.

not and do not want to be Google substitutes, but aim to use its technology in a more defined context. Moreover, it is possible then to grasp the positive meaning of a "partial" universe of resources to which the research tools are applied: a space that is always selected and controlled, mediated by libraries or, better still, by the library service.

This technological evolution has led to various changes that may constitute the future nature of information discovery, for example, as the author points out, innovations in librarianship vocabulary, decisive for evolving a paradigm shift, and a new theory which is respectful of past and present paradigms. Many changes have also affected professional practice, reflecting each other in the structuring of libraries and services, pushing librarians to conquer a new operational dimension.[28] Finally, all these changes have been documented by the literature, even if they are often practical evaluation interventions, dictated by "emergencies," with few reflections that either pose the question at theoretical level, or try to evaluate the principles for which this series of impulses transformation can be accepted with a scientific reason in LIS.[29]

Despite the positivity of their adequate implementation and appropriate use, WSDS seem, however, to remain limited, even now, to being basic tools for a first univocal search and discovery of resources mediated by a library. Each library, therefore, must first of all be concerned with establishing and instructing users about the potential usefulness of the new tools in relation to the traditional ones, highlighting the differences that still make them useful for different purposes, as well as inform about search strategies, critical evaluation of results, and the risks of excessive disintermediation.[30]

The objective that discovery tools operate at their best, deploying their functionalities, which can be complementary to those of the other peculiar tools of the library, depends in any case—as for OPACs or databases—on the quality of the metadata and data to which such systems are applied. Well-

[28] On the first debate related to new technological changes in the professions see, for example: Mary L. Chute, *A core for flexibility*, "Information services & use," 32 (2012), no. 3/4, p. 143—147, https://content.iospress.com/articles/information-services-and-use/isu668; Maria Cassella [et al.], *Le professioni* per *le biblioteche accademiche di ricerca*, "AIB studi," 53 (2013), no. 1, p. 63—100, https://aibstudi.aib.it/article/view/8876.

[29] These papers are reviewed by the author: H. A. H. Richardson, *Revelations from the literature* cit., p. 15—16.

[30] For a first examination of the need for a renewed information literacy, cf.: J. Condit Fagan, *Discovery tools and information literacy* cit.; N. Fawley; N. Krysak, *Information literacy opportunities within the discovery tool environment* cit.

structured, controlled, and reliable metadata are needed[31] to structure really useful guides aimed at orientating oneself in the wide range of references found and proposed by the search system, or to create faceted filters able to collect references by subject, classification, author, series, publisher, etc.

Faceted filters, often offered in orientation columns alongside the long list of search results, have the potential to be one of the richest and most useful tools in the WSDS, capable of guiding ordinary people as well as experienced users. These tools follow and enhance the browsing logic of OPACs and databases and are based on the availability of excellent cataloging and bibliographic data, extracted and verified with care and experience.[32] The quality of the search or faceted navigation of a discovery tool, therefore, is strictly dependent on the quality of the metadata work on the resources to which it is applied, on the richness, completeness, and reliability of the elements with which the resources are then indexed. This is true even if the overall quality of the faceted navigation is still linked to the capabilities of the index treatment algorithms of each system. The limit of the faceted guides, therefore, is the kind of resource to which they are applied: even if the filter applies to all the resources treated in the single index of the discovery tool, many of them may not present all the useful and correct data needed for effective grouping and faceted browsing.

Furthermore, the degree of accuracy of faceted browsing and its reliability are also linked to the possibility of "sharing" schemes and thesauri among the various indexed resources to attain metadata that are as qualitatively consistent as possible. Not only is it important to reach a high the percentage of resources with complete metadata, especially with respect to subjects or classes, but also to ensure that a classification system, for example, can be used at the same time for different collections of resources, and, finally, that a general thesaurus born from the "fusion" of other more

[31] See for example: Susan C. Wynne; Martha J. Hanscom, *The effect of next-generation catalogs on catalogers and cataloging functions in academic libraries*, "Cataloging & classification quarterly," 49 (2011), no. 3, p. 179—207, https://www.tandfonline.com/doi/full/10.1080/01639374.2011.559899; Michael Kelley, *Coming into focus: Web-Scale Discovery Services face growing need for best practices*, «Library journal», 137 (2012), no. 17, p. 34—40; David Nelson; Linda Turney, *What's in a word? Rethinking facet headings in a discovery service*, "Information technology and libraries," 34 (2015), no. 2, p. 76—91, https://ejournals.bc.edu/index.php/ital/article/view/5629.

[32] See also: Eliane Blumer [et al.], *The usability issues of faceted navigation in digital libraries*, "JLIS.it," 5 (2014), no. 2, p. 85—100, https://www.jlis.it/article/view/10072.

specific ones can be adopted.[33] The lack of common schemes for creating metadata hinders the development of valid faceted search functions. Discovery tools that index complete and accurate metadata can allow an effective combination of recall and precision in the search strategy. On the other hand, functional filters and groupings of results, reliable dynamic browsing and effective serendipity in information discovery, and "mixing" in the index of different classification or subjecting schemes can return confused search results and lists of resources decontextualized from the disciplinary field, thus disorienting the researcher rather than guiding his discovery.[34]

Therefore, in addition to the ease of use and the "superficial" uniqueness of the WSDS, a new in-depth structure is required, which enables one of the most important functions of the discovery tools and makes it really effective and reliable: the guided and faceted-filtered search. A common effort is still needed today between all those involved in the processes of resource production, collection, treatment, indexing, and research, to deeply understand the reasons and functions for the creation and use of resource metadata that allow to represent them at semantical level.

Among the efforts aimed at creating shared infrastructures to support large and rich semantic research systems, those for the fine-tuning of the linked data architecture are prominent. In fact, this system aims at the creation of a shared, enhanced, and transparent complex of links among data, which make its semantics automatically explicit, without the mediation of metadata capable of capturing the meanings or subject areas. This is the same effort through which libraries also aim to integrate catalog data into the Web, sharing rich and authoritative data and "meanings" that can form the basis for a reliable information discovery system.[35]

[33] Cf. J. C. Fagan, *Discovery tools and information literacy* cit.

[34] William Breitbach, *Web-scale discovery: a library of Babel?* In: *Planning and implementing resource discovery tools in academic libraries* cit., p. 637—645.

[35] Among the various writings that first addressed the question: Marshall Breeding, *Linked data: the next big wave or another tech fad?* "Computers in libraries," 33 (2013), no. 3, p. 20—22, http://www.infotoday.com/cilmag/apr13/Breeding-Linked-Data-The%20-Next-Big-Wave-or-Another-Tech-Fad.shtml; Lorcan Dempsey, *Thirteen ways of looking at libraries, discovery, and the catalog: scale, workflow, attention*, "Educause review online," 10 December 2012, http://www.educause.edu/ero/article/thirteen-ways-looking-libraries-discovery-and-catalog-scale-workflow-attention; Library of Congress, *Bibliographic framework as a web of data* cit.; Karen Coyle, *Library data in a modern context*, "Library technology reports," 46 (2010), no. 1, p. 5—13, https://journals.ala.org/index.php/ltr/article/view/4630.

Until a given level of metadata richness and interoperability, or the diffusion of a solid and shared linked data architecture is achieved,[36] discovery tools will tend to qualify as first access tools to all kinds of information and resources, and information discovery will be limited to a preliminary survey, to be deepened with the use of specific research tools, typical of information retrieval. Like the overall exploration of a potentially infinite set of resources, even univocal search in a very wide area is not easily reached until different tools, albeit of high quality, are applied to differently processed data, albeit with very reliable methods. Although it is still a distant goal—bearing the connotations of an utopia—a "common, standardized, open, and integrated" data and metadata environment, extended to the Web, can represent the right, "universal" space for application of unique and "all-encompassing" research and discovery systems, adequate and useful for all people, for all information, and knowledge needs."[37]

Therefore, library contexts, also defined from their own point of view, can really be a "safer" partition not to lose context awareness and to orientate oneself among the information and knowledge resources in a potentially infinite data universe. In this perspective, the hypothetical "contrast" between information retrieval and information discovery would, in any case, be of little tenor. Obviously, this "mitigation" is not to be intended in the sense that the WSDS applied to the library field can definitively replace advanced research tools, while discovery tools and the like remain—at least as currently conceived—"first entry" tools to the heritage of information and resources mediated by libraries, archives, museums, galleries, and so on.

Probably, there is a wider solution to the maybe only apparent opposition between information retrieval and information discovery, and this might reside in the technological-cultural revolution that can be expected from WSDS, linked data, the Semantic Web, and even open access. Thus, only "information professionals" can weigh which type of search and retrieval tools are to be provided or recommended to different categories of people to allow data and resources exploitation. There will be those who

[36] On this issue, cf. Erik Mitchell, *Leveraging metadata to create better web services*, "Journal of Web librarianship," 6 (2012), no. 2, p. 136–139, https://www.tandfonline.com/doi/full/10.1080/19322909.2012.671653.

[37] In this sense, the conclusions of the review by N. P. Ellero, *Integration or disintegration* cit.

need a quick search for general information, as well as those who need a guide to start a study, those who require advanced assistance for scientific research, and those who possess excellent Web skills but lack a correct approach to critically evaluate resources.

One of the achievements in the development of knowledge resources may be the "independence" of information from the search tool, and the ability to find and evaluate quality information with any tool. If catalogs, databases, institutional repositories, open-access archives, and portals will "express" themselves through linked data, if they will "expose" the knowledge resources they own or mediate through the new Semantic Web method, and if all valid resources will be accessible with the new system, then search, discovery, retrieval, and sharing tools may be more or less specialized, more or less professional, more or less reliable, but none will have the exclusivity of quality information, and consequently of access to quality resources. In that case, from the point of view of their affordability and evaluability, will all be on the same level: an excellent resource will be reached from the OPAC or from the Web. Excellence will be guaranteed by the OPAC but not by the search engine. The OPAC will have a reliable guide and those who use a search engine will have to find their own way. Those who are not interested in quality assurance, or know how to frame what they are looking for, may prefer the engine to the OPAC, etc.

Catalogs, databases, repositories, etc., must open their own contents, or rather, must deal with contents that shall be open to the Web and to the various search engines, but this does not mean that they must also be transformed into generic search systems. This would imply that specialized tools, created by an institution and defined for its specific users, would not be clearly recognized from other useful even if less reliable tools, available to all. However, apart from this "special" distinction, based on the selected application space and the tools that can be applied to it, there is no reason for libraries to cherish a sort of "jealousy" for the quality of their ownership, since they have already lost it. The "added value" of libraries, as well as of specialized database producers, will not change in substance and principles and will always consist in the ability to evaluate, select, and mediate between the available resources, as well as the competence to know and describe them appropriately for their users.

As a corollary to all this, in a space where contents are equally accessible regardless of the search system, there will no longer be room for producers of "closed" systems—nor for databases designed to be efficient only with discovery tools distributed by the same manufacturer. The competition space will be the "democratic" Web—prodigal and fearful as a popular stream—and to compare and develop better research systems and proprietary interfaces than those freely available, one will really need to care for the quality of possible information operations, developing them technologically, but only striving, at different levels, toward the best research achievements using data and contents that can no longer be monopolized.[38] What the producers will charge, therefore, will only be the result of this highly specialized activity of collection, selection, description, and mediation, that is, the same that libraries do for free, or rather, thank to investments connected to other essential services paid by the community of citizens, until this will be sustainable.

5.2 Discovery tools and information literacy

The sharing, interoperability, and reuse of data appear, therefore, as a goal that may be sometimes close, sometimes more difficult to achieve. If linked data concerning the many different available and useful resources can really populate the Web and the indexes of the library databases as well, then the Web could represent the space in which search engines will be free to carry out their "boundless" investigation, and the spaces of libraries would represent those in which discovery tools can develop research within the boundaries drawn in designing a given library and its specific mission, despite this is not easy to define or theorize, but rather remarkable in its logical and technical essence. Nongeneralist search systems, therefore, would "work" in a more controlled and reliable universe of resources but should still have the same "capacity" and versatility of a large network search engine, together with specific tools for advanced search. These features would allow broad but "safe," as well as structured, research, and discovery. Expanding the boundaries of this universe, then, would be simple, and nothing new: the discovery tools should be applied to the databases of "allied" libraries, and also to those of other cultural institutions, sharing a given disciplinary field or belonging to a functional typology, nationally or internationally.

[38] About the intentions of some commercial producers, cf. A. Kaschte, *Linked open data on its way into next generation library management and discovery solutions* cit. Also, see: John J. Regazzi, *The battle for mindshare: a battle beyond access and retrieval*, "Information services & use," 24 (2004), no. 2, p. 83–92, https://content.iospress.com/articles/information-services-and-use/isu426.

Without building a universe of data and resources parallel to that of the Web, libraries can offer all people—scholars, professionals, citizens in general—the possibility of choosing a specific "point of view," a line from which to start and to delve into information and knowledge. Furthermore, the point of view offered by libraries does not necessarily have to be that of a more "accomplished" research, a safer of one's own steps or more assisted one. Libraries can also guide to a more or less adventurous, "serendipitous" path to the discovery of resources, which takes place following intuitions, loaded with unpredictability, creativity, and leading to results that are as unexpected as well as precious.[39] During these discovery paths, new ideas can be conceived that originate from the unpredictable meeting of information and knowledge, which emerge as totally new creations in the context of a research aimed not only at finding given information, but also at sifting through the many possible relationships involved in this path.[40]

Consequently, much must be invested in the activities and principles of information literacy, which must be further studied as a method for instruction in the use and evaluation of all information retrieval and discovery tools, and above all the evaluation of the resources individuals have reached.[41] The new tools can be easily approached and their use can be learned, and then more time remains available to instill "critical thinking" on the results often too easily obtained. It is necessary that all information professionals are prepared to always guide individuals, whatever level of information competence they have, toward choosing and critically

[39] Among the others, see: Tammera M. Race, *Resource discovery tools: supporting serendipity*. In: *Planning and implementing resource discovery tools in academic libraries* cit., p. 139–152. In addition, the behavior and the fortuitous search path, based on serendipity, can also be modeled, like other user behaviors: cf. Stephann Makri; Ann Blandford, *Coming across information serendipitously*, "Journal of documentation," 68 (2012), no. 5, p. 684–724, https://www.emerald.com/insight/content/doi/10.1108/00220411211256030/full/html.

[40] Regarding the emergence of new ideas in information discovery processes, see: Andruid Kerne [et al.], *An experimental method for measuring the emergence of new ideas in information discovery*, "International journal of human-computer interaction," 24 (2008), no. 5, p. 460–477, https://www.tandfonline.com/doi/full/10.1080/10447310802142243; Andruid Kerne [et al.], *combinFormation: mixed-initiative composition of image and text surrogates promotes information discovery*, "ACM transactions on information systems," 27 (2009), no. 1, p. 5:1–5:45, https://dl.acm.org/citation.cfm?id=1416955.

[41] On this point, see again: J. C. Fagan, *Discovery tools and information literacy* cit.; N. Fawley; N. Krysak, *Information literacy opportunities within the discovery tool environment* cit.

evaluating information, resources, research, and discovery tools, even in areas other than those of libraries, also and above all on the Web.[42]

In defining the better system to "instruct" people how to reach a viewpoint inside the universe of information and knowledge, it is impossible not to notice that information literacy has undergone continuous changes and evolutions, due to the technological development of society. In particular, the development of various new forms of information literacy in relation to the various evolutions of technologies and the information society highlights how it is necessary, in the library environment, to adapt to new situations.[43] The most striking trend is the overcoming of the traditional hierarchy of information sources, the diminishing importance of sources classically appointed to support the development of knowledge, such as those of libraries. Without perceiving the need for assistance and mediation, users grasp directly the infinite sources and resources accessible through the Web. Nonetheless, in this interactive, accessible, and friendly universe, specific skills and abilities are necessary to handle information tools and information itself, but almost everything can be reached by self-taught people or with "peers."[44]

In its about 50 years of tradition,[45] information literacy that libraries have taken on has always been aimed at giving people the necessary skills to use

[42] Although oriented toward information literacy only in the university context, it is useful to see: Lisa M. Rose-Wiles; Melissa A. Hofmann, *Still desperately Cf.king citations: undergraduate research in the age of web-scale discovery*, "Journal of library administration," 53 (2013), no. 2/3, p. 147–166, https://www.tandfonline.com/doi/full/10.1080/01930826.2013.853493; Nina Exner, *Research information literacy: addressing original researchers' needs*, "The journal of academic librarianship," 40 (2014), p. 460–466, https://www.sciencedirect.com/science/article/pii/S0099133314000901.

[43] There are, of course, other opinions, which, unlike extolling information literacy, claim the value of the traditional reference service: Anthony Verdesca, *What's in a word: coming to terms with reference*, "Reference librarian," 56 (2015), no. 1, p. 67–72, https://www.tandfonline.com/doi/full/10.1080/02763877.2015.976467.

[44] An interesting approach to information literacy as a nonformally structured system is the one that understands it as a "participatory" process: Annemarie Lloyd, *No man (or woman) is an island: information literacy, affordances and communities of practice*, "Australian library journal," 54 (2005), no. 3, p. 230–237, https://www.tandfonline.com/doi/abs/10.1080/00049670.2005.10721760.

[45] The expression "information literacy" was coined in: Paul G. Zurkowski, *The information service environment: relationships and priorities*. Washington: National commission on libraries and information science, 1974, http://files.eric.ed.gov/fulltext/ED100391.pdf.

information resources for their activities, to be able to use the different primary information tools, in particular catalogs, databases, and other kinds of reliable repertories. The developments of the Web that we have witnessed so far, in any case, require rethinking information as a continuous, dynamic, and pervasive flow, which cannot simply be stored in a classic "silos" of data waiting to be recovered, neither quantitatively nor for its new qualities of updating and development. Information is, therefore, "the world we live in and that [...] we help to build": this is why libraries can take into full consideration the new Web of interaction, sharing, creating, developing, and deepening one's own field of existence through information literacy, to give to each individual's action a renewed and specific formative value.[46]

For more than 20 years, we have been talking about digital literacy as a vast field that would interact with information literacy, and be able to grasp the new identity of all the resources present on the network, textual and multimedia, static and dynamic, authoritative or ephemeral, and to establish the right skills and the appropriate tools to allow use for each of them, in a way appropriate to their nature, without preconceptions related to the hierarchy of sources.[47] Clearly, information literacy cannot become a simple subset of digital literacy, because there are classic or new information skills that have nothing to do with digital ones. Learning digital technologies, in any case, is not linked only to information and is considered increasingly crucial for the development of citizens' knowledge, skills, and freedom. Important international organizations such as the UNESCO, the European Union, or even the American Library Association (ALA) have placed digital literacy at the center of numerous projects, reserving libraries an important role in its realization, which can reach further expand the concept of competence up to media information literacy (MIL), which indicates not only the ability to evaluate information content but also that

[46] An in-depth analysis of these issues is contained in: Laura Testoni, *Quali literacy al tempo dei social network?*, "Biblioteche oggi," 32 (2014), 4, p. 28–36, http://www.bibliotecheoggi.it/rivista/article/view/94.

[47] On this topic, cf. P. Gilster, *Digital literacy* cit.

of creating them by mastering the different tools that have this function[48] (Fig. 5.20).

Libraries must, therefore, take on the task of developing information literacy, toward the perspectives of digital literacy and MIL, including in the training program all the skills that can really be used by individuals to orientate themselves in the new world of information and technologies. Information literacy becomes an all-round education to experience the world of the Web, not limited to the search for information, or to library instruction. Just as information retrieval extends to information discovery, while maintaining the peculiarities of its quality tools without replacing them entirely with new tools, in the same way information literacy can only evolve toward new skills, including non—library-related ones, while maintaining its peculiar ability to develop critical thinking around each object of application, favoring the all-round development of individuals and citizens, both as users and as creators of the new society that surrounds them.[49]

By limiting the discussion on information literacy to academic libraries and research institutes—as most of the literature on the subject actually does—the specific principles deepen and become even more decisive. Just

[48] Some documents that indicate these specific choices are: Unesco, *Fez declaration on Media and information literacy*. 2011, http://www.unesco.org/new/fileadmin/MULTIMEDIA/HQ/CI/CI/pdf/news/Fez%20Declaration.pdf; European Commission. Directorate-General for Education and Culture, *Better eLearning for Europe*. Luxembourg: Office for official publications of the European Communities, 2003, https://www.jyu.fi/hum/laitokset/solki/en/research/projects/tolp/betterelearningforeurope.pdf; American Library Association. Office for Information Technology Policy. Digital Literacy Task Force, *Digital literacy, libraries and public policy*. 2013, http://www.districtdispatch.org/wp-content/uploads/2013/01/2012_OITP_digilitreport_1_22_13.pdf. Furthermore, in this perspective, one cannot fail to mention the *Lyon declaration* cit.

[49] On this issue, see also: Thomas P. Mackey; Trudi E. Jacobsen, *Metaliteracy: reinventing information literacy to empower learners*. London: Facet, 2014.

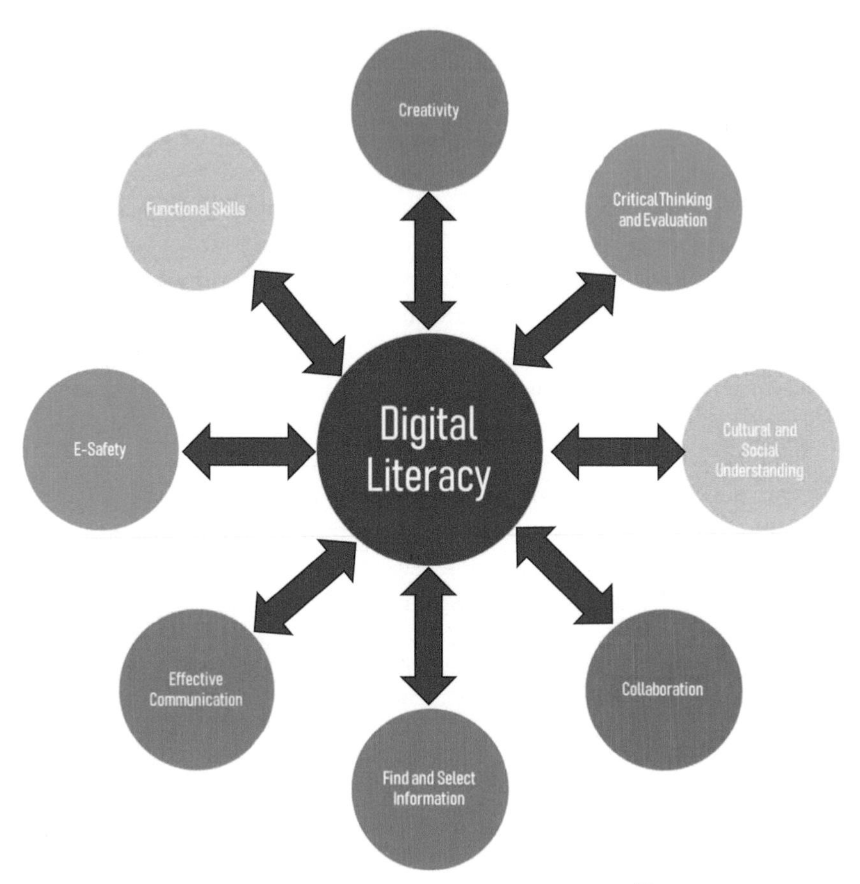

Figure 5.20 Components of *digital literacy*.[50]

as various literacies have necessarily developed as a result of information technologies, to empower citizens to act in today's society, so also academic information literacy is required to follow developments and updates of research methodologies, which in turn follow technological developments,

[50] Image inspired by the work of Payton and Hague. Cf.: Cassie Hague; Sarah Payton, *Digital literacy across the curriculum*. Futurelab, 2010, p. 19, https://www.nfer.ac.uk/publications/FUTL06/FUTL06.pdf.

to empower researchers and university students, as well as scholars in general.[51] In fact, however, the problem of the relationship between information discovery and information literacy is perceived and discussed mainly in the academic field, where the new Web-scale services are more used, and this is also confirmed by the first reviews of the literature on the subject.[52]

The discussion on the acceptance of WSDS, therefore, and the consequent greater attention to the education of the people who must use them, begins early in the context of academic and research libraries. The principle is that the tools, discovery tools, and the search logic or information discovery are welcomed in a productive and "safe" way, without prejudice but without blind enthusiasm, first of all by librarians and immediately consequently by the users of the services offered by libraries.[53] Information literacy is the link to questions and their solution. Only by fully understanding the advantages and limitations of the new tools can librarians be able to integrate them perfectly into research services and thus propose and explain them to researchers, who often demonstrate that they need clear guidance, whether direct or mediated by the library's website.[54] Still in the academic field, information literacy must be developed into different degrees when not addressed toward students in general, but professional researchers, professors, and PhDs, engaged in the development of theories and experiments.[55]

[51] See for example: Tibor Koltay [et al.], *The shift of information literacy toward research 2.0*, "Journal of academic librarianship," 41 (2015), no. 1, p. 87–93, https://www.sciencedirect.com/science/article/pii/S0099133314001979. See also: Michelle Dalton, *The form of search tool chosen by undergraduate students influences research practices and the type and quality of information selected*, "Evidence based library & information practice," 9 (2014), no. 2, p. 19–21, https://journals.library.ualberta.ca/eblip/index.php/EBLIP/article/view/21327.

[52] See B. Thomsett-Scott; P. E. Reese, *Academic libraries and discovery tools* cit.

[53] In support, see: *The discovery tool cookbook: recipes for successful lesson plans*, edited by Nancy Fawley, Nikki Krysak. Chicago: ALA, 2016; Natasha Danae Allen, *Utilizing discovery tools for classrooms: how do librarian attitudes on discovery impact tools they teach?* "Library Hi Tech news," 32 (2015), no. 1, p. 8–12, https://www.emerald.com/insight/content/doi/10.1108/LHTN-09-2014-0078/full/html.

[54] Cf. Darren Chase [et al.], *The perfect storm: examining user experience and conducting a usability test to investigate a disruptive academic library web site redevelopment*, "Journal of web librarianship," 10 (2016), no. 1, p. 28–44, https://www.tandfonline.com/doi/full/10.1080/19322909.2015.1124740.

[55] On this topic, cf. N. Exner, *Research information literacy* cit.

In this regard, Jody Fagan discusses to what extent the implementation of a discovery tool as the core searching tool for information influences the possibility of becoming really "information literate," despite the risk of concealing too much of the complexities that constitute research by adopting an apparently simple, but as such potentially misleading, action.[56] Therefore, proposing adequate information literacy to service users becomes a necessity and, at the same time, a great "virtue" for libraries, which in this way can ensure an understanding of the differences, potential, and usefulness of all new and traditional research tools, as well as an understanding of new research strategies and meeting the increased need for critical evaluation of results.

In support of these views, Fagan refers to the principles according to which an information literate person must be able to recognize his or her own information needs, and then know how to locate, evaluate, and effectively use the resources necessary to meet these needs.[57] Therefore, the author proposes a careful analysis of the first two of the five standards proposed in 2000 by the Association of College and Research Libraries (ACRL), which refer to the aforementioned principles,[58] to verify when the use of discovery tools can support information literacy, and why preferring them over more traditional tools "hinders" in other cases a correct learning and instructional process. Fagan's article refers to the ACRL standard in force in the period in which the author writes, replaced in 2015 by a more innovative framework,[59] but it remains in principle still a valid reading, since it represents some issues still present today.

The first standard of the ACRL relates to the ability to determine the nature and extent of the information needed by a researcher. In this, the author argues discovery tools can offer partial help. The system allows the user to easily explore a large number of different sources, without having to previously choose a given database or catalog, contributing to familiarize with the research object, and to define key concepts and terms more precisely. For a more advanced definition, however, the specific tools

[56] J. C. Fagan, *Discovery tools and information literacy* cit.

[57] The definition of these principles is in: American Library Association. Presidential Committee on Information Literacy, *Final Report*. Chicago: American Library Association, 1989.

[58] Association of College and Research Libraries, *Information literacy competency standards for higher education*. Chicago: ALA, 2000, https://alair.ala.org/handle/11213/7668.

[59] Association of College and Research Libraries, *Framework for information literacy for higher education*. 2015, http://www.ala.org/acrl/standards/ilframework.

of a given sector are more useful. Moreover, again due to its all-encompassing nature that mixes collections, metadata, and thesauri, the discovery tool does not allow to evaluate how knowledge is divided into disciplines, and how sources of information differ between disciplines and within each domain. The filters and limiters of the discovery tools do not work with the consistency of those of databases and catalogs, because they do not arise from a unique and "competent" structuring of resource representation schemes. It is necessary, however, to underline the value of the WSDS as a tool for retrieving resources, once identified, precisely because of the extent of their application space, even if, on the other hand, this simplicity of retrieving the first resources found does not lead to review further research objectives and seek other sources of information.[60]

For the second ACRL standard, the information literate must know how to access the desired information effectively and efficiently. The researcher's ability is primarily related to knowing how to choose the specific tool that can provide him with the most suitable and reliable information, whether it is a database, an institutional repository, an open archive, or a specialist catalog. Besides, choice strategies and methodologies of research also vary according to the disciplinary field of action. A discovery tool, through its simplifying and misleading single search box, tarnishes or masks the differences between the access tools and between the reasons for choosing based on the fields represented and makes it unnecessary to refine the search strategy within it. On the contrary, the library website or portal can show, list and describe these tools, guide the choice, and explain the research methodology for each of them. The advantage of the single system, on the other hand, is certainly found in all subsequent activities relating to the processing, organization, and citation of the results list.[61]

Given the partial correspondence of the use of information discovery systems with the objectives of correct information literacy, librarians must engage on various issues relating to how to compensate for the shortcomings of these tools and exploit new opportunities, both in the processes of acceptance, parameterization, and integration between the other tools of the library and in training and guiding people to use them. It is equally necessary, moreover, to reflect on the development and updating of the same standards for assessing the skills of information literate, which have now changed according to the new technologies that must be mastered. Only by evaluating

[60] J. C. Fagan, *Discovery tools and information literacy* cit., p. 171–174.
[61] *Ivi*, p. 175–177.

which skills are no longer effective in the current information universe, and which ones must take their place, can a proper information literacy program be established to assist people in using old and new research tools—and in this Fagan already feels the need for the new framework launched in 2015.[62]

The new framework for information literacy of the ACRL starts from the assumption that it is possible to create a real "movement of educational reform," based on the development of information competence, through the coordination and dissemination of a series of basic principles. Many of these principles, and many practices and guidelines, were developed by librarians in academic libraries, and then used in various study and research institutes, starting with the first standards of the ACRL itself.[63] However, it is necessary to keep up with the times, to update the image of students and researchers, present in the minds of those who have to deal with their education in the use of information, and for this purpose, the new ACRL document looks more like to a reference framework, in fact, rather than a rigid set of rules or standards to be followed, dynamically opening up to innovations and adaptations. The role of librarians, teachers, and students must be well understood and interpreted in the sense of the maximum interaction of skills and needs.[64]

The framework is structured as a series of interconnected "key concepts," with different and flexible options for implementation and use. The basic conceptualizations of the framework develop a series of different ideas and

[62] With regard to this need to update information literacy standards, "old" by a decade, the ACRL has, in fact, produced the new dynamic framework: ACRL, *Framework for information literacy for higher education* cit.

[63] ACRL, *Information literacy competency standards for higher education* cit. Consider also: Jesús Lau, *Guidelines on information literacy for lifelong learning: final draft*. IFLA, 2006, https://www.ifla.org/ES/publications/guidelines-on-information-literacy-for-lifelong-learning.

[64] Among the various studies on the ACRL framework: Sara D. Miller, *Diving deep: reflective questions for identifying tacit disciplinary information literacy knowledge practices, dispositions, and values through the ACRL Framework for Information Literacy*, "Journal of academic librarianship," 44 (2018), no. 3, p. 412–418, https://www.sciencedirect.com/science/article/pii/S0099133317302720; Bethany Wilkes, *Framing Digital Literacy: the ACRL Framework*, «Singapore journal of Library & information management», 45 (2016), p. 11–19, https://www.las.org.sg/wp/sjlim/framing-digital-literacy-the-acrl-framework/; Colleen Burgess, *Teaching students, not standards: the new ACRL Information Literacy Framework and threshold crossings for instructors*, "Partnership," 10 (2015), no. 1, p. 1–6, https://journal.lib.uoguelph.ca/index.php/perj/article/view/3440.

concepts on information, research, and study, which are connected to each other and can represent the mandatory and essential "threshold concepts" to enter a discipline and begin to understand it.[65] To this, the task force curating the framework has added two elements that define some important learning objectives related to the concepts presented: the "knowledge practices," which represent skills or abilities of those who become experts in dealing with information, developed through understanding of threshold concepts, and "attitudes," which express attitudes, preferences, and ways characteristic of a given tendency to "move" among information.

The framework is organized into six "frames," and each of these defines a central concept for the development of information literacy. For each of them, there is a set of knowledge practices and a set of attitudes. The frames are listed and discussed simply in alphabetical order and do not define an a priori fixed sequence. Obviously, none of the practices or attitudes, nor the overall structuring of each frame, must be considered an immutable standard; each user must calibrate and rebalance the tools according to their own needs for intervention, analysis, or educational action in their own context of reference.

The concept of the first frame is: "Authority is the result of a construction and is contextual." That is, the various information resources are characterized by the experience and credibility of their creators, as well as by the context of use and also by the information need itself. Consequently, the "construction" of authority varies not only based on the constituent factors of the information itself, but also based on the characteristics deemed relevant in the "context" of use. The second frame defines: "The creation of information is a process." In fact, information, whatever the type and format, is the tool to convey a message through an established and shared communication process which, in its phases, influences and "shapes" the message itself.

The third frame has as its principle: "Information has value." In fact, information can take on different dimensions of value, including material, as it can be an economic asset, a tool for education, an element of influence, and as an element for understanding the scope of action and also of existence. Skipping the fourth, the fifth frame represents the concept "Scientific knowledge is a conversation." In fact, knowledge and progress are shared

[65] The *framework* cites: Grant Wiggins; Jay McTighe, *Understanding by design*. Alexandria: Association for supervision and curriculum development, 2004; *Threshold concepts and transformational learning*, edited by Jan H. F. Meyer [et al.]. Rotterdam: Sense publishers, 2010.

and uninterrupted discursive practices, in which ideas are born, developed, and then discussed; they disappear, return, are reevaluated, and are disseminated, across centuries through the communities of scholars or among ordinary people.

The fourth frame—like the sixth—is a frame that is very well suited to the discussion of the principles of information discovery and discovery tools: "Research is an investigation." By focusing on this principle, much can be explained about WSDS and their usage strategies. Research, in fact, is defined as an iterative process, based on the growing complexity of the questions to be satisfied, which increase quantitatively and qualitatively as the answers and results are found. From all the answers obtained, other starting questions and new research paths often develop. The investigation moves from one field to another, involves different skills, and either extends beyond the scientific sphere in which it was generated or enters the scientific sphere after having been generated in everyday life. In the sharing and collaboration of investigations, whether directly or indirectly, strong affinities or violent disagreements can arise, which the knowledge community must cope with, to reach progress and common goods. In these contexts, the levels of investigation vary greatly, from exploratory and initial, to very in-depth or revolutionary ones, and for each of them, a competence is needed to identify and use the most suitable methods and tools to conduct one's own investigations with the best strategy.

Finally, the sixth frame concerns the necessary deepest principles of strategy searching to use discovery services: "Searching is a strategic exploration." Given that the search and above all the discovery of information are often iterative and nonlinear processes, it is necessary to be able to evaluate a very wide and varied series of sources, as well as to have flexibility and interaction skills such as to be able to guess and pursue alternative paths, considering that the level of knowledge deepens and the number of acquired knowledge increases. Research is described as "a mixture of investigation, discovery, and serendipity," which allows us to understand the possible relevant sources as well as the ways to access them. In these "paths," research is a complex and complete experience, which involves both the rational and cognitive sphere and the affective, social, and sensitivity one.

5.3 Information literacy and individual needs

Another analysis of the need for information literacy, carried out by Nancy Fawley and Nikki Krysak, also written in the period of the first debates on discovery tools, begins with people's lack of technological competence.[66] Digital natives are scarcely competent in the research of information both for what concerns library tools, as for the tools of the Web themselves. People use Google and other general search engines all the time, but they ignore the basics of how these tools work and what even a simple search strategy is.[67] The discovery tools adopted by libraries, with their single Google-like interface, aim to simplify the search and make it more intuitive by approaching the normal habits of Web users, but end up worsening the situation of their technological incompetence. These tools work as long as it is a question of starting a research, even at university level, but users should be clarified about their validity and the moment in which they should switch to more specific tools, even if they are to be checked one by one and with specific methods.

In academic libraries, the debate focuses precisely on these limitations, before which information discovery systems are useful for accompanying students and researchers to the start of their investigation, or to an interdisciplinary "inspection," after which it is necessary to move on to not only more traditional, but more suited to the furthering and deepening of the search for information. Libraries must rethink user education criteria to the new skills needed to master information technologies and then provide a renewed information literacy capable of clarifying ideas about the different moments of current research methodologies and the different tools to address it. If with new technologies librarians have to invest less time to teach the basic use of an instrument—it is often repeated in this period—more time remains at their disposal to educate them in the evaluation and critical choice of the tools to use, as well as to develop "critical thinking" in people regarding the results and contents obtained. Users themselves tend to focus more on what they have found than what is the way and the tool to find it, first evaluating the search concepts and objectives against the type of resource to be looking for.[68] Obviously, the simplicity of the discovery tool search method—it is repeated again—must not completely mask the complexity of the process itself, and the importance of using the right tools.[69]

[66] N. Fawley; N. Krysak, *Information literacy opportunities within the discovery tool environment* cit.

[67] Cf. Andrew D. Asher; Lynda M. Duke, *Searching for answers: student research behavior at Illinois Wesleyan University*. In: *College libraries and student culture: what we now know*, edited by Lynda M. Duke, Andrew D. Asher. Chicago: ALA, 2011, p. 71–85.

[68] Some conclusions on this matter are in: J. Luther; M. C. Kelly, *The next generation of discovery* cit.; M. Breeding, *The state of the art in library discovery 2010* cit.

[69] Fawley and Krysak cite: J. C. Fagan, *Discovery tools and information literacy* cit.

Based on the results of some studies on the reception of new systems by users,[70] Fawley and Krysak draw a portrait of digital natives, which confirms the lack of any methodology for conducting research or a critical awareness in evaluating resources. Therefore, their study confirms the need for a structured and updated activity of education in skills in digital technologies, and information and critical thinking in research heuristics. In this regard, they suggest a model and some best practices for the development of information literacy courses that academic libraries must implement,[71] which should focus on some specific objectives: the development and evaluation of useful keywords in a "multithesaurus" environment; the effectiveness and "limitedness" of facet filters; the development of a critical thinking on tools, resources, research strategy; and the usefulness of the unique interfaces limited to the start of research and interdisciplinary research.[72]

Also at the time of the first academic implementations of discovery systems, Lisa Rose-Wiles and Melissa Hofmann began their analysis of the necessary literacy by complaining about the low level of competence of people, specifically university students: if they are always desperate searching for information to use and cite, they have almost no idea how to find it and even why they need it.[73] The problem of the poor ability to understand and use the information retrieval systems made available by university libraries may depend on the complexity of the systems themselves, but the habit of searching with Web engines, and similar discovery tools, hinders even more the learning—and the willingness to learn—of the appropriate skills to process and use information, or to patiently structure a good research strategy.

Some considerations of the authors are taken from the literature review—nothing new—and concern, for example, the preference given to discovery tools over other tools, due not only to the similarity to generalist

[70] In particular: Sarah C. Williams; Anita K. Foster, *Promises fulfilled? An EBSCO Discovery Service usability study*, "Journal of web librarianship," 5 (2011), no. 3, p. 179–198, https://www.tandfonline.com/doi/full/10.1080/19322909.2011.597590; D. Way, *The impact of web-scale discovery on the use of a library collection* cit.

[71] Regarding other promising practices that are still emerging, see: S. Buck; C. Steffy, *Promising practices in instruction of discovery tools* cit.

[72] Cf. N. Fawley; N. Krysak, *Information literacy opportunities within the discovery tool environment* cit., p. 211–213.

[73] L. M. Rose-Wiles; M. A. Hofmann, *Still desperately Cf.king citations* cit.

engines for simplicity and speed, but also to single search box that acts on different databases and catalogs, filters, and guides for searching and linking functions and tools for saving and processing results.[74] The widespread considerations also concern the negative aspects, of course, such as that for which the simplification of the search is reflected in the loss of precision, in the proposal of too many results and irrelevant results, as well as in the coverage gap, in the scarce possibility of limiting or refining the results, in the unreliability of relevance ranking.[75]

A frequently recurring problem is that of the contrast between the untrained use of discovery tools and the development of the ability to conduct research critically, all the more necessary in a large information discovery system. In this, we can claim the importance of information literacy, whose objectives coincide with those in general of university professors, who support the development of a capacity to think and think critically, not impeded by any system or technological tool that simplifies too much the processes of seeking knowledge.[76] Not to mention—again—the need for information literacy to be able to evaluate the results, the sources, the resources, and their areas of belonging, the tools, and their right place in a research strategy, as well as to set up and master the strategies same of a more precise information retrieval and a broader information discovery.[77]

Therefore, since the early days of the experimentation of discovery tools in the libraries of universities and research centers, many studies and opinions agree in establishing that the WSDS, if not properly introduced and explained, negatively affect on the ability to conduct information searches and that this situation is worsened by the growing diffusion of digital

[74] See B. Thomsett-Scott; P. E. Reese, *Academic libraries and discovery tools* cit.

[75] See Roberta F. Woods, *From federated search to the universal search solution*, "Serials librarian," 58 (2010), no. 1/4, p. 141–148, https://www.tandfonline.com/doi/full/10.1080/03615261003622957.

[76] Will Wheeler, *The role of reference in discovery systems: effecting a more literate search*. In: *Something's gotta give: Charleston conference proceedings, 2011*. West Lafayette: Purdue University Press, 2011, http://docs.lib.purdue.edu/cgi/viewcontent.cgi?article=1229&context=charleston.

[77] Cfr. L. M. Rose-Wiles; M. A. Hofmann, *Still desperately Cf.king citations* cit., p. 153–155; 157–161.

information and the more typical methods of managing it. It is even possible to speak of a specific "library anxiety," a phenomenon already known for some time in the context of less technologized libraries than it is now, but which may recur with greater resurgence in the users of current research systems, who are unable to understand them and keep them in check.[78]

The time saved in the use of the new tools, thanks to their speed and simplicity, should therefore be used by people to better and more critically frame the needs and objectives of the research, as well as to reflect on the role and methods of the tools that, although they are also technologically simpler, they require a greater patience of application in exchange for a more precise correspondence to the research itself.[79]

If necessary, a part of the most recent literature moves to defend the importance of not neglecting information discovery in setting up information literacy programs, which emphasizes the harmfulness of an a priori attitude of underestimating this system. The exclusion of the role of

[78] For further information, cf. Erin L. McAfee, *Shame: the emotional basis of library anxiety*, "College and research libraries," 79 (2018), no. 2, p. 237–256, https://crl.acrl.org/index.php/crl/article/view/16604/18604.

[79] For an idea of users' awareness of these possibilities, see: Joel Tonyan; Christi Piper, *Discovery tools in the classroom: a usability study and implications for information literacy instruction*, "Journal of web librarianship," 13 (2019), no. 1, p. 1–19, https://www.tandfonline.com/doi/full/10.1080/19322909.2018.1530161?src=recsys; Asim M. Qayyum; David Smith, *Changing research behaviors of university students with progression throughout a course*, "Journal of the Australian Library & Information Association," 67 (2018), no. 3, p. 256–277, https://www.tandfonline.com/doi/full/10.1080/24750158.2018.1502243; Megan Dempsey; Alyssa M. Valenti, *Student use of keywords and limiters in web-scale discovery searching*, "The journal of academic librarianship," 42 (2016), no. 3, p. 200–206, https://www.sciencedirect.com/science/article/pii/S0099133316300027.

discovery tools is as harmful as excessive centralization, both in the organization of research services and in education for the critical evaluation of research tools and resources found.[80]

There are many reasons and opportunities to invest in the activities and principles of information literacy, which must be further studied in terms of education in the use and evaluation of all information retrieval and discovery tools, and above all for education to evaluation of the resources they have reached. From librarians and other information professionals, further help is needed more than ever to people, digital natives or not, to learn how to choose and critically evaluate both information and resources, and research and discovery tools, above all, when information, resources, and tools belong to areas other than libraries and cultural institutions, especially when the research space and the results obtained potentially expand indefinitely.

Without prejudice to the individual differences among people, who are individually more or less inclined to the critical deepening of their practical and intellectual action, an accurate reflection on the renewed technological

[80] Among other papers: Alexandra Hamlett; Helen Georgas, *In the wake of discovery: student perceptions, integration, and instructional design*, "Journal of web librarianship," 13 (2019), no. 3, p. 230–245, https://www.tandfonline.com/doi/full/10.1080/19322909.2019.1598919?src=recsys; Steven Shapiro, *Academic librarians, information overload, and the Tao of discovery*, «The journal of academic librarianship», 44 (2018), no. 5, p. 671–673, https://www.sciencedirect.com/science/article/pii/S0099133318302210; Ellen L. Rubenstein [et al.], *ARL instruction librarians and the one-box: a follow-up study*, "Reference services review," 45 (2017), no. 3, p. 368–381, https://www.emerald.com/insight/content/doi/10.1108/RSR-12-2016-0084/full/html; Nancy Fawley; Nikki Krysak, *Learning to love your discovery tool: strategies for integrating a discovery tool in face-to-face, synchronous, and asynchronous instruction*, "Public services quarterly," 10 (2014), no. 4, p. 283–301, https://www.tandfonline.com/doi/full/10.1080/15228959.2014.961110?af=R; Alison J. Head, *Learning the ropes: how freshmen conduct research once they enter college. Project information literacy research report: the passage studies (2013, December 5)*. 2013, https://papers.ssrn.com/sol3/papers.cfm?abstract_id=2364080. See also: Guihua Li; Longlong Wu, *New service system as an information-Cf.king context: investigation of an unfamiliar discovery service*, "Journal of Documentation," 73 (2017), no. 5, p. 1082–1098, https://www.emerald.com/insight/content/doi/10.1108/JD-08-2016-0102/full/html; Kimberly Copenhaver; Alyssa Koclanes, *Impact of web-scale discovery on reference inquiry*, "Reference services review," 44 (2016), no. 3, p. 266–281, https://www.emerald.com/insight/content/doi/10.1108/RSR-11-2015-0046/full/html; Valeria E. Molteni; Emily K. Chan, *Student confidence/overconfidence in the research process*, "Journal of academic librarianship," 41 (2015), no. 1, p. 2–8, https://www.sciencedirect.com/science/article/pii/S0099133314002420.

situation of libraries and their social context, and the consequent preparation of an adequate educational path to information literacy, can help the library community as a whole, and not just academics, to find and use the power that knowledge provides to act for development, progress, and well-being, both for individuals and for society as a whole.

CHAPTER 6

Conclusions: since we have Google and Sci-Hub, what need is there for libraries?

It will not be possible to have truly revolutionary Web-scale discovery services until there are profound changes in the handling of the data to which they must be applied. As long as the catalogs, databases, repositories, and other mediation and research tools each have their own schema for the creation of descriptions and metadata, the discovery tools will have to create an index, however unique, generated from different elements. The result will always be the 'simplification' of the research system, made consistent at the lowest level of the elements that can be found in common, and this, mixed with gaps of various kinds and an inevitable confusion of the data extracted from different schemes—not to mention decontextualization—it will make the reliability and scientificity of research and discovery tools scarce, like that of many Web tools.

It is therefore essential, while maintaining the rigor in the analysis and description of the resources—and, indeed, introducing it for those tools that are not very equipped with them—that at the end of the process they can be either exported, published, or communicated, according to one simple but rigorous scheme, shared but authoritative, the 'real' data of the resources treated. According to the method currently proposed by linked data, in the Semantic Web all the data of information and knowledge resources would be found, they could be linked to identify the resources and their "meanings," and they could be collected, processed, and proposed from search and discovery tools of all kinds: from generic search engines to refined OPAC interfaces.

Currently, the excessive availability of information and resources, in addition to confusing people, already makes them turn to the infinite whole of the Web, considering it as a single and comprehensive source, without posing the problem of identifying the boundaries between different search and discovery systems, and not even those of resources that are not

Web-Scale Discovery Services
ISBN 978-0-323-90298-4
https://doi.org/10.1016/B978-0-323-90298-4.00006-9

searchable on the Web: in the abundance of the offer there is often something, even regarding 'quality'," which meets their expectations. The generalist search engines, for their part, tend to confirm this situation, giving apparent consistency to results coming from absolutely diverse sources, not only structurally, but also considering original purposes. The boundless universe, therefore, is made unique in a 'forced' way, even if apparently simple, while the truly unique universe designed, at the moment, by the Semantic Web—really 'one-way'—can be better divided into confined partitions but contextualized, given that they remain in solid relationships with the 'rest'," in which the discovery services of libraries and other cultural organizations can conduct their research.

With the exponential increase in available information, therefore, the main objective of library-type search systems is even more to ensure the right balance between precision and recall.[1] Within its own borders—wonderous, but present, changeable, dynamic, and alive like the mission of the library, but safe—the research and discovery space of libraries can also prove to be sure of its own 'diversity'," governed by 'mapping' tools that allow a single look without hiding the contexts of origin of the different resources. In this 'ordered' space, specific research tools, traditional and Web-scale ones, implemented and provided by libraries and other cultural organizations, can lead people to better clarify and satisfy their knowledge needs.

These navigation maps cannot and must not only be taken care of by librarians, or other information experts, but each person must be able to conceive the space of one's own research, to use the correct investigation tools, and to evaluate the achievements of their own discoveries. Everyone must be information literate, and the information literacy that can be acquired must also enable everyone to build their own maps and follow them with the appropriate tools, until they reach what they can satisfy and then go on, exploring further needs and reaching new paths for discovery.

Even if a reasoned and adequate implementation and a careful and appropriate use make Web-scale discovery services a useful tool to promote and teach in libraries, they still seem to remain limited, at least in current technological development, to being basic, start-up tools, apt for a first and univocal search and discovery of the available resources, for an unfinished information discovery activity. Each library will have to carefully establish the potential and usefulness of the new tools in relation to the traditional

[1] See: P. Saffo, *It's the context, stupid* cit.

ones, making them available and explaining to users the specific differences that make all the tools remain distinct and organized for different purposes. In the same way, specific research strategies, the necessary critical evaluation of the results, and the risks of excessive disintermediation for the inexperienced will have to be taught.

As much as they may have the tendency, the Semantic Web, data, and research tools are not 'generated' aside from the outside world. Necessary for people, the whole thing must be created and developed by people: specifically in libraries, the preparation is up to the diverse identifiable information professionals. Without the updating of theoretical models and practical methodologies, without the development of professions and the will of professionals to 'develop', even the simple hypothesis of adjustments to reality, renovations, improvements, growths, and revolutions is useless.[2] The new librarians will be those who, always drawing lessons from their own history, dotted with crises and revolutions, will know how to fit into a system centered on new paradigms developed from the previous ones, in a new bibliographic universe no longer 'book-centered' for a long time. They will be professionals able to process and organize information and resources wherever they are and whatever aspect they have, making their own, always essential, part of universally open and connected data.[3]

In conclusion, this book can answer some unsettled questions—whatever or informative they may be—that increasingly ask what we need libraries for, since there are now Google Scholar, Google Books, Unpaywall, Sci-Hub, arXiv, Medline, and so on?

Let us just remember that Google Scholar, although it is based on selective abilities of academic material, compared with generalist Google, still applies to 'what it finds" on the Web, although there are some programmatic enrichment projects with the most suitable resources. Sci-Hub, in addition to the fact that the legitimacy of the population criteria of its archive is not yet clear, still remains a 'good opportunity' not yet exploited,

[2] In support of these conclusions, one cannot fail to mention: John Palfrey, *BiblioTech: why libraries matter more than ever in the age of Google*. New York: Basic Books, 2015.

[3] On the ongoing debate on professions, cf. M. L. Chute, *A core for flexibility* cit. Two other points, among the many discussions in this regard, are represented by: Maria Cassella [et al.], *Le professioni per le biblioteche accademiche di ricerca*, "AIB studi," 53 (2013), no. 1, p. 63–100, <https://aibstudi.aib.it/article/view/8876>; Antonio Sgobba, *I bibliotecari in crisi e la rivoluzione (attesa) degli open data*, "Corriere della sera," 6 June 2013, <http://nuvola.corriere.it/2013/06/06/i-bibliotecari-in-crisi-e-la-rivoluzione-attesa-degli-open-data>.

given that it seems to have chosen more the path of the aggregate 'frond' to act with spirit of contrast and protest, rather than being a 'normal' open archive of international collaboration that acts in compliance with the disputable but still 'Socratically' respecting laws on the rights of authors—and publishers.

It is hoped, at least, to have set up a critical response, however long the whole book, through this study, which presents a succession of topics that need to be questioned again, which combine with each other in a mutual discourse, to fully reflect on the feasibility of a balanced development of mediation and information search tools, which embraces the advantages of a conscious updating of methods and principles, and avoids the negative effects of a too immediate and enthusiastic search for novelties to themselves.

What must be implemented is an effective innovation of the information management and research systems and of all knowledge resources, but which is profound, organic, and balanced, and not only for the catalog and the OPAC, but also for databases, institutional repositories, open-access archives, and related interfaces. This is linked to an overall technological innovation for the future of information and cultural services to people, and for the progress of society.

Should we simply surrender to the natural principle of affirming the most suitable mediation tool at the moment, or should we impose a cultural principle for the development of the most absolutely reliable systems? The virtuous solution could be, as for a thousand other things, in the middle of a reasoned path partly of listening and partly of addressing the reality that surrounds us. In this path, libraries can still be identified as the 'designated' places for the mediation of information and knowledge, those that have an irreplaceable and specific "quid" that has always made them the most suitable institutions in all ages for this mission, but they must equip themselves to really develop, and really maintain this primacy in the face of the other tools that technology and society offer as alternatives to libraries themselves.[4]

[4] A series of essays that deal with the importance of always balancing between the old and the new, between conservation and innovations, in the choice of dynamic models to propose and follow, is contained in the monographic issue: *I modelli biblioteconomici*, "Biblioteche oggi Trends," 4 (2018), no. 1, <http://www.bibliotecheoggi.it/trends/issue/view/60>.

The conclusions can only be provisional and problematic. However, we are not moving toward the creation of a parallel system where machines will organize the world and things for us. The idea of "a network of things in the world, described by data on the Web"[5] may be just a cultural superstructure that will allow to see the world from one of the possible perspectives we can imagine it might just be. The important thing is not to lose a thoughtful and critical vision of this whole system, to always go back to the cultural and human basis of this representation, and not to be blinded, trivially, by the 'subculture' that often governs the clichés of the network and the uncritical vision of its potential and its qualities. The spirit of progress has always pushed to innovate everything that surrounds the human being. To find the most suitable line for the 'survival' of all that is produced by action, one must simply be careful not to lose oneself.

[5] C. Bizer [et al.], *Linked data: the story so far* cit., p. 2.

Bibliography and further readings

Access to Research. http://www.accesstoresearch.org.uk/.

African Open Science Platform. http://africanopenscience.org.za/.

Alper, A., et al., 2012. A novel Semantic Web browser for user centric information retrieval: person. Exp. Syst. Appl. 39 (15), 12001–12013. https://www.sciencedirect.com/science/article/pii/S0957417412005799?via%3Dihub.

AmeLICA. http://www.amelica.org/en/.

American Library Association, 1989. Presidential Committee on Information Literacy, Final Report. American Library Association, Chicago.

American Library Association, 2013. Office for Information Technology Policy. Digital Literacy Task Force, Digital Literacy, Libraries and Public Policy. http://www.districtdispatch.org/wp-content/uploads/2013/01/2012_OITP_digilitreport_1_22_13.pdf.

Anobii. http://www.anobii.com.

AquaBrowser. https://www.proquest.com/products-services/AquaBrowser.html.

Arena Discovery. https://www.axiell.co.uk/arena-discovery/.

Arnold Stephen, E., 2009. Real-time search: where retrieval and discovery collide. Online 33 (6), 40–41.

Asher Andrew, D., Duke Lynda, M., 2011. Searching for answers: student research behavior at Illinois Wesleyan University. In: Duke, L.M., Asher, A.D. (Eds.), College Libraries and Student Culture: What We Now Know. ALA, Chicago, pp. 71–85.

Association of College and Research Libraries, 2000. Information Literacy Competency Standards for Higher Education. ALA, Chicago. https://alair.ala.org/handle/11213/7668.

Association of College and Research Libraries, 2015. Framework for Information Literacy for Higher Education. http://www.ala.org/acrl/standards/ilframework.

Azadbakht, E., et al., 2017. Everyone's Invited: a website usability study involving multiple library stakeholders. Inf. Technol. Libr. 36 (4), 34–45. https://ejournals.bc.edu/index.php/ital/article/view/9959.

Azpiazu, I., et al., 2017. Online searching and learning: YUM and other search tools for children and teachers. Inf. Retr. J. 20 (5), 524–545. https://www.springerprofessional.de/en/online-searching-and-learning-yum-and-other-search-tools-for-chi/13321940.

Baeza-Yates, R., Berthier, R.-N., 2000. Modern Information Retrieval. Longman, New York.

Balaji, B.P., et al., 2019. Web 2.0 use in academic libraries of top ranked Asian universities. Electron. Libr. 37 (3), 528–549. https://www.emerald.com/insight/content/doi/10.1108/EL-12-2018-0248/full/html.

Bambini, C., Tatiana, W., 2014. La Biblioteca Diventa Social. Bibliografica, Milano.

Bardelli, A., Francesca, V., 2019. The Discovery tool is a growing organism. JLIS.it 10 (3), 97–124. https://www.jlis.it/article/view/12575.

Basile, P., et al., 2019. Bridging the gap between linked open data-based recommender systems and distributed representations. Inf. Syst. 86, 1–8. https://www.sciencedirect.com/science/article/pii/S0306437918302436?dgcid=rss_sd_all.

Bates, M.J., 1989. The design of browsing and berry picking techniques for the online search interface. Online Rev. 13 (5), 407–424. https://www.emerald.com/insight/content/doi/10.1108/eb024320/full/html.

Battelle, J., 2005. The Search: How Google and its Rivals Rewrote the Rules of Business and Transformed Our Culture. Brealey, London.

Beall, J., 2007. The value of alphabetically-sorted browser displays in information discovery. Libr. Collect. Acquisit. Tech. Serv. 31 (3/4), 184–194. https://www.tandfonline.com/doi/full/10.1080/14649055.2007.10766164.

Bergamin, G., 2008. OPAC: migliorare l'esperienza degli utenti. Biblio 11 (1). http://www.aib.it/aib/sezioni/emr/bibtime/num-xi-1/bergamin.htm.

Berners-Lee, T., 1998. Semantic Web Road Map. http://www.w3.org/DesignIssues/Semantic.html.

Berners-Lee, T., 2000. Semantic Web – XML2000. http://www.w3.org/2000/Talks/1206-xml2k-tbl.

Berners-Lee, T., et al., 2001. The Semantic Web: a new form of web content that is meaningful to computers will unleash a revolution of new possibilities. Sci. Am. 284 (5), 34–43. https://www.scientificamerican.com/article/the-semantic-web/.

Berners-Lee, T., 2006. Linked Data. http://www.w3.org/DesignIssues/LinkedData.html.

Berners-Lee, T., 2009. The Next Web. https://www.ted.com/talks/tim_berners_lee_on_the_next_web.

Berners-Lee, T., 2010. The Year Open Data Went World Wide. https://www.ted.com/talks/tim_berners_lee_the_year_open_data_went_worldwide.

Berners-Lee, T., 2010. Long live the web: a call for continued open standards and neutrality. Sci. Am. 303 (6), 80–85. https://www.scientificamerican.com/article/long-live-the-web/.

Berners-Lee, T., 2013. The Many Meanings of Open. http://en.blogthinkbig.com/2013/10/09/tim-berners-lee-telefonica-open-agenda/. Available also at the URL: http://www.w3.org/DesignIssues/Open.html.

Berners-Lee, T., 2014. A Magna Carta for the Web. https://www.ted.com/talks/tim_berners_lee_a_magna_carta_for_the_web/reading-list?curator=MediaREDEF.

Berners-Lee, T., March 12 , 2017. Three challenges for the web, according to its inventor. Web Found. http://webfoundation.org/2017/03/web-turns-28-letter/.

Berners-Lee, T., Mark, F., 1999. Weaving the Web: The Original Design and Ultimate Destiny of the World Wide Web by its Inventor. Harper Collins, San Francisco.

Bertot, J.C., et al., 2012. Assessing the usability of WorldCat Local: findings and considerations. Libr. Q. 82 (2), 207–221. https://www.journals.uchicago.edu/doi/abs/10.1086/664588?mobileUi=0&journalCode=lq.

Biagetti, M.T., 2010. Nuove funzionalità degli OPAC e relevance ranking. Boll. AIB 50 (4), 339–356. https://bollettino.aib.it/article/view/5340.

Biagetti, M.T., 2014. Sviluppi e trasformazioni delle biblioteche digitali: dai repositories di testi alle semantic digital libraries. AIB Studi 54 (1), 11–34. https://aibstudi.aib.it/article/view/9955.

Biagetti, M.T., 2019. Le biblioteche digitali: tipologie, funzionalità e modelli di sviluppo, con scritti di Roberto Raieli, Antonella Iacono, Antonella Trombone, Simona Turbanti. Angeli, Milano.

Bianchini, C., 2010. Futuri scenari: RDA, REICAT e la granularità dei cataloghi. Boll. AIB 50 (3), 219–238, pp. 224–238. https://bollettino.aib.it/article/view/5319.

Bianchini, C., 2012. Dagli OPAC ai library linked data: come cambiano le risposte ai bisogni degli utenti. AIB Studi 52 (3), 303–323. https://aibstudi.aib.it/article/view/8597.

Bianchini, C., 2017. «Funziona come Google, vero?». Prima indagine sull'interazione utente-catalogo nella biblioteca del Dipartimento di musicologia e beni culturali (Cremona) dell'Università di Pavia. AIB Studi 57 (1), 23–49. https://aibstudi.aib.it/article/view/11557.

BIBFRAME. http://www.loc.gov/bibframe.

BiblioCommons. https://www.bibliocommons.com/.

BiblioCore. https://www.bibliocommons.com/products/bibliocore/.

Bibliographic Enrichment Advisory Team. http://www.loc.gov/catdir/beat.

BiblioWeb. https://www.bibliocommons.com/products/biblioweb.
Bizer C. [et al.], Linked data: the story so far. Int. J. Semantic Web Inf. Syst., 5 (2009), no. 3, p. 1- 22. https://www.igi-global.com/article/linked-data-story-far/37496.
Blumer, E., et al., 2014. The usability issues of faceted navigation in digital libraries. JLIS.it 5 (2), 85–100. https://www.jlis.it/article/view/10072.
Boccone, A., Tania, M., 2020. Biblioteche e bibliotecari nel Wikiproject Covid-19: authority control, contenuti di qualità e linked open data. AIB Studi 60 (2), 269–291. https://aibstudi.aib.it/article/view/12189.
Bonner, S., Williams, G., 2016. A small academic library and the power of EBSCO discovery service. Ser. Rev. 42 (3), 187–191. https://www.tandfonline.com/doi/full/10.1080/00987913.2016.1205428.
Bossaller, J.S., 2017. Heather Moulaison Sandy, Documenting the conversation: a systematic review of library discovery layers. Coll. Res. Libr. 78 (5), 602–619. https://crl.acrl.org/index.php/crl/article/view/16714.
Bradford, R., 2016. Discoverability in self-publishing. Libr. J. 141 (14), pp. 24–24.
Breeding, M., 2008. Progress on the DLF ILS discovery interface API: the Berkeley accord. Inf. Stand. Q. 20 (3), 18–19. https://groups.niso.org/apps/group_public/download.php/5637/ISQv20no3.pdf.
Breeding, M., 2010. The state of the art in library discovery 2010. Comput. Libr. 30 (1), 31–35. https://librarytechnology.org/repository/item.pl?id=14574.
Breeding, M., 2013. Linked data: the next big wave or another tech fad? Comput. Libr. 33 (3), 20–22. http://www.infotoday.com/cilmag/apr13/Breeding–Linked-Data–The%20Next-Big-Wave-or-Another-Tech-Fad.shtml.
Breeding, M., 2014. Library resource discovery products: context, library perspectives, and vendor positions. Libr. Technol. Rep. 50 (1), 5–58.
Breeding, M., 2015. The Future of Library Resource Discovery: A White Paper Commissioned by the NISO Discovery to Delivery (D2D) Topic Committee. NISO, Baltimore. https://www.niso.org/publications/future-library-resource-discovery.
Breeding, M., et al., 2016. Sharing metadata across discovery systems. In: Spiteri, L.F. (Ed.), Managing Metadata in Web-Scale Discovery Systems. Facet, London, pp. 113–135.
Breeding, M., 2016. Privacy and security for library systems. published also in. In: Library Technology Reports, vol. 52. ALA, Chicago (2016), no. 4.
Breitbach, W., 2012. Web-scale discovery: a library of babel? In: Planning and Implementing Resource Discovery Tools in Academic Libraries, Edited by Mary Pagliero Popp, Diane Dallis. IGI global, Hershey, pp. 641–649.
Breitbach, W., 31 . Web-scale discovery: utopian dream or dystopian nightmare (or maybe something in between)? In: Paper Presented at the "California Academic & Research Libraries 2016 Conference" Costa Mesa, California. http://conf2016.carl-acrl.org/wp-content/uploads/2016/05/Breitbach-Web-scale-discovery-FINAL.pdf.
Brickley, D., Ramanathan, V., W3C, G. (Eds.), 2014. RDF Schema 1.1. http://www.w3.org/TR/rdf-schema.
Brigham, T.J., et al., 2016. Web-scale discovery service: is it right for your library? Mayo clinic libraries experience. J. Hosp. Librarian. 16 (1), 25–39. https://www.tandfonline.com/doi/full/10.1080/15323269.2016.1118280.
British museum, 1841. Department of Printed Books, Catalogue of Printed Books in the British Museum. London (with Antonio Panizzi's Rules).
Brown, C.C., 2017. Google scholar. Charlest. Advis. 19 (2), 31–34. https://www.ingentaconnect.com/content/charleston/chadv/2017/00000019/00000002/art00009.
Browne, O., et al., 2019. Distributed data and ontologies: an integrated semantic web architecture enabling more efficient data management. J. Assoc. Inf. Sci. Technol. 70 (6), 575–586. https://asistdl.onlinelibrary.wiley.com/doi/abs/10.1002/asi.24144.
Buck, S., Christina, S., 2013. Promising practices in instruction of discovery tools. Commun. Info. Liter. 7 (1), 66–80. https://pdxscholar.library.pdx.edu/comminfolit/vol7/iss1/6/.

Bulock, C., 2021. Finding open content in the library is surprisingly hard. Ser. Rev. 47 (2), 68–70. https://www.tandfonline.com/doi/full/10.1080/00987913.2021.1936416.

Burgess, C., 2015. Teaching students, not standards: the new ACRL Information Literacy Framework and threshold crossings for instructors. Partnership 10 (1), 1–6. https://journal.lib.uoguelph.ca/index.php/perj/article/view/3440.

Burke, E., 1985. Inchiesta sul bello e il sublime. Aesteticha, Palermo (original ed.: Id., A philosophical enquiry into the origin of our ideas of the sublime and beautiful. London: Dodsley, 1759).

Burke, T., January 20, 2004. Burn the Catalog. http://www.swarthmore.edu/SocSci/tburke1/perma12004.html.

Bush, V., 1945. As we may think. Atl. Mon. 176 (1), 101–108.

Byrum John, D., 14-18 August 2005. Recommendations for urgently needed improvement of OPAC and the role of the National bibliographic agency in achieving it. In: Presented at the "71th IFLA General Conference and Council". Oslo. http://www.ifla.org/IV/ifla71/papers/124e-Byrum.pdf.

Byrum John, D., 2005. Raccomandazioni per miglioramenti urgenti dell'OPAC: il ruolo delle agenzie bibliografiche nazionali. Bibl. Oggi 23 (10), 5–14. http://www.bibliotecheoggi.it/2005/20051000501.pdf.

Calhoun, K., 2006. The Changing Nature of the Catalog and its Integration with Other Discovery Tools: Final Report. Library of Congress, Washington. http://www.loc.gov/catdir/calhoun-report-final.pdf.

Calhoun, K., et al., 2009. Online Catalogs: What Users and Librarians Want. OCLC, Dublin. http://www.oclc.org/content/dam/oclc/reports/onlinecatalogs/fullreport.pdf.

California digital library, 2006. The Melvyl Recommender Project Final Report. http://www.cdlib.org/services/publishing/tools/xtf/melvyl_recommender/report_docs/Mellon_final.pdf.

Candela, G., et al., 2019. A linked open data framework to enhance the discoverability and impact of culture heritage. J. Inf. Sci. 45 (6), 756–766. https://journals.sagepub.com/doi/full/10.1177/0165551518812658.

Caplan, P., 2012. On discovery tools, OPACs and the motion of library language. Libr. Hi Technol. 30 (1), 108–115. https://www.emerald.com/insight/content/doi/10.1108/07378831211213247/full/html.

Case Donald, O., Given Lisa, M., 2016. Looking for Information: A Survey of Research on Information Cf.King, Needs, and Behavior, fourth ed. Emerald, Bingley.

Cassella, M., et al., 2013. Le professioni per le biblioteche accademiche di ricerca. AIB Studi 53 (1), 63–100. https://aibstudi.aib.it/article/view/8876.

Castellucci, P., 2009. Dall'ipertesto Al Web: Storia Culturale Dell'informatica. Laterza, Roma.

Castellucci, P., 2017. Formiche virtuali o virtuose? Verso un'etica dell'accesso. AIB Studi 57 (1), 51–62. https://aibstudi.aib.it/article/view/11555.

Castellucci, P., 2017. Carte del nuovo mondo: banche dati e open access. il Mulino, Bologna.

Castellucci, P., e massa, T., 2011. Una nuova energia nella comunicazione scientifica. Boll. AIB 51 (3), 237–244. https://bollettino.aib.it/article/view/5428.

Castellucci, P., George, B., 2004. Il pensiero dietro la maschera. In: L'organizzazione del sapere: studi in onore di Alfredo Serrai, a cura di Maria Teresa Biagetti. Bonnard, Milano, pp. 55–69.

Lo Castro Valeria, 2015. Linked data nelle biblioteche digitali e di ricerca. Bibl. Oggi 33 (1), 36–44. http://www.bibliotecheoggi.it/rivista/article/view/5.

Ceroti, M., 2012. Rassegna critica della letteratura scientifica italiana sugli OPAC. Bibl. Oggi 30 (9), 15–27.

Chase, D., et al., 2016. The perfect storm: examining user experience and conducting a usability test to investigate a disruptive academic library web site redevelopment. J. Web Librar. 10 (1), 28–44. https://www.tandfonline.com/doi/full/10.1080/19322909.2015.1124740.

Chickering, F.W., Yang Sharon, Q., 2014. Evaluation and comparison of discovery tools: an update. Inf. Technol. Libr. 33 (2), 5–30. https://ejournals.bc.edu/index.php/ital/article/view/3471.

Chute Mary, L., 2012. A core for flexibility. Inf. Serv. Use 32 (3/4), 143–147. https://content.iospress.com/articles/information-services-and-use/isu668.

Ciccone, K., John, V., Summon, 2015. EBSCO Discovery Service, and Google Scholar: a comparison of search performance using user queries. Evid. Base Libr. Inf. Pract. 10 (1), 34–49. https://journals.library.ualberta.ca/eblip/index.php/EBLIP/article/view/23845.

cOAlition S. https://www.coalition-s.org/.

Cohen Rachael, A., Thorpe Pusnik Angie, 2018. Measuring query complexity in web-scale discovery: a comparison between two academic libraries. Ref. User Serv. Q. 57 (4), 274–284. https://journals.ala.org/index.php/rusq/article/view/6705.

Colleu, G., 2011. Editori Indipendenti & Bibliodiversità. Fidare-Federazione italiana editori indipendenti, Torino.

Comeaux, D.J., 2012. Usability testing of a web-scale discovery system at an academic library. Coll. Undergrad. Libr. 19 (2–4), 189–206. https://www.tandfonline.com/doi/full/10.1080/10691316.2012.695671.

Convegno AIB CILW, 2016. La rinascita delle risorse dell'informazione: granularità, interoperabilità e integrazione dei dati (Roma, 21 October 2016). https://www.aib.it/attivita/congressi/aib-cilw-2016-conference/2016/56896-convegno-aib-cilw-2016-programma/.

Cooper Gregory, F., 2015. The center for causal discovery of biomedical knowledge from big data. J. Am. Med. Inf. Assoc. 22 (6), 1132–1136. https://academic.oup.com/jamia/article/22/6/1132/2357622.

Copenhaver, K., Koclanes, A., 2016. Impact of web-scale discovery on reference inquiry. Ref. Serv. Rev. 44 (3), 266–281. https://www.emerald.com/insight/content/doi/10.1108/RSR-11-2015-0046/full/html.

Corrado Edward, M., Jaffe, R., 2014. Transforming and enhancing metadata for enduser discovery: a case study. JLIS.it 5 (2), 33–48. https://www.jlis.it/article/view/10069.

Coyle, K., 2010. Library data in a modern context. Libr. Technol. Rep. 46 (1), 5–13. https://journals.ala.org/index.php/ltr/article/view/4630.

Coyle, K., 2013. Library linked data: an evolution. JLIS.it 4 (1), 53–61. http://leo.cineca.it/index.php/jlis/article/view/5443.

Cutter Charles, A., 1876. Rules for a Printed Dictionary Catalogue. Government printing office, Washington.

Dalton, M., 2014. The form of search tool chosen by undergraduate students influences research practices and the type and quality of information selected. Evid. Base Libr. Inf. Pract. 9 (2), 19–21. https://journals.library.ualberta.ca/eblip/index.php/EBLIP/article/view/21327.

Danae, A.N., 2015. Utilizing discovery tools for classrooms: how do librarian attitudes on discovery impact tools they teach? Libr. Hi Tech News 32 (1), 8–12. https://www.emerald.com/insight/content/doi/10.1108/LHTN-09-2014-0078/full/html.

Dublin Core Metadata Initiative (DCMI). http://dublincore.org/.

Deana, D., 2019. I vestiti nuovi dell'imperatore. Bibl. Oggi 37 (1–2), 18–27.

Delsey, T., 1998. Modelling the logic of AACR. In: Jean Weihs (Ed.), The Principles and Future of AACR: Proceedings of the International Conference on Principles and Future of AACR. Canadian Library Association, Ottawa, pp. 1–16.

DeMars, J.M., 2017. Discovering our users: a multi-campus usability study of Primo. In: Presented at "IFLA WLIC 2017. Libraries. Solidarity. Society. Satellite Meeting: Reference and Information Services and Information Technology Sections". Wrocław, Poland. http://library.ifla.org/id/eprint/1810.

Dempsey, L., 2009. Always on: libraries in a world of permanent connectivity. Clin. Hemorheol. Microcirc. 14 (1/5). http://firstmonday.org/article/view/2291/2070.

Dempsey, L., December 10 , 2012. Thirteen Ways of Looking at Libraries, Discovery, and the Catalog: Scale, Workflow, Attention,. Educause review online. http://www.educause.edu/ero/article/thirteen-ways-looking-libraries-discovery-and-catalog-scale-workflow-attention.

Dempsey, M., Valenti Alyssa, M., 2016. Student use of keywords and limiters in web-scale discovery searching. J. Acad. Librar. 42 (3), 200–206. https://www.sciencedirect.com/science/article/pii/S0099133316300027.

DeZelar-Tiedman Christine, A., 2016. Redefining library resources in discovery systems. In: Spiteri, L.F. (Ed.), Managing Metadata in Web-Scale Discovery Systems. Facet, London, pp. 91–112.

Dhara, A., 2016. A personalised discovery service using Google custom search engine. Ann. Libr. Inf. Stud. 63 (4), 298–305. http://op.niscair.res.in/index.php/ALIS/article/view/13880.

Digital Library Federation, 2004. In: Timothy, D.J., et al. (Eds.), Electronic Resource Management: Report of the DLF ERM Initiative. DLF, Washington. https://old.diglib.org/pubs/dlf102.

Digital Library Federation, 2008. DLF Electronic Resource Management Initiative, Phase II: Final Report. December 30th, 2008. DLF, Washington. http://old.diglib.org/standards/ERMI2_Final_Report_20081230.pdf.

Ding, L., et al., 2005. Tracking RDF Graph Provenance Using RDF Molecules (Technical Report TR-CS-05-06, Computer Science and Electrical Engineering. University of Maryland. Baltimore County, 30 April 2005). ftp://www.ksl.stanford.edu/local/pub/KSL_Reports/KSL-05-06.pdf.

Dinotola, S., 2016. I sistemi per la gestione delle risorse elettroniche. AIB Studi 56 (1), 59–73 (Part one). http://aibstudi.aib.it/article/view/11411. http://aibstudi.aib.it/article/view/11412, 56 (2016), no. 2, pp. 205–218 (Part two).

Discovery tools: A bibliography, edited by François Renaville. https://discoverytoolsbibliography.wordpress.com/.

Discovery tools, 2012. The next generation of library research. Coll. Undergrad. Libr. 19 (2/4).

Dodds, L., November 5, 2018. Sir Tim Berners-Lee Launches 'Magna Carta for the Web' to Save Internet from Abuse,. The telegraph. https://www.telegraph.co.uk/technology/2018/11/05/sir-tim-berners-lee-launches-magna-carta-web-save-internet-abuse/.

Di Domenico Giovanni, 2015. Un'identità plurale per la biblioteca pubblica. AIB Studi 55 (2), 235–246. https://aibstudi.aib.it/article/view/11197.

Donlan, R., Anna, C., 2007. A sheep in wolf's clothing: discovery tools and the OPAC. Ref. Libr. 48 (2), 67–71. https://www.tandfonline.com/doi/abs/10.1300/J120v48n02_10.

Dotta, G., August 30, 2019. Siamo ancora capaci di cercare? Puntoinformatico. https://www.punto-informatico.it/siamo-ancora-capaci-a-cercare/.

Dougan, K., 2018. The 'black box': how students use a single search box to search for music materials. Inf. Technol. Libr. 37 (4), 81–106. https://ejournals.bc.edu/index.php/ital/article/view/10702.

Doyle, L., Joseph, B., 1975. Information Retrieval and Processing. Los Angeles: Melville.

Dulle Frankwell, W., 2016. Alphonce Alex, Addressing online information resources' access challenges: potentials of resource discovery tools' application. Ann. Libr. Inf. Stud. 63 (4), 266–273. http://op.niscair.res.in/index.php/ALIS/article/view/14454.

EBSCO, Relevance ranking. https://www.ebscohost.com/discovery/technology/relevance-ranking.

EBSCO Dicovery Service (EDS). https://www.ebscohost.com/discovery.

EDM (Europeana Data Model). http://pro.europeana.eu/page/edm-documentation.

Ketterman, E., Inman Megan, E., 2014. Discovery tool vs. PubMed: a health sciences literature comparison analysis. J. Electron. Resour. Med. Libr. 11 (3), 115–123. https://www.tandfonline.com/doi/full/10.1080/15424065.2014.938999.

Ellero Nadine, P., 2013. Integration or disintegration: where is discovery headed? J. Libr. Metadata 13 (4), 311–329. https://www.tandfonline.com/doi/full/10.1080/19386389.2013.831277.

Encore. https://www.iii.com/products/sierra-ils/encore-discovery/.

Enterprise. http://www.sirsidynix.com/products/enterprise.

European Commission, 2003. Directorate-General for Education and Culture, Better eLearning for Europe. Office for official publications of the European Communities, Luxembourg. https://www.jyu.fi/hum/laitokset/solki/en/research/projects/tolp/betterelearningforeurope.pdf.

Europeana. http://www.europeana.eu.

Ex Libris, Summon: Relevance Ranking. https://www.exlibrisgroup.com/products/primo-library-discovery/.

Ex Libris, 2015. Primo Discovery: Search, Ranking, and beyond. Ex Libris. https://files.mtstatic.com/site_11811/26778/0?Expires=1539105246&Signature=eLqOUxxUsVQ22ve5-anrQp4uzk5hdVg4kuw3h526I0I00euYi4AlgvW9LGST8ZOVbT1~IaYMaL25yiPjwyQtcXZ2-iQV-iUKYc4YLmznV31Z-EgME~S3gETfgyVCAZjQ91LjLv9nF3MAJAbFbNXbsiJbd-51Y4wT-iRC3wFRAZ4_&Key-Pair-Id=APKAJ5Y6AV4GI7A555NA.

Exner, N., 2014. Research information literacy: addressing original researchers' needs. J. Acad. Librar. 40, 460–466. https://www.sciencedirect.com/science/article/pii/S0099133314000901.

Extensible Catalog Organization: https://www.extensiblecatalog.org/.

Fagan Jody, C., Mandernach Meris, A., 2011. A roadmap for discovery service implementation at an academic library. In: Presented at "ACRL 2011 Conference", (Philadelphia, 30 March-2 April, 2011). http://www.lib.jmu.edu/documents/discovery/roadmap.aspx.

Fagan Jody Condit, 2011. Discovery tools and information literacy. J. Web Librar. 5 (3), 171–178. https://www.tandfonline.com/doi/full/10.1080/19322909.2011.598332.

Fagan Jody Condit, 2012. Top 10 discovery tool myths. J. Web Librar. 6 (1), 1–4. https://www.tandfonline.com/doi/full/10.1080/19322909.2012.651417?scroll=top&needAccess=true.

Fagan Jody Condit, et al., 2012. Usability test results for a discovery tool in an academic library. Inf. Technol. Libr. 31 (1), 83–112. https://ejournals.bc.edu/index.php/ital/article/view/1855.

Falvey memorial library. Villanova University: https://library.villanova.edu/Find.

Faster, smarter and richer. Reshaping the library catalogue. In: International Conference" (Roma, 27-28 February 2014), 2014. FSR. http://www.aib.it/attivita/congressi/c2014/fsr2014.

Fawley, N., Krysak, N., 2012. Information literacy opportunities within the discovery tool environment. Coll. Undergrad. Libr. 19 (2/4), 207–214. https://www.tandfonline.com/doi/full/10.1080/10691316.2012.693439.

Fawley, N., Krysak, N. (Eds.), 2016. The Discovery Tool Cookbook: Recipes for Successful Lesson Plans. ALA, Chicago.

Feliciati, P., 2018. La qualità dell'universo documentario digitale: dai contenuti al servizio. AIB Studi 58 (1), 53–63. https://aibstudi.aib.it/article/view/11740.

Feliciati, P., Alfier, A., 2017. Online archives for users: premises for a quality reference model. JLIS.it 8 (1), 22–38. https://www.jlis.it/article/view/12269.

Fitzgerald Sarah Rose, 2020. Toward a conceptual framework for scholarly information seeking. J. Acad. Librar. 46, 6. https://www.sciencedirect.com/science/article/pii/S0099133320301506.

Floridi, L., 2012. Hyperhistory and the philosophy of information policies. Philos. Technol. 25 (2), 129–131. https://link.springer.com/article/10.1007/s13347-012-0077-4.

FOLIO. https://www.folio.org/.

Frame Michael, T., 2004. Information discovery and retrieval tools. Inf. Serv. Use 24 (4), 187–193. https://content.iospress.com/articles/information-services-and-use/isu445.

Francese, E., 2013. Test di usabilità sul discovery tool Primo all'Università di Torino. Bibl. Oggi 31 (10), 10–17. http://www.bibliotecheoggi.it/rivista/article/view/342.

Functional Requirements: The FRBR Family of Models, 2014. http://www.ifla.org/node/2016.

FSR 2014, 2014. Special issue. JLIS.it 5 (2). http://leo.cineca.it/index.php/jlis/issue/view/651.

Galeffi, A., 2017. Se il catalogo parlasse, lo capiremmo? Cinque assiomi della comunicazione catalografica. AIB Studi 57 (2), 239–252. https://aibstudi.aib.it/article/view/11648.

Galeffi, A., Sardo, L., 2013. FRBR. AIB, Roma.

Galeffi, A., Weston, P.G., 2020. Varcare la soglia: il digitale nel catalogo, alcune riflessioni. AIB Studi 60 (2), 345–360. https://aibstudi.aib.it/article/view/12260.

George, K., 2021. Accessibility and discoverability: a report on the ALCTS CaMMS catalog form and function interest group meeting. Tech. Serv. Q. 38 (1), 92–96. https://digitalscholarship.unlv.edu/lib_articles/709/.

Gewirtz Sarah, R., et al., 2014. Evaluating the intersection between WorldCat Local and student research. J. Web Librar. 8 (2), 113–124. https://www.tandfonline.com/doi/full/10.1080/19322909.2014.877312.

Gil-Leiva, I., et al., 2020. The abandonment of the assignment of subject headings and classification codes in university libraries due to the massive emergence of electronic books. Knowl. Organ. 47 (8), 646–667. https://www.ergon-verlag.de/isko_ko/downloads/ko_47_2020_8_4.pdf.

Global Interoperability and Linked Data in Libraries, 18-19 June 2012. Florence. http://www.linkedheritage.eu/linkeddataseminar.

Global interoperability and linked data in libraries: special issue. JLIS.it 4 (1), 2013. http://leo.cineca.it/index.php/jlis/issue/view/536.

Goldfinger Rebecca, K., 2017. WorldCat UMD Usability Final Report. University of Maryland. https://drum.lib.umd.edu/handle/1903/19604?show=full.

Goodreads: https://www.goodreads.com.

Google Knowledge Graph. https://www.google.it/intl/it/insidesearch/features/search/knowledge.html. Google Scholar. https://scholar.google.it/.

Gorman, M., 2000. Our Enduring Values: Librarianship in the 21st Century. American Library Association, Chicago.

Gorman, M., 2015. Our Enduring Values Revisited: Librarianship in an Ever-Changing World. American Library Association, Chicago.

Gorman, M., 2015. Revisiting enduring values. JLIS.it 6 (2), 13–33. https://www.jlis.it/article/view/10907.

Gramatica, R., Ruth, P., 2017. Yewno: an AI-driven path to a knowledge-based future. Insights 30 (2), 107–111. https://insights.uksg.org/articles/10.1629/uksg.369/.
Grigson, A., et al., 2015. Information without frontiers: barriers and solutions. Insights 28 (1), 62–72, pp. 64–68. https://insights.uksg.org/articles/10.1629/uksg.176/.
Gritten T.; Comer Alberta, Venturing across the borders: collaborating on a new discovery system between academic and public libraries, Presented at "IFLA WLIC 2017. Libraries, solidarity, society. Section S10, Satellite Meeting: Reference and Information Services and Information Technology Sections". http://library.ifla.org/id/eprint/1813.
Gross, J., Lutie, S., 2011. Web scale discovery: the user experience. New Libr. World 112 (5–6), 236–247. https://www.emerald.com/insight/content/doi/10.1108/03074801111136275/full/html.
Guercio, M., Cecilia, C., 2015. The research archives in the digital environment: the Sapienza Digital Library project. JLIS.it 6 (No. 1), 1–19. https://www.jlis.it/article/view/10989.
Guerrini, M., 2014. BIBFRAME. Un'ipotesi di ambiente bibliografico nell'era del web. In: Il libro al centro. Percorsi fra le discipline del libro in onore di Marco Santoro. Liguori, Napoli, pp. 103–115.
Guerrini, M., 2017. La filosofia open: paradigma del servizio contemporaneo. Bibl. Oggi 35 (4), 12–21.
Guerrini, M., 2018. Sardo Lucia, IFLA Library Reference Model (LRM): un modello concettuale per le biblioteche del XXI secolo. Bibliografica, Milano.
Guerrini, M., Possemato, T., 2013. Linked data: a new alphabet for the semantic web. JLIS.it 4 (1), 67–90. https://www.jlis.it/article/view/6305.
Guerrini, M., Possemato, T., 2015. Linked data per biblioteche, archivi e musei. Bibliografica, Milano.
Guthrie, A., Rhonda, M.C., 2012. A glimpse at discovery tools within the HBCU library landscape. Coll. Undergrad. Libr. 19 (2/4), 297–311. https://www.tandfonline.com/doi/full/10.1080/10691316.2012.693437.
Guy, M., Emma, T., 2006. Folksonomies tidying up tags? D-lib Magazine 12 (1). http://www.dlib.org/dlib/january06/guy/01guy.html.
Hague, C., Payton, S., 2010. Digital Literacy across the Curriculum. Futurelab. https://www.nfer.ac.uk/publications/FUTL06/FUTL06.pdf.
Hamlett, A., Georgas, H., 2019. In the wake of discovery: student perceptions, integration, and instructional design. J. Web Librar. 13 (3), 230–245. https://www.tandfonline.com/doi/full/10.1080/19322909.2019.1598919.
Han-Yu, S., Yu-Liang, C., 2021. Applications of semantic web in integrating open data and bibliographic records: a development example of an infomediary of Taiwanese indigenous people. Electron. Libr. 39 (2), 337–353. https://www.emerald.com/insight/content/doi/10.1108/EL-09-2020-0258/full/html?skipTracking=true.
Hanneke, R., O'Brien Kelly, K., 2016. Comparison of three web-scale discovery services for health sciences research. J. Med. Libr. Assoc. 104 (2), 109–117. https://www.ncbi.nlm.nih.gov/pmc/articles/PMC4816486/.
Harris, C., June 14 , 2007. Catalog manifesto. Infomancy. http://schoolof.info/infomancy/?p=388.
Head, A.J., 2013. Learning the Ropes: How Freshmen Conduct Research once They Enter College. Project Information Literacy Research Report: The Passage Studies (2013, December 5). https://papers.ssrn.com/sol3/papers.cfm?abstract_id=2364080.
Heath, T., Christian, B., 2011. Linked Data: Evolving the Web into a Global Data Space. Morgan & Claypool, New York.

Hendry David, G., et al., 2006. Collaborative bibliography,. Inf. Process. Manag. 42 (3), 805–825. https://www.sciencedirect.com/science/article/pii/S0306457305000683?via%3Dihub.

Hoeppner, A., 2012. The ins and outs of evaluating Web-Scale Discovery Services. Comput. Libr. 32 (3), 6–10. http://www.infotoday.com/cilmag/apr12/Hoeppner-Web-Scale-Discovery-Services.shtml.

Holman, L., 2011. Millennial students' mental models of search: implications for academic librarians and database developers. J. Acad. Libr. 37 (1), 19–27. https://www.sciencedirect.com/science/article/pii/S0099133310002545.

van Hooland, S., Verborgh, R., 2014. Linked Data for Libraries, Archives and Museums: How to Clean, Link and Publish Your Metadata. Facet, London.

Houser, J., 2009. The VuFind implementation at villanova university. Libr. Hi Technol. 27 (1), 93–105. https://www.emerald.com/insight/content/doi/10.1108/07378830910942955/full/html.

Hull, D., et al., 2008. Defrosting the digital library: bibliographic tools for the next generation Web. PLoS Comput. Biol. 4 (10). http://www.ploscompbiol.org/article/info%3Adoi%2F10.1371%2Fjournal.pcbi.1000204.

Iacono, A., 2010. Opac, utenti, rete. Prospettive di sviluppo dei cataloghi elettronici. Boll. AIB 50 (1/2), 69–88, pp. 75–81. https://bollettino.aib.it/article/view/5295.

Iacono, A., 2013. Verso un nuovo modello di OPAC. Dal recupero dell'informazione alla creazione di conoscenza. JLIS.it 4 (2), 85–107. https://www.jlis.it/article/view/8903.

Iacono, A., 2014. Linked Data. AIB, Roma.

Iacono, A., 2014. Dal record al dato. Linked data e ricerca dell'informazione nell'OPAC. JLIS.it 5 (1), 77–102. https://www.jlis.it/article/view/9095.

Iacono, A., 2017. L'impatto dei linked data bibliografici nella Library catalog analysis: nuove opportunità per la valutazione scientifica. In: Maria Teresa Biagetti, Valutare la ricerca nelle scienze umane e sociali, con scritti di Antonella Iacono e Antonella Trombone. Bibliografica, Milano, pp. 149–174.

IFLA/UNESCO Public Library Manifesto, 1994. https://www.ifla.org/publications/iflaunesco-public-library-manifesto-1994.

IFLA, 2009. cataloguing principles: statement of International cataloguing principles (ICP) and its glossary. In: Tillett, B., Cristán, A.L. (Eds.), München: Saur. http://www.ifla.org/files/assets/cataloguing/icp/icp_2009-en.pdf.

Imodelli, 2018. biblioteconomici. Biblioteche oggi Trends 4 (1). http://www.bibliotecheoggi.it/trends/issue/view/60.

International Federation of Library Associations and Institutions, 1998. Study Group on the Functional Requirements for Bibliographic Records, Functional Requirements for Bibliographic Records: Final Report. München: Saur the current text is available at: the URL: http://www.ifla.org/publications/functional-requirements-for-bibliographic-records.

International Federation of Library Associations and Institutions, 2005. Guidelines for Online Public Access Catalogue (OPAC) Displays: Final Report. München: Saur.

International Federation of Library Associations and Institutions, 2013. Riding the Waves or Caught in the Tide? http://trends.ifla.org/insights-document.

International Federation of Library Associations and Institutions, 2016. Cataloguing section; international federation of library Associations and institutions. In: Meetings of Experts on an International Cataloguing Code, Statement of International Cataloguing Principles (ICP). https://www.ifla.org/publications/node/11015.

International Federation of Library Associations and Institutions. Libraries, Archives, Museums, Monuments & Sites (LAMMS). http://www.ifla.org/lamms.

Jantzi, L., et al., 2016. Managing discovery and linking services. Ser. Libr. 70 (1–4), 184–197. https://www.tandfonline.com/doi/abs/10.1080/0361526X.2016.1153331.

Järvelin, K., 2003. Information retrieval (IR). In: Feather, J., Paul, S. (Eds.), International Encyclopedia of Information and Library Science. Routledge, London, pp. 293–295.

Jia, J., 2021. From data to knowledge: the relationships between vocabularies, linked data and knowledge graphs. J. Doc. 77 (1), 93–105. https://www.emerald.com/insight/content/doi/10.1108/JD-03-2020-0036/full/html?skipTracking=true.

Jiang, T., et al., 2017. A clickstream data analysis of Chinese academic library OPAC users' information behavior. Libr. Inf. Sci. Res. 39 (3), 213–223. https://www.sciencedirect.com/science/article/pii/S0740818816301451.

John, A., 2017. Discovery systems: are they now the library? Learn. Publ. 30 (1), 87–89. https://onlinelibrary.wiley.com/doi/full/10.1002/leap.1085.

Joint, N., 2010. The one-stop shop search engine: a transformational library technology? Libr. Rev. 59 (4), 241–248. https://www.emerald.com/insight/content/doi/10.1108/00242531011038550/full/html.

Joint steering committee for development of RDA, et al., 2014. RDA: Resource Description & Access. American Library Association, Chicago.

Kalita, D., Deka, D., 2021. Searching the great metadata timeline: a review of library metadata standards from linear cataloguing rules to ontology inspired metadata standards. Libr. Hi Technol. 39 (1), 190–204. https://www.emerald.com/insight/content/doi/10.1108/LHT-08-2019-0168/full/html.

Karolina, A., 2017. Fatti alternativi e fake news: la verificabilità nella società dell'informazione. AIB Studi 57 (1), 5–6. https://aibstudi.aib.it/article/view/11618.

Kaschte, A., 2013. Linked open data on its way into next generation library management and discovery solutions. JLIS.it 4 (1), 313–323. https://www.jlis.it/article/view/5492.

Katagi, S., Bhakti, G., 2020. Social tags of select books written by Mahatma Gandhi: a comparative study of library thing tags and OCLC fast subject headings. DESIDOC J. Libr. Inf. Technol. 40 (1), 34–39. https://publications.drdo.gov.in/ojs/index.php/djlit/article/view/15138.

Kelley, M., 2012. Coming into focus: web-Scale Discovery Services face growing need for best practices. Libr. J. 137 (17), 34–40.

Kerne, A., et al., 2008. An experimental method for measuring the emergence of new ideas in information discovery. Int. J. Hum. Comput. Interact. 24 (5), 460–477. https://www.tandfonline.com/doi/full/10.1080/10447310802142243.

Kerne, A., et al., 2009. combinFormation: mixed-initiative composition of image and text surrogates promotes information discovery. ACM Trans. Inf. Syst. 27 (1), 5:1–5:45. https://dl.acm.org/citation.cfm?id=1416955.

Kliewer, G., et al., 2016. Using Primo for undergraduate research: a usability study. Libr. Hi Technol. 34 (4), 566–584. https://www.emerald.com/insight/content/doi/10.1108/LHT-05-2016-0052/full/html.

Koltay, T., et al., 2015. The shift of information literacy towards research 2.0. J. Acad. Libr. 41 (1), 87–93. https://www.sciencedirect.com/science/article/pii/S0099133314001979.

Kortekaas, S., Kramer, B., 2014. Thinking the unthinkable: doing away with the library catalogue. Insights 27 (3), 244–248. https://insights.uksg.org/articles/10.1629/2048-7754.174/.

Kortekaas, S., 2012. Thinking the unthinkable: a library without a catalogue. Reconsidering the future of discovery tools for Utrecht University library. In: Report Submitted to "LIBER 41st Annual Conference", (27-30 June 2012. Tartu, Estonia. http://www.uttv.ee/naita?id=12538.

Kroeger Angela, 2013. The road to BIBFRAME: the evolution of the idea of bibliographic transition into a post-MARC future. Catal. Classif. Q. 51 (8), 873–890. https://www.tandfonline.com/doi/full/10.1080/01639374.2013.823584.

Fawley, N., Krysak Nikki, 2014. Learning to love your discovery tool: strategies for integrating a discovery tool in face-to-face, synchronous, and asynchronous instruction. Publ. Serv. Q. 10 (4), 283–301. https://www.tandfonline.com/doi/full/10.1080/15228959.2014.961110?af=R.

Kuali OLE. https://openlibraryenvironment.org/.

Lancaster Frederick, W., 2003. Indexing and Abstracting in Theory and Practice. University of Illinois. Graduate school of LIS, Urbana Champaign.

Landow George, P., 2006. Hypertext 3.0: Critical Theory and New Media in an Era of Globalization. The Johns Hopkins University, Baltimore.

Lankes, R.D., et al., 2007. Participatory Networks: The Library as Conversation, vol. 12. Information Research. http://www.informationr.net/ir/12-4/colis/colis05.html. no. 4.

Lankes, R.D., 2011. The Atlas of New Librarianship. MIT, Cambridge.

Lapôtre, R., 2017. Library Metadata on the web: the example of data.bnf.fr. JLIS.it 8 (3), 58–70. https://www.jlis.it/article/view/12402.

Lashkari, F., et al., 2019. Neural embedding-based indices for semantic search. Inf. Process. Manag. 56 (3), 733–755. https://www.sciencedirect.com/science/article/pii/S0306457318302413.

Lau, J., 2006. Guidelines on Information Literacy for Lifelong Learning: Final Draft. IFLA. https://www.ifla.org/ES/publications/guidelines-on-information-literacy-for-lifelong-learning.

Lawton, A., 2015. Use of ESBCO discovery tool at one university reveals increased use of electronic collections but decreased use in circulation of print collections. Evid. Base Libr. Inf. Pract. 10 (4), 244–246. https://journals.library.ualberta.ca/eblip/index.php/EBLIP/article/view/25473.

Lee, B., Chung, E.K., 2016. An analysis of web-scale discovery services from the perspective of user's relevance judgment. J. Acad. Libr. 42 (5), 529–534. https://www.sciencedirect.com/science/article/pii/S0099133316301021.

Lei, Z.M., 2019. Semantic enrichment for enhancing LAM data and supporting digital humanities. El Prof. Inf. 28 (1), 1–35. http://www.elprofesionaldelainformacion.com/contenidos/2019/ene/03.pdf.

Levine-Clark, M., 2014. Access to everything: building the future academic library collection. Portal 14 (3), 425–437. https://muse.jhu.edu/article/549201.

Levy, R., 2014. Open web V the library. inCite 35 (10), 19.

Li, G., Wu, L., 2017. New service system as an information-Cf.king context: investigation of an unfamiliar discovery service. J. Doc. 73 (5), 1082–1098. https://www.emerald.com/insight/content/doi/10.1108/JD-08-2016-0102/full/html.

Library Consortium of Vigo County OPAC. https://indsu.iii.com/*eng.

Library of Congress Working Group on the Future of Bibliographic Control, on the Record, 2008. Library of Congress, Washington. http://www.loc.gov/bibliographic-future/news/lcwg-ontherecord-jan08-final.pdf.

Library of Congress, 2012. Bibliographic Framework as a Web of Data: Linked Data Model and Supporting Services. Library of Congress, Washington. http://www.loc.gov/bibframe/pdf/marcld-report-11-21-2012.pdf.

Library thing. http://www.librarything.com.

Jones (Ed.), 2016. Linked Data for Cultural Heritage. Michele Seikel. ALA.

Lloyd, A., 2005. No man (or woman) is an island: information literacy, affordances and communities of practice. Aust. Libr. J. 54 (3), 230–237. https://www.tandfonline.com/doi/abs/10.1080/00049670.2005.10721760.

Long Bradley, A., 2017. Addressing a discovery tool's shortcomings with a supplemental health sciences-specific federated search engine. J. Electron. Resour. Med. Libr. 14 (3), 101–113. https://www.tandfonline.com/doi/full/10.1080/15424065.2017.1368425.

Louise, T., Kidder, M., 2016. Exploring discovery @ Rosenberg Library: what happens when a library, a museum, and an archive get together to share a single discovery tool? In: Varnum, K.J. (Ed.), Exploring Discovery: The Front Door to Your Library's Licensed and Digitized Content. ALA, Chicago, pp. 35–43.

LS2 PAC. https://tlcdelivers.com/ls2-pac/.

Lubetzky, S., 1953. Cataloging Rules and Principles: A Critique of the A.L.A. Rules for Entry and a Proposed Design for Their Revision. Library of Congress, Washington.

L'universo delle risorse culturali: lampi di genio e azioni concrete. Lightning talks presentati al Convegno AIB CILW 2016, a cura del Gruppo di studio AIB CILW. AIB Studi 57 (1), 2017, 91–117. https://aibstudi.aib.it/article/view/11569.

Luther, J., Kelly Maureen, C., 2011. The next generation of discovery. Libr. J. 136 (5), 66–71. https://www.libraryjournal.com/?detailStory=the-next-generation-of-discovery.

Lynch Clifford, A., 1995. Networked information resource discovery: an overview of current issues. IEEE J. Select. Areas Commun. 13 (8), 1505–1522. https://ieeexplore.ieee.org/document/464719.

Lyon Declaration on Access to Information and Development, 2014. http://www.lyondeclaration.org.

Machetti, C., 2016. Biblioteche e discovery tool: il caso OneSearch e l'ateneo di Siena. AIB Studi 56 (3), 391–408. https://aibstudi.aib.it/article/view/11501.

Mackey Thomas, P., Jacobsen Trudi, E., 2014. Metaliteracy: Reinventing Information Literacy to Empower Learners. Facet, London.

Magi Trina, J., 2019. Why discovery tools and information literacy are not enough: reconnecting with reference sources. Coll. Res. Libr. News 80 (10), 573–574. https://crln.acrl.org/index.php/crlnews/article/view/24047/31763.

Maheshwari, S., November 20, 2016. How Fake News Goes Viral: A Case Study. The New York Times. https://www.nytimes.com/2016/11/20/business/media/how-fake-news-spreads.html.

Maiello, R., 2017. Le biblioteche per la convergenza digitale. Bibl. Oggi 53 (4), 22–29.

Makri, S., 2012. Blandford Ann, coming across information serendipitously. J. Doc. 68 (5), 684–724. https://www.emerald.com/insight/content/doi/10.1108/00220411211256030/full/html.

Spiteri, L.F. (Ed.), 2016. Managing Metadata in Web-Scale Discovery Systems. Facet, London.

Mann, T., 2006. Il catalogo e gli altri strumenti di ricerca: un punto di vista dalla Library of Congress. Boll. AIB 46 (3), 186–206 testo originale inglese. https://bollettino.aib.it/article/view/5154. http://www.guild2910.org/AFSCMECalhounReview.pdf.

Mann, T., 2006. What Is Going on at the Library of Congress? http://www.guild2910.org/AFSCMEWhatIsGoingOn.pdf.

Manning Christopher, D., et al., 2008. Introduction to Information Retrieval. Cambridge University press, Cambridge.

Marchitelli, A., 2012. Frigimelica Giovanna, OPAC. AIB, Roma, pp. 34–54.

Marchitelli, A., Tessa, P., 2008. OPAC, SOPAC e social networking: cataloghi di biblioteca 2.0? Bibl. Oggi 26 (2), 82–92. http://www.bibliotecheoggi.it/2008/20080208201.pdf.

Marcum Deanna, B., 2006. The future of cataloging. Libr. Resour. Tech. Serv. 50 (1), 5–9. https://www.questia.com/library/journal/1G1-141577373/the-future-of-cataloging.

Martinelli, L., 2016. Wikidata: la soluzione wikimediana ai linked open data. AIB Studi 56 (1), 75–85. https://aibstudi.aib.it/article/view/11434.

Matthews, B., et al., 2010. An evaluation of enhancing social tagging with a knowledge organization system. ASLIB Proc. 62 (4/5), 447–465. https://www.emerald.com/insight/content/doi/10.1108/00012531011074690/full/html.

McAfee Erin, L., 2018. Shame: the emotional basis of library anxiety. Coll. Res. Libr. 79 (2), 237–256. https://crl.acrl.org/index.php/crl/article/view/16604/18604.

McCallum, S., 2017. BIBFRAME development. JLIS.it 8 (3), 71–85. https://www.jlis.it/article/view/12415.

McCrae John, P., 2020. The Linked Open Data Cloud. http://lod-cloud.net/.

Meehan, T., 2014. BibFrame. Catal. Index (174), 43–52. https://archive.cilip.org.uk/sites/default/files/documents/Catalogue%20and%20Index%20issue%20174%2C%20March%202014.pdf.

Memento project. http://mementoweb.org/about/.

Martínez-González, M., Mercedes, A.-D., María-Luisa, 2020. A semantic web methodological framework to evaluate the support of integrity in thesaurus tools. J. Inf. Sci. 46 (3), 378–391. https://journals.sagepub.com/doi/full/10.1177/0165551519837195.

Metitieri, F., 2009. L'OPAC collaborativo, tra folksonomia e socialità. Bibl. Oggi 27 (2), 7–12. http://www.bibliotecheoggi.it/2009/20090200701.pdf.

Michetti, G., 2009. Ma è poi tanto pacifico che l'albero rispecchi l'archivio? Archivi Comput. 19 (1), 85–95.

Michetti, G., 2016. Oltre l'interdisciplinarità? AIB Studi 56 (3), 409–420. https://aibstudi.aib.it/article/view/11513.

Michetti, G., 2017. Linked data nel dominio archivistico: rischi e opportunità. In: Progressi dell'informazione e progresso delle conoscenze: granularità, interoperabilità e integrazione dei dati, a cura di Roberto Raieli. AIB, Roma, pp. 255–277.

Microsoft Academic. https://academic.microsoft.com/.

Miller Eric, J., 2001. An introduction to the resource description framework. J. Libr. Adm. 34 (3/4), 245–255. https://www.tandfonline.com/doi/abs/10.1300/J111v34n03_04.

Miller Sara, D., 2018. Diving deep: reflective questions for identifying tacit disciplinary information literacy knowledge practices, dispositions, and values through the ACRL Framework for Information Literacy. J. Acad. Libr. 44 (3), 412–418. https://www.sciencedirect.com/science/article/pii/S0099133317302720.

Mitchell, E., 2012. Leveraging metadata to create better web services. J. Web Libr. 6 (2), 136–139. https://www.tandfonline.com/doi/full/10.1080/19322909.2012.671653.

Mitchell Erik, T., 2016. Library Linked Data: Early Activity and Development. ALA, Chicago.

Molteni Valeria, E., Chan Emily, K., 2015. Student confidence/overconfidence in the research process. J. Acad. Libr. 41 (1), 2–8. https://www.sciencedirect.com/science/article/pii/S0099133314002420.

Moore, M., 2016. But is my resource included? How to manage, develop, and think about the content in your discovery tool. Ser. Libr. 70 (1–4), 149–157. https://www.tandfonline.com/doi/full/10.1080/0361526X.2016.1147877.

Moore Kate, B., Greene, C., 2012. Choosing discovery: a literature review on the selection and evaluation of discovery layers. J. Web Libr. 6 (3), 145–163. https://www.tandfonline.com/doi/full/10.1080/19322909.2012.689602.

Morgan Eric Lease, 2007. Next Generation Library Catalog. http://infomotions.com/musings/ngc/.

Musei Archivi Biblioteche (MAB). http://www.mab-italia.org.

Nelson, D., Turney, L., 2015. What's in a word? Rethinking facet headings in a discovery service. Inf. Technol. Libr. 34 (2), 76–91. https://ejournals.bc.edu/index.php/ital/article/view/5629.

Nelson Theodor Holm, 1990. Literary Machines. Mindful, Sausalito.

Nichols Aaron, F., et al., 2014. Kicking the tires: a usability study of the Primo discovery tool. J. Web Libr. 8 (2), 172–195. https://www.tandfonline.com/doi/full/10.1080/19322909.2014.903133.
Nichols Aaron, F., et al., 2017. What does it take to make discovery a success? A survey of discovery tool adoption, instruction, and evaluation among academic libraries. J. Web Libr. 11 (2), 85–104. https://www.tandfonline.com/toc/wjwl20/11/2?nav=tocList.
Nikesh, N., Byers Dorothy Furber, 2017. Improving web scale discovery services. Ann. Libr. Inf. Stud. 64 (4), 276–279. http://op.niscair.res.in/index.php/ALIS/article/view/19348.
OA2020. https://oa2020.org/.
Old wine, new bottle? Principi e metodi per una reale innovazione nelle prospettive LIS. Il parere di Marshall Breeding. Mauro Guerrini, David Weinberger, Paul Gabriele Weston, Maja Žumer, a cura di Roberto Raieli [et al.] AIB Studi 55 (3), 2015, 385–403. https://aibstudi.aib.it/article/view/11384.
Oliveira, M.L.M., et al., 2019. Semantic web or web of data? A diachronic study (1999 to 2017) of the publications of Tim Berners-Lee and the world Wide web Consortium. J. Assoc. Inf. Sci. Technol. 70 (7), 701–714. https://asistdl.onlinelibrary.wiley.com/doi/abs/10.1002/asi.24111.
Oliver, G., Harvey, R., 2016. Digital Curation, second ed. Facet, London.
Olson Tod, A., 2007. Utility of a faceted catalog for scholarly research. Libr. Hi Technol. 25 (4), 550–561. https://www.emerald.com/insight/content/doi/10.1108/07378830710840509/full/html.
Online Computer Library Center, 2005. Perceptions of Libraries and Information Resources: A Report to the OCLC Membership. OCLC, Dublin. http://oclc.org/reports/2005perceptions.en.html.
Online Computer Library Center, 2007. Sharing, Privacy and Trust in Our Networked World: A Report to the OCLC Membership. OCLC, Dublin. https://eric.ed.gov/?id=ED532599.
Online Computer Library Center, 2011. Perceptions of Libraries, 2010: Context and Community. A Report to the OCLC Membership. OCLC, Dublin. http://oclc.org/reports/2010perceptions.en.html.
Open annotation collaboration. http://www.openannotation.org.
Open data commons. http://opendatacommons.org.
Open Knowledge Foundation. https://okfn.org. Open Library Foundation. http://www.openlibraryfoundation.org/.
Open library project. https://openlibrary.org.
OpenAIRE. https://www.openaire.eu.
OWL (Web Ontology Language). https://www.w3.org/OWL/.
Padmavathi, T., Krishnamurthy, M., 2017. Semantic web tools and techniques for knowledge organization: an overview. Knowl. Organ. 44 (4), 273–290.
Palfrey, J., 2015. BiblioTech: Why Libraries Matter More than Ever in the Age of Google. Basic Books, New York.
Paliaga Simone, January 23, 2018. Big data. Ecco perché le discipline umanistiche governeranno il digitale. Avvenire.it. https://www.avvenire.it/agora/pagine/algoritm-c69cd26cfb864b589e128b2611bc932f.
Pandey, S., Sahoo, S., 2020. Research collaboration and authorship pattern in the field of semantic digital libraries. DESIDOC J. Libr. Inf. Technol. 40 (6), 375–381. https://publications.drdo.gov.in/ojs/index.php/djlit/article/view/15680.
Park, H., 2019. Kipp margaret, library linked data models: library data in the semantic web. Catal. Classif. Q. 57 (5), 261–277. https://www.tandfonline.com/doi/full/10.1080/01639374.2019.1641171.

Pasqui, V., 2009. Evoluzione dei sistemi di gestione bibliotecaria tra vecchi e nuovi paradigmi. Boll. AIB 49 (3), 289–306. https://bollettino.aib.it/article/view/5455.

Paul, G., 1997. Digital Literacy. Wiley, New York.

Petrucciani, A., 2006. La catalogazione, il mercato e la fiera dei luoghi comuni. Boll. AIB 46 (3), 177–185. https://bollettino.aib.it/article/view/5153.

Pinkas María, M., et al., 2014. Selecting and implementing a discovery tool: the university of Maryland health sciences and human services library experience,. J. Electron. Resour. Med. Libr. 11 (1), 1–12. https://www.tandfonline.com/doi/full/10.1080/15424065.2013.876574.

Planning and Implementing Resource Discovery Tools in Academic Libraries, Edited by Mary Pagliero Popp, Diane Dallis, 2012. IGI global, Hershey.

Possemato, T., Delle, D.R., 2017. SHARE Catalogue: un'esperienza di cooperazione. Bibl. Oggi 35 (1), 21–29.

Potter, W.G., 1989. Expanding the online catalog. Inf. Technol. Libr. 8 (2), 99–104. https://www.questia.com/library/journal/1G1-13823201/expanding-the-online-catalog.

Precision and recall. In: Wikipedia, the free enciclopedia. https://en.wikipedia.org/wiki/Precision_and_recall.

Progressi dell'informazione e progresso delle conoscenze: granularità, interoperabilità e integrazione dei dati, a cura di Roberto Raieli, 2017. AIB, Roma.

Proper Henderik, A., Bruza Peter, D., 1999. What is information discovery about? J. Am. Soc. Inf. Sci. 50 (9), 737–750. https://asistdl.onlinelibrary.wiley.com/doi/10.1002/%28SICI%291097-4571%281999%2950%3A9%3C737%3A%3AAID-ASI2%3E3.0.CO%3B2-C.

Public Knowledge Project. https://pkp.sfu.ca/.

Qayyum Asim, M., Smith, D., 2018. Changing research behaviours of university students with progression throughout a course. J. Australian Libr. Inf. Assoc. 67 (3), 256–277. https://www.tandfonline.com/doi/full/10.1080/24750158.2018.1502243.

Qiao, C., Hu, X., 2019. Text classification for cognitive domains: a case using lexical, syntactic and semantic features. J. Inf. Sci. 45 (4), 516–528. https://journals.sagepub.com/doi/full/10.1177/0165551518802522.

Quan, D., Karger David, R., 2004. How to make a semantic web browser. In: WWW '04. Proceedings of the 13th International Conference on World Wide Web. ACM, New York, pp. 255–265.

Quint, B., 2014. Attacking our problems. Inf. Today 31 (2), 8.

Race Tammera, M., 2012. Resource discovery tools: supporting serendipity. In: Planning and Implementing Resource Discovery Tools in Academic Libraries, Edited by Mary Pagliero Popp, Diane Dallis. IGI global, Hershey, pp. 139–152.

Raieli, R., 2010. Nuovi metodi di gestione dei documenti multimediali. Bibliografica, Milano.

Raieli, R., 2016. Introducing multimedia information retrieval to libraries. JLIS.it 7 (3), 9–42. https://www.jlis.it/article/view/11530.

Raieli, R., 2017. Oltre i termini dell'information retrieval: information discovery e multimedia information retrieval. Bibliothecae.it 6 (1), 178–232. https://bibliothecae.unibo.it/article/view/7028.

Raieli, R., 2017. La comunità della conoscenza: senso e possibilità del progetto LOD-Semantic Web. In: Progressi dell'informazione e progresso delle conoscenze: granularità, interoperabilità e integrazione dei dati, a cura di Roberto Raieli. AIB, Roma, pp. 37–76.

Ramelli, A. In: Wikipedia, the free enciclopedia. https://en.wikipedia.org/wiki/Agostino_Ramelli.

Ramelli, A., 1981. Le diverse et artificiose machine del capitano Agostino Ramelli dal Ponte della Tresia ingegniero del christianissimo re di Francia e di Pollonia. Maestri, Milano (original ed. 1588).

Rasmussen, P.D., Laura, C., 2019. Connecting the silos: implementations and perceptions of linked data across European libraries. J. Doc. 75 (3), 643—666. https://www.emerald.com/insight/content/doi/10.1108/JD-07-2018-0117/full/html.

Raza, M., 2019. Application of linked data technologies in digital libraries: a review of literature. Libr. Hi Tech News 36 (3), 9—12. https://www.emerald.com/insight/content/doi/10.1108/LHTN-10-2018-0067/full/html.

RDA, 2016. Resource description and access: the metamorphosis of cataloguing, edited by Carlo Bianchini, mauro Guerrini,. JLIS.it 7 (2). https://www.jlis.it/issue/view/753.

RDA, 2018. An overview on RDA in Europe: EURIG2017, edited by Carlo Bianchini, Mauro Guerrini, Tiziana Possemato,. JLIS.it 9 (1). https://www.jlis.it/issue/view/787.

RDA Toolkit. www.rdatoolkit.org.

Resource Description Framework (RDF). http://www.w3.org/RDF.

ReadersFirst. http://www.readersfirst.org/.

Regazzi John, J., 2004. The battle for mindshare: a battle beyond access and retrieval. Inf. Serv. Use 24 (2), 83—92. https://content.iospress.com/articles/information-services-and-use/isu426.

Rentier, B., 2019. Open Science: The Challenge of Transparency. Académie Royale de Belgique, Bruxelles.

Revelli, C., 2004. Il Catalogo. Bibliografica, Milano.

Riccardo, R., 2018. Livelli di verità: post-verità, fake news e neutralità intellettuale in biblioteca. AIB Studi 58 (3), 455—477. https://aibstudi.aib.it/article/view/11833.

Riccardo, R., 2019. La piramide dell'informazione: una introduzione. AIB Studi 59 (1—2), 69—96.

Richardson Hillary, A.H., 2013. Revelations from the literature: how web-scale discovery has already changed us. Comput. Libr. 33 (4), 12—17. http://www.infotoday.com/cilmag/may13/Richardson–How-Web-Scale-Discovery-Has-Already-Changed-Us.shtml.

Riding the Waves or Caught in the Tide?, 2013. http://trends.ifla.org/insights-document.

Riva, P., 2016. Il nuovo modello concettuale dell'universo bibliografico: FRBR library reference model. AIB Studi 56 (2), 265—275. https://aibstudi.aib.it/article/view/11480.

Riva, P., Patrick, Le B., Maja, Ž., 2017. IFLA Library Reference Model: A Conceptual Model for Bibliographic Information. IFLA. https://www.ifla.org/publications/node/11412.

De Robbio, A., 2007. Analisi citazionale e indicatori bibliometrici nel modello open access. http://eprints.rclis.org/10686/1/valutazione-23gennaio2008.pdf.

De Robbio, A., 2012. Forme e gradi di apertura dei dati: i nuovi alfabeti dell'Open Biblio tra scienza e società. Bibl. Oggi 30 (6), 11—24.

Roncaglia, G., 2018. Fake news: bibliotecario neutrale o bibliotecario attivo? AIB Studi 58 (1), 83—93. https://aibstudi.aib.it/article/view/11772.

Roncaglia, G., 2018. L'età della frammentazione: cultura del libro e scuola digitale. Laterza, Roma.

De Rosa, C., et al., 2011. Perceptions of Libraries, 2010: Context and Community. OCLC, Dublin. https://www.oclc.org/research/publications/2010/2010perceptions.html.

Rose-Wiles Lisa, M., Hofmann Melissa, A., 2013. Still desperately Cf.king citations: undergraduate research in the age of web-scale discovery. J. Libr. Adm. 53 (2/3), 147—166. https://www.tandfonline.com/doi/full/10.1080/01930826.2013.853493.

Rossana, M., 2019. Blockchain, intelligenza artificiale e internet delle cose in biblioteca. AIB Studi 59, 1–2 p. [in corso di pubblicazione].
Roy, B.K., et al., 2018. Designing web-scale discovery systems using the VuFind open source software. Libr. Hi Tech News 35 (3), 16–22. https://www.emerald.com/insight/content/doi/10.1108/LHTN-12-2017-0088/full/html.
Rubenstein Ellen, L., et al., 2017. ARL instruction librarians and the one-box: a follow-up study. Ref. Serv. Rev. 45 (3), 368–381. https://www.emerald.com/insight/content/doi/10.1108/RSR-12-2016-0084/full/html.
Sadeh Tamar, 2015. From search to discovery. Bibliothek 39 (2), 212–224. https://www.degruyter.com/view/j/bfup.2015.39.issue-2/bfp-2015-0028/bfp-2015-0028.xml?format=INT.
Saffo, P., 1994. It's the context, stupid. Wired 2 (3), 74–75. https://www.wired.com/1994/03/context-2/.
Salarelli, A., 2012. Introduzione Alla Scienza Dell'informazione. Bibliografica, Milano.
Salarelli, A., 2014. Sul perché, anche nel mondo dei Linked Data, non possiamo rinunciare al concetto di documento. AIB Studi 54 (2/3), 279–293. https://aibstudi.aib.it/article/view/10128.
Salarelli, A., Tammaro, A.M., 2006. La Biblioteca Digitale. Bibliografica, Milano.
Sara, C.R., et al., 2021. The impact of COVID-19 on the use of academic library resources. Inf. Technol. Libr. 40 (2), 1–20. https://ejournals.bc.edu/index.php/ital/article/view/12629.
Sardo, L., 2017. La Catalogazione: Storia, Tendenze, Problemi Aperti. Bibliografica, Milano.
Scardilli, B., 2016. Working together toward an open source future. Inf. Today 33 (9), 25–27.
Scardilli, B., 2016. ILS product roundup: choosing among the top discovery services. Comput. Libr. 36 (2), 34–39. http://www.infotoday.com/cilmag/mar16/Scardilli–ILS-Product-Roundup.shtml.
Schneider, K.G., April 3, 2006. How OPACs Suck, Part 2: The Checklist of Shame. ALA TechSource. http://www.alatechsource.org/blog/2006/04/how-opacs-suck-part-2-the-checklist-of-shame.html.
SciELO. https://www.scielo.org/.
Serrai, A., 2016. In Conrad Gesner l'origine dell'era della informazione. Bibliothecae.it 5 (2), 354–357. https://bibliothecae.unibo.it/article/view/6397.
Serrai, A., 2019. Linguaggi, codici e informazione. Bibliothecae.it 8 (1), 1–3. https://bibliothecae.unibo.it/article/view/9495/9283.
Serrai, A., 2017. Biblioteche, archivi, musei. Bibliothecae.it 6 (1), 361–369. https://bibliothecae.unibo.it/article/view/7041.
Sgobba, A., June 6 , 2013. I bibliotecari in crisi e la rivoluzione (attesa) degli open data. Corriere Della Sera. http://nuvola.corriere.it/2013/06/06/i-bibliotecari-in-crisi-e-la-rivoluzione-attesa-degli-open-data.
Shadbolt, N., et al., 2006. The semantic web revised. IEEE Intell. Syst. 21 (3), 96–101. https://ieeexplore.ieee.org/document/1637364.
Shapiro, S., 2018. Academic librarians, information overload, and the Tao of discovery. J. Acad. Librar. 44 (5), 671–673. https://www.sciencedirect.com/science/article/pii/S0099133318302210.
SirsiDynix Enterprise: http://www.sirsidynix.com/products/enterprise.
SKOS (Simple Knowledge Organization System). http://www.w3.org/2004/02/skos/.
SNAC (Social networks and archival context). http://socialarchive.iath.virginia.edu.
Solimine, G., 1995. Introduzione allo studio della biblioteconomia: riflessioni e documenti. Manziana: Vecchiarelli.
Solimine, G., 2004. La biblioteca: scenari, culture, pratiche di servizio. Laterza, Roma.

Solimine, G., 2007. Verso una biblioteconomia 2.0? Boll. AIB 47 (4), 433–434. https://bollettino.aib.it/article/view/5250.

Solimine, G., 2013. Nuovi appunti sulla interpretazione della biblioteca pubblica. AIB Studi 53 (3), 261–271. https://aibstudi.aib.it/article/view/9132.

Spärck, J.K., 1972. A statistical interpretation of term specificity and its application in retrieval. J. Doc. 28 (1), 11–21. https://www.emerald.com/insight/content/doi/10.1108/eb026526/full/html.

SPARQL Protocol And RDF Query Language. http://www.w3.org/TR/sparql11-overview/.

Spiteri Louise, F., 2016. Managing user-generated metadata in discovery systems. In: Spiteri, L.F. (Ed.), Managing Metadata in Web-Scale Discovery Systems. Facet, London, pp. 165–193.

Sridevi, S., et al., 2021. Investigation on Blockchain technology for Web service composition: a case study. Int. J. Web Serv. Res. 18 (1), 1–23. https://www.igi-global.com/article/investigation-on-blockchain-technology-for-web-service-composition/261592.

Stock Wolfgang, G., Stock, M., 2013. Handbook of Information Science. De Gruyter Saur, Berlin.

Summers, E., Dorothea, S., 2013. Linking Things on the Web: A Pragmatic Examination of Linked Data for Libraries, Archives and Museums. http://arxiv.org/abs/1302.4591.

Sweet, M., 2012. There's nothing wrong with discovery services that can't be fixed by the reference layer. In: The Fiesole Collection Development Retreat, April 12, 2012. http://www.casalini.it/retreat/2012_docs/sweet.pdf.

iPods in the sauna or kids these days. In: Tallent (Ed.), Inter. Ref. Serv. Q. 16 (3), 83–89. https://www.tandfonline.com/doi/full/10.1080/10875301.2011.602602.

Tallerås, K., 2013. From many records to one graph: heterogeneity conflicts in the linked data restructuring cycle. Inf. Res. 18, 3. http://InformationR.net/ir/18-3/colis/paperC18.html.

Taniguchi, S., 2018. Is BIBFRAME 2.0 a suitable schema for exchanging and sharing diverse descriptive metadata about bibliographic resources? Catal. Classif. Q. 56 (1), 40–61. https://www.tandfonline.com/doi/full/10.1080/01639374.2017.1382643.

Tay, A., 2014. Four Possible Web Scale Discovery Future Scenarios. http://musingsaboutlibrarianship.blogspot.com/2014/12/four-possible-web-scale-discovery.html#.Vvrov-IrJpg.

Tay, A., 2016. Managing volume in discovery systems. In: Spiteri, L.F. (Ed.), Managing Metadata in Web-Scale Discovery Systems. Facet, London, pp. 113–135.

Tennant, R., 2002. MARC must die. Libr. J. 127 (17), 26–27. https://www.libraryjournal.com/?detailStory=marc-must-die.

Tennant, R., 2005. Lipstick on a pig. Libr. J. 130 (7), 34–37.

Tennant, R., 2006. Fixing library discovery. Libr. J. 131 (11), 30–31.

Testoni, L., 2014. Quali literacy al tempo dei social network. Bibl. Oggi 32 (4), 28–36. http://www.bibliotecheoggi.it/rivista/article/view/94.

The OPAC Sucks. http://www.youtube.com/watch?v=tJD-safYEb0.

The Summon service. https://www.proquest.com/products-services/the-summon-service.html.

The University of California libraries, 2005. Bibliographic Services Task Force, Rethinking How We Provide Bibliographic Services for the University of California: Final Report. University of California, Berkeley. http://libraries.universityofcalifornia.edu/groups/files/bstf/docs/Final.pdf.

Thompson JoLinda, L., et al., 2018. Discovery assessment and improvement at an academic health sciences library: health Information @ Himmelfarb five years later. J. Electron. Resour. Med. Libr. 15 (1), 7–25. https://www.tandfonline.com/doi/abs/10.1080/15424065.2018.1433093.

Thomsett-Scott, B., Reese, P.E., 2012. Academic libraries and discovery tools: a survey of the literature. Coll. Undergrad. Libr. 19 (2/4), 123–143. https://www.tandfonline.com/doi/full/10.1080/10691316.2012.697009.

Time travel. http://timetravel.mementoweb.org/.

Todd, E., 2018. Tracking down the problem: the development of a web-scale discovery troubleshooting workflow. Ser. Libr. 74 (1–4), 234–239. https://www.tandfonline.com/doi/full/10.1080/0361526X.2018.1427984.

Tonyan, J., Christi, P., 2019. Discovery tools in the classroom: a usability study and implications for information literacy instruction. J. Web Libr. 13 (1), 1–19. https://www.tandfonline.com/doi/full/10.1080/19322909.2018.1530161?src=recsys.

Trombone, A., 2014. New displaying models of bibliographic data and resources: cataloguing/resource description and search results. JLIS.it 5 (2), 19–32. https://www.jlis.it/article/view/10063.

Trombone, A., 2015. Il progetto BIBFRAME della Library of Congress: come stanno cambiando i modelli strutturali e comunicativi dei dati bibliografici. AIB Studi 55 (2), 215–226. https://aibstudi.aib.it/article/view/11100.

Trombone, A., 2018. Principi di catalogazione e rappresentazione delle entità bibliografiche. AIB, Roma.

Trombone, A., 2019. Formare e gestire collezioni con i discovery tools. Bibl. Oggi 37 (3), 11–19.

Turbanti, S., 2016. La visibilità – e l'impatto? – nel Web ai tempi dei social: i principali strumenti di altmetrics. AIB Studi 56 (No. 1), 41–58. https://aibstudi.aib.it/article/view/11410.

Turbanti, S., 2016. REICAT. AIB, Roma.

Tyson, A.F., Dinneen, J.D., 2020. A cross-discipline comparison of subject guides and resource discovery tools. Inf. Res. 25 (3) paper 871. http://informationr.net/ir/25-3/paper871.html.

Unesco, 2011. Fez Declaration on Media and Information Literacy. http://www.unesco.org/new/fileadmin/MULTIMEDIA/HQ/CI/CI/pdf/news/Fez%20Declaration.pdf.

University College London, 2008. Information Behaviour of the Researcher of the Future. University College, London. http://www.jisc.ac.uk/media/documents/programmes/reppres/gg_final_keynote_11012008.pdf.

Utrecht University Library. https://www.uu.nl/en/university-library.

Uzwyshyn Raymond, J., 2018. Academic libraries and technology: an environmental scan towards future possibility. In: Holbrook, G.J. (Ed.), Academic and Digital Libraries: Emerging Directions and Trends. Nova, New York, pp. 63–86.

Vassallo, S., 2013. L'integrazione tra archivi e biblioteche alla prova del web semantico. In: Biblioteche in cerca di alleati. Oltre la cooperazione, verso nuove strategie di condivisione. Bibliografica, Milano, pp. 430–454.

Vaughan, J., 2011. Web Scale Discovery Services, vol. 47. American library association, Chicago (published also as: «Library technology reports. (2011), no. 1).

Verdesca, A., 2015. What's in a word: coming to terms with reference. Ref. Libr. 56 (1), 67–72. https://www.tandfonline.com/doi/full/10.1080/02763877.2015.976467.

VIAF (Virtual International Authority File). https://viaf.org/.

Vivarelli, M., 2015. C'è bisogno di collezioni? Teorie, modelli, pratiche per l'organizzazione di spazi documentari connessi e condivisi. Biblioteche oggi trends 1 (1), 18–29. http://www.bibliotecheoggi.it/trends/article/view/38.

VuFind. https://vufind.org/vufind/.

World Wide Web Consortium (W3C). http://www.w3.org/.

Walker, J., 2015. The NISO Open Discovery Initiative: promoting transparency in discovery. Insights 28 (1), 85–90. https://insights.uksg.org/articles/10.1629/uksg.186/.

Way, D., 2010. The impact of web-scale discovery on the use of a library collection. Ser. Rev. 36 (4), 214–220. https://www.sciencedirect.com/science/article/pii/S0098791310000882.

Weinberger, D., November 13 , 2005. Crunching the metadata. What Google print really tells us about the future of books. Boston Globe (MA). http://www.boston.com/ae/books/articles/2005/11/13/crunching_the_metadata.

Weinberger, D., 2012. Too Big to Know: Rethinking Knowledge Now that the Facts Aren't the Facts, Experts Are Everywhere, and the Smartest Person in the Room Is the Room. Basic books, New York.

Weston, P.G., 2017. Sardo Lucia, Metadati. AIB, Roma.

Weston, P.G., Salvatore, V., 2007. "…e il navigar m'è dolce in questo mare": linee di sviluppo e personalizzazione dei cataloghi. In: La biblioteca su misura: verso la personalizzazione del servizio, a cura di Claudio Gamba, Maria Laura Trapletti. Bibliografica, Milano, pp. 130–167.

Weston Paul Gabriele, et al., 2017. Authority data and cross-domain intersection within aggregation portals: the case of BeWeb. JLIS.it 8 (1), 139–154. https://www.jlis.it/article/view/12127.

Wheeler, W., 2011. The role of reference in discovery systems: effecting a more literate search. In: Something's Gotta Give: Charleston Conference Proceedings, 2011. Purdue University Press, West Lafayette. http://docs.lib.purdue.edu/cgi/viewcontent.cgi?article=1229&context=charleston.

Wiggins, G., Jay, M.T., 2010. Understanding by design. In: Meyer, Jan H.F., et al. (Eds.), Alexandria: Association for Supervision and Curriculum Development, 2004; Threshold Concepts and Transformational Learning. Sense Publishers, Rotterdam.

Wikicite. https://meta.wikimedia.org/wiki/WikiCite.

Wikidata. https://www.wikidata.org.

Wikidata: WikiProject Source MetaData. https://www.wikidata.org/wiki/Wikidata:WikiProject_Source_MetaData.

Wikipedia, 2018. Libraries and archives. In: Catalani, L., Feliciati, P. (Eds.), JLIS.it, vol. 9 no. 3. https://www.jlis.it/issue/view/789.

Wilkes, B., 2016. Framing digital literacy: the ACRL framework. Singapore J. Libr. Inf. Manag. 45, 11–19. https://www.las.org.sg/wp/sjlim/framing-digital-literacy-the-acrl-framework/.

Williams Sarah, C., Foster Anita, K., 2011. Promises fulfilled? An EBSCO Discovery Service usability study. J. Web Libr. 5 (3), 179–198. https://www.tandfonline.com/doi/full/10.1080/19322909.2011.597590.

Wolff-Eisenberg, C., et al., 2016. US Faculty Survey 2015. In: Ithaka S+R. https://sr.ithaka.org/publications/ithaka-sr-us-faculty-survey-2015/.

Wolff-Eisenberg, C., et al., 2019. US Faculty Survey 2018. In: Ithaka S+R. https://sr.ithaka.org/blog/new-questionnaire-for-the-us-faculty-survey-2018-now-available/.

Woods Roberta, F., 2010. From federated search to the universal search solution. Ser. Libr. 58 (1/4), 141–148. https://www.tandfonline.com/doi/full/10.1080/03615261003622957.

World Wide Web Consortium, Category: Semantic Web Browser. https://www.w3.org/2001/sw/wiki/Category:Semantic_Web_Browser.

World Wide Web Consortium, 2011. Library Linked Data Incubator Group, Library Linked Data Incubator Group Final Report. W3C. http://www.w3.org/2005/Incubator/lld/XGR-lld-20111025.

World Wide Web Foundation. http://webfoundation.org/.

WorldCat Discovery. https://www.oclc.org/en/worldcat-discovery.html.

Wynne, S.C., Hanscom Martha, J., 2011. The effect of next-generation catalogs on catalogers and cataloging functions in academic libraries. Catal. Classif. Q. 49 (3), 179–207. https://www.tandfonline.com/doi/full/10.1080/01639374.2011.559899.

Xu, A., et al., 2018. From MARC to BIBFRAME 2.0: crosswalks. Catal. Classif. Q. 56 (2–3), 224–250. https://www.tandfonline.com/doi/full/10.1080/01639374.2017.1388326.

Yang Sharon, Q., 2012. Tagging for subject access. Comput. Libr. 32 (9), 19–23. https://www.questia.com/magazine/1P3-2816646581/tagging-for-subject-access.

Yang Sharon, Q., Kurt, W., 2010. Evaluating and comparing discovery tools: how close are we towards next generation catalog? Libr. Hi Technol. 28 (4), 690–709. https://www.emerald.com/insight/content/doi/10.1108/07378831011096312/full/html.

Yu, H., Young, M., 2004. The impact of Web search engines on subject searching in OPAC. Inf. Technol. Libr. 23 (4), 168–181. https://ejournals.bc.edu/index.php/ital/article/view/9658.

Zapounidou, S., et al., 2017. Representing and integrating bibliographic information into the Semantic Web: a comparison of four conceptual models. J. Inf. Sci. 43 (4), 525–553. https://journals.sagepub.com/doi/full/10.1177/0165551516650410.

Zeng, M.L., Philipp, M., 2019. Knowledge organization systems (KOS) in the semantic web: a multi-dimensional review. Int. J. Digit. Libr. 20 (3), 209–230. https://link.springer.com/article/10.1007%2Fs00799-018-0241-2.

Zhu, J., 2017. Should publishers work with library discovery technologies and what can they do? Learn. Publ. 30 (1), 71–80. https://onlinelibrary.wiley.com/doi/abs/10.1002/leap.1079.

Zhu, J., Kelley, J., 2015. Collaborating to reduce content gaps in discovery: what publishers, discovery service providers, and libraries can do to close the gaps. Sci. Technol. Libr. 34 (4), 315–328. https://www.tandfonline.com/doi/full/10.1080/0194262X.2015.1102677.

Zickuhr, K., et al., 2013. Library Services in the Digital Age. In: Pew Internet & American life project, Washington. http://libraries.pewinternet.org/2013/01/22/library-services.

Zurkowski Paul, G., 1974. The Information Service Environment: Relationships and Priorities. National Commission on Libraries and Information Science, Washington. http://files.eric.ed.gov/fulltext/ED100391.pdf.

Index

Note: 'Page numbers followed by "f" indicate figures and "t" indicate tables.'

W

Printed in the United States
by Baker & Taylor Publisher Services